TALES
from the
CASTING COUCH

An Unprecedented Candid Collection
of Stories, Essays, and Anecdotes
by and about Legendary Hollywood Stars,
Starlets, and Wanna-bes. . .

─────────────── ✦ ───────────────

Compiled by Michael Viner and Terrie Maxine Frankel

DOVE
BOOKS

Dove Books, Inc.
301 N. Canon Drive
Beverly Hills, CA 90210

ISBN 0-7871-0226-1

Printed in the United States of America

Dove Books
301 North Cañon Drive
Beverly Hills, CA 90210

Distributed by Penguin USA

Jacket, text design, and layout by Michele Lanci-Altomare

First Printing: October 1995

10 9 8 7 6 5 4 3 2 1

TABLE OF CONTENTS

FOREWORD

When Michael Viner, president of Dove Books, first had the concept for *Tales from the Casting Couch*, he approached his friends for casting stories, to see if it was an idea that would work. I was asked to submit a story. After reading my casting story about David Letterman, he asked if I would help him compile the book! We began a year-long effort of compiling, interviewing, and editing what has now become an important work and an embarrassment of riches. Our one-year odyssey has taken us from one lone story by Michael York, to several hundred casting stories by and about some of Hollywood's most famous and influential people.

We originally sought the blessings and participation of the highly regarded Casting Society of America in compiling this book. We even invited them to write an introduction. To our surprise, we found resistance from some of its members to the title *Tales from the Casting Couch*. The CSA's belief is that the name perpetuates a Hollywood myth they have been saddled with since the first want-to-be's stepped off of the bus from Iowa and found themselves lured into unsavory situations with unfulfilled promises of stardom in exchange for sexual favors. In all of our interviews, that type of situation was rarely brought to light. Certainly these seedy stories do exist—however to our knowledge they are rare. And those few stories that we heard—some included for your curiosity—involved despicable self-proclaimed producers, certainly not any legitimate professionals in the business. Fortunately, many CSA members have contributed to these pages, and to them we are grateful.

This anthology is historic. It is a work that should be passed down from generation to generation. *Tales from the Casting Couch* is more than just never-before-told casting stories about the entertainment industry's most fascinating people. It is a blueprint for going after the things you want, reserving the right to take no for an answer, knowing that every cloud has a silver lining ... It is a guide to life!

I would like to thank my sister, Jennie Louise Frankel, for the tireless work she has put forth in helping us to pull this book together. Her creative input has been invaluable and we are grateful to have such an extraordinary talent on our team.

This book would also not have been as successful without the help of the following people who gave so enthusiastically of their support: Mary Aarons, Ethan Addis, Jessica Algazi, Elizabeth Bersanetti, Laramy Blohm, MaryAnn Camarillo, Vera and Paul Chow, Paul Craig, Zhen Zhong Dai, Sharon M. Ferritto, Michael Francis, Jewell Frankel, Clive Fox, Sandi Gilbert, Cindy Jo Hinkelman, Peter Hoffman, Warren Imus, Tao Kang, Li Ke, Karrie Komaru, Michele Lanci-Altomare, Jeff Lasley, Samantha Leffel, JoAnn Leto, Gina Misiroglu, Bill Moody, Dan Musselman, Ned Neddervile, Laura Neimi, Vicki Neimi, Mitch Plessner, Vicky Preminger, Faye Resnick, Mindy Richmond, Diane Robison, Randi Rotwein, Stefan Rudnicki, Christian Schlosser, David Seymour, Cynthia Shahian, Karen Silverman, Carol Smith, Leona Smith, John Tinkel, Charles Tolbert, Robert Troy, Sam Trust, Wendy Walker, Lori Williams, Carole Ita White, Carol Wynans, and, of course, co-founder of Dove Books, Deborah Raffin.

All stories in *Tales from the Casting Couch* are written by the people who experienced them. Enjoy!

—Terrie Maxine Frankel, Producer/Writer

INTRODUCTION

Making a movie can be compared to preparing a meal—the script is the recipe; the set is the kitchen; the chef is the director; and the ingredients are the cast. With the right ingredients, a fine experience can be had by all—those who make it and those who taste it. Choosing these ingredients takes care, understanding, insight, and imagination as to how it will all turn out. This is why casting right is so essential.

For the actor, casting represents two issues: a chance to act and thus show his skill; and a chance to get a job. When the latter is in the forefront the actor usually doesn't show his best. This is particularly true in what are termed "callbacks," when the actor is asked to return to meet with the director and/or producers a second and even third time. In callbacks the actor knows that he or she is being considered for the role, seriously, and therefore might get the job. Often these second performances in the casting room are not as good as the first, since now the actor is conscious of the future job potential rather than concentrating on the moment of performing. And this is the lesson that many actors learn. To be in the casting session, particularly if they are asked to perform in some way is, in fact, to be acting. And this is what an actor does. Whether you get the job or not, in the casting session you get to do your work. To act.

What is being examined in casting is the relationship between actor and director, and whether each can support the other in the realization of a vision of the story. But the power is in the mind and hand of the director. If he or she doesn't feel the actor is right for the part, then it won't work, even if the actor gets the part. This happens sometimes when the real power in casting is in the hands of the producers or financiers, an often dangerous situation. On the set, it is the interpersonal dynamics of the director and the actor—how they relate to each other—that determines the quality of the performance.

And casting is fun. No wonder the financiers, writers, producers, associate producers, and personal assistants all want to attend the casting sessions. Oftentimes an actor will come to a casting session and find so many people in the room that she or he doesn't know who he is performing for or who in the room is in fact the director.

So, what's the right way to run a casting session? Ask many famous directors and you will get many contradictory answers. It depends on the personality and habits of the director. For some in this age of electronics, they only look at videotapes, and don't even meet the actors in person! For others it's the one-to-one contact that makes the difference; sometimes not in the casting room, but in a more relaxed environment, at a meal, or just hanging together. Some directors require the actor to read scenes from the script. Some ask for more improvisational work, setting up situations in the casting session where the director is looking for the actor's more spontaneous responses. Some ask actors to read with other actors who either already have a part in the film or are hired to perform that part for the casting sessions. Some directors like to read the roles themselves and have the actor read with them. Some ask personal questions to see how in touch with the flow of emotion the actor is; even in the pressurized situation of the casting session. Others like to videotape the sessions and study the tapes later. Most have their casting people screen many actors for the smaller roles before they see who the casting person thinks are the best candidates. Others demand to see everyone and anyone themselves, if they have the time.

Casting is a microcosm of the filmmaking process. It is a combination of talent, judgment, chemistry, timing, and magic. It is the first and crucial step in turning a script into a movie. And it has been said that once the film is cast, 80 percent of the work is done. Not quite true. But the wrong cast can ruin a movie—or spoil the meal. So great care—both creative and commercial—rests on these decisions. As you will feast in the following pages. . . .

—Jeremy Kagan, Writer/Producer/Director

CHAPTER I

STAR SEARCH!

☆

"I used to think as I looked out on
the Hollywood night—
there must be thousands of girls
sitting alone like me,
dreaming of becoming a movie star.
But I'm not going to worry about them.
I'm dreaming the hardest!"

—MARILYN MONROE
Legend

First Big Breaks

Actors may have the rocket ship and the launching pad. But the flight can't be made without the fuel supplied by the visionaries who give them their first break . . . and the agents, managers, and friends who keep them on their course.

THE "OTHER" MICHAEL DOUGLAS

———— ☆ ————

By Charlie Hauck
Writer/Producer/Author

There was a young man named Mike Douglas on the floor crew of a public television station I worked at in Pittsburgh. He was very funny and very appealing, and he had an interest in doing comedy. When I went out to Hollywood in 1974 to write and later produce "Maude," I kept in touch with young Mike Douglas, and encouraged him to try his hand in Los Angeles.

He came out and started getting on stage at the Comedy Store. I sent a manager friend of mine to see him, and he signed Mike up. I gave Mike a small part on a "Maude" episode, and that led to a regular role on a half-hour comedy "All's Fair," with Richard Crenna and Bernadette Peters. And I think he's done pretty well since then.

Early on, Mike had to come up with a new name for himself. There were already Screen Actors Guild members called

Mike Douglas and Michael Douglas. He bounced a few names off me, and I liked the one he finally chose . . . Michael Keaton.

I GET A KICK OUT OF JODIE FOSTER

By James Komack
Producer

Jodie Foster was six years old when I was doing a show called "The Courtship of Eddie's Father." Jodie came in to audition with her mother, Brandy. I looked at Jodie and said, "Are you an actress?" She said, "Yes." I said, "Well, we need a tough little girl. Are you a tough little girl?" She then kicked me in the shins . . . and I gave her the part!

"MAGNUM" LANDS SHARON STONE

By Charles Floyd Johnson
Producer

In 1985, Donald Bellisario, the creator and executive producer of "Magnum, P.I.," had just written a two-hour script entitled *Echoes of the Mind* as the season opener for the fifth year of the series. His script called for a stunningly beautiful young woman who could play the dual role of a schizophrenic who believed she was both herself and her less outgoing sister. We attempted to cast several established actresses and kept coming up empty-handed for a variety of reasons; so, we decided to look for a newer, fresher face, which is always a tall order for very challenging roles.

Our casting director, Donna Dockstader, sent us numerous tapes in Honolulu and among them was a stunningly beautiful young actress at whom she suggested we "take a very serious look." One viewing and we understood why Donna made the suggestion; even with few credits on her resumé. She possessed extraordinary grace and style in her work. Hands down, we decided to cast her, but there was a hitch—her agents wanted more for her services than our budget could afford, and no one wanted to justify spending money that we didn't have for a little-known talent with no marquee value. But, as usual with television schedules, the eleventh hour was upon us with no decision and no actress.

In an effort to expedite the decision-making process, not to mention the production schedule, I furiously started calling everyone involved and insisted that they were missing the chance to not only cast the right actress for the part but clearly an actress who was going to be a big star in the future. Well, it worked; she got the part, we got our actress, and I can happily say that Sharon Stone went on to prove how accurate my crystal ball was that day.

SALLY FIELD
Under the Right Street Lamp
at the Right Time!

———— ★ ————

By Eddie Foy III
Casting Director

This happened when I first started casting at Screen Gems, a subsidiary of Columbia Pictures. Executive producer Harry Ackerman had the most impossible project I ever had to cast. For four months I looked at every teenager in town—interviewed and read over five thousand girls. I went all over Southern California to plays and workshops, looking for this girl. The prerequisites were that she had to be cute, tiny, and able to play comedy.

Four days before we were going to shoot the pilot for ABC I told Millie Gussey, the head of casting at Screen Gems, "We don't have her." And then she told me, "Keep looking." That night I went back to a workshop at Columbia Pictures—it was called the Film Industry's Workshop. I retold Tony and Pat Miller, who were in charge of the workshop, about the role I was trying to cast. Then they told me about a "kid" who had just started working with them. I said I'd like to meet her. They said, "She just left!" I said, "I'm going to go find her!"

So I ran out and looked up Beachwood Drive and saw what appeared to be a big furry animal under the street lamp. I walked up, cleared my throat, and when she turned around I asked, "Are you Sally Field?" She said, "Yes." I said, "Would you like to play Gidget?" She was flabbergasted.

To make a long story short, she came in to read and did something very cute. At one point she crossed her eyes. It was the most instinctive move . . . the next day she started shooting "Gidget."

I have a picture in my office, "To Tootles—the one who started it all!" She used to call me Tootles.

YOUNG, RESTLESS, AND BROKE

By Eileen Davidson
Actress

Before I landed my first well-paying job on "The Young and the Restless," I didn't even know how I was going to make my rent. I was feeling disillusioned at the time and kind of beaten down by Hollywood. I had been waiting tables and, after paying for acting lessons, I had three hundred dollars in my bank account.

A friend of mine was in the South of France and he said, "Why don't you just fly over to France, I'll pay for the ticket." I stayed there for two weeks and when I came back, I didn't have any money—but I did have more confidence. I was feeling like I didn't want to be an actress anymore. Then "The Young and the Restless" hit. I read for the casting agent and was called back for the producers. During my screen test I lost one of my contact lenses and was blind in one eye. I was bumping into furniture and having to feel my way around. It was horrible. . . . When my agent told me I got the job I screamed! It changed my life.

GRAB ALEC BALDWIN

———————— ✸ ————————

By Jane Jenkins, Janet Hirshenson, and Michael Hirshenson
Casting Directors, The Casting Company

Often, actors have only one chance to do the best job they can in a room filled with strangers. This can be a nerve-wracking experience. When Alec Baldwin read for the John Hughes film, *She's Having a Baby*, we knew he was nervous and was not going to get the job. We believed he could do better and were discussing among ourselves, "Should we let him go?" By this time Alec was disappearing at the end of the parking lot. . . .

Michael ran after Alec while Janet went into the room and asked John if he would give him a second chance. John agreed.

We brought Alec in to read again—and this time the part was his! As casting directors, it's gratifying to know our instincts are right. Alec has since gone on to become a major motion picture star.

BOB NEWHART,
AN OVERNIGHT SENSATION

By Bob Finkel
Director/Producer

I was producing the Emmy Awards, hosted by Fred Astaire. The sponsor happened to be Lilt. I had booked Elaine May and Mike Nichols who wanted to do a brilliant satire on a Lilt hair product commercial. The network came to me and said, "Lilt does not want that satire." When I told Mike Nichols, he said, "We're either doing that or nothing." They left and returned to New York.

The show was just two days away and I had to find a replacement for Nichols and May. On my desk was one of those demonstration acetate records of a young comic from Chicago. His name was Bob Newhart and he was just hysterical. There were two comedy pieces we could use. One was *The Khrushchev Landing*. The next was about a German submarine that came up off the coast of Miami. I brought the acetate to Hal Kemp, then vice-president of programming, and asked if we could fly this guy in from Chicago. We flew him to Los Angeles and he did the two pieces for the show. The day after the Emmys Bob Newhart was the biggest name in show business!

I "BELTED" RICHARD ROUNDTREE

By Joel Freeman
Producer

Richard Roundtree was a model who was also starring in a play in Philadelphia, *The Great White Hope*. He had never been in a film before and when he came in on a cattle call, we knew he had the qualities we were looking for. We wanted to create a new Black hero image, and here he was. He was likeable, very cool, had some sophistication—and never forgot his roots.

We wanted to give Richard a screen test, but we didn't have a lot of money to spend and there wasn't anyone available to do the test with him . . . so we shot it in 16 mm, in our New York office, and I played the scene opposite him. Gordon Parks directed, and Richard did very well. When he arrived that day, he didn't have a belt, so he borrowed mine. Well, he had it framed and I never got the belt back! Once Richard got the role of John Shaft, I said, "Now, I want you to go to the gym . . . here's some money, eat plenty of steak, get yourself in top form." Not that he wasn't in good shape, we just wanted him to be in great shape.

MICKEY ROURKE ON THE ROAD
TO *BODY HEAT*

———— ★ ————

By Fern Champion
Casting Director

Once in a while an actor comes in who has something special. When I was casting a film called *Fade to Black*, Mickey Rourke came in and totally blew me away with his reading. He was incredible. I brought him in to read for the part of the best friend. My director, who was also the writer of the screenplay, took notes as Mickey read. Mickey stopped him and said, "Listen to me, you (CENSORED)! I'm here to read! I want a part! Either you're going to listen to me, or you're going to write!" Mickey does have a power to him . . . always has. The director put down his pen and said, "I'm going to listen."

Mickey Rourke got the part. As a result, he also got his Screen Actors Guild card. The rest is history.

JOHN STAMOS, TEEN IDOL

———— ☆ ————

By Marvin Paige
Casting Director

During the nine and a half years I cast "General Hospital," we were constantly looking for interesting new talent with star potential. One such instance was when we needed to find a young actor to develop into a *teen idol*. After a long search, I found a young, then unknown eighteen-year-old named John Stamos. For his lack of experience, he gave a very intelligent reading and had tremendous appeal.

John had previously done some minor commercials and plays and was in his high school band. I called in the head writer, Norma Monty, to see him. John ran through some more scenes and they decided to take a chance. He was only on the show for two weeks when the mail started to pour in and all the other soaps were trying to steal him. I recommended that "General Hospital" put him under contract immediately, which they did. The character of Blackie became one of the most popular on the show and John did become a teen idol. He eventually went on to become the popular star of the TV series "Full House."

ALFRE WOODARD—YOU CAN'T JUDGE AN ACTRESS BY HER "COVER"

By Robert B. Radnitz
Producer

One evening during the period that director Marty Ritt and I were casting *Cross Creek*—the autobiography of Marjorie Kinnan Rawlings, who also wrote *The Yearling*—I went down to the Mark Taper to see a play entitled *For Colored Girls Who Have Considered Suicide When the Rainbow Is Enuf.* I was struck by a young actress, Alfre Woodard. I turned to my companion and said, "She's the perfect girl to play Geechee in *Cross Creek.*" The following morning I had breakfast with Marty and said to him, "I think I've found our Geechee."

Alfre came in to read for us, and we were totally wiped out. She read with Mary Steenburgen—who played Marjorie Kinnan Rawlings in the film—and with Peter Coyote and Rip Torn, who were other major characters. I think all of us were floored by Alfre's performance. I am frequently told, "You like to cast people on the actual location." I do. I like the indigenous quality they bring. With *Cross Creek*, some were sure I found Alfre in the swamps of Florida. "Not exactly," I replied. "Alfre graduated from Brown University, where she studied acting." What particularly stands out in my mind about Alfre, and still does, is that she has a quality wherein, if you took thirty disparate people and put them in a room, by the end of the evening—with Alfre's persona—they'd all love each other . . . a very rare gift.

The greatness of Alfre is an ability to bring to her roles something that is innately hers—and at the same time lose herself in her performance. I have enormous respect for her as an actress and a human being. When *Cross Creek* was released, Alfre's performance was lauded and she was nominated for an Academy Award.

ANDY GRIFFITH DISCOVERS JIM NABORS

By Sheldon Leonard
Producer

There was a nightclub that specialized in giving people the opportunity to stand up on stage and show what they could do. Andy Griffith had been there and had seen this young man who had a gorgeous voice—inconsistent with his country appearance. Andy suggested I go and see him, which I did. We were so very much impressed with him we decided to build a character for him into "The Andy Griffith Show." We called the character Gomer Pyle. And Gomer Pyle became such a success that eventually he wound up with a show of his own.

DEMI MOORE AND JANINE TURNER SOAP UP

By Marvin Paige
Casting Director

We were looking for a couple of new characters on "General Hospital" to replace the Genie Francis character of Laura. Agent Edgar Small brought in Demi Moore, then an unknown actress. My producer, Gloria Monty, met with them and then brought me into the room. Here was this wonderfully interesting girl with this husky voice. She hadn't done very much, except for a horror film, but we decided to take a chance and put her under contract.

Demi played a character called Jackie Templeton, and she was marvelous. Now, we needed another actress to play her sister, another new character named Laura. One particular actress gave a very impressive reading, and so I took her to meet Gloria Monty. Because we didn't make the decision right away, this actress decided to go back to Texas to be with her family. When I got the call from the producer saying, "Let's go with her," I suddenly remembered she was at the airport about to take off on a plane! I picked up the phone and tracked her down at the airport just in time. She came back to play the role of Laura. Her name . . . Janine Turner, who, of course, is one of the stars of the television show "Northern Exposure."

Janine Turner was on "General Hospital" for a couple of years and did such a great job she received Emmy nominations. It's very rewarding when we help young actors get started and they later become superstars.

CHUCK McCANN
The Heart Is a Lonely Hunter

———— ☆ ————

By Joel Freeman
Producer

When I was asked to become involved in *The Heart Is a Lonely Hunter*, the only actor that had been cast was Alan Arkin. We had to find someone to play opposite him—the character of Antonapolis. Alan Arkin's son had seen a clown on television and brought him to our attention. So Robert Ellis Miller and I went up to the William Morris office in New York and they ran some footage for us of this actor who played this clown on television. His name was Chuck McCann. He had never done a feature film. The qualities that we saw in him were many. We knew he could play a mute magnificently, because he mimed very well, and that was the key. He was stocky and seemed sympathetic, much like a child, which is what we were looking for . . . kind of immature. And he had this great aura of humor about him. It was good casting and an experience I will never forget.

THE DONKEY THAT CAME BETWEEN ALLEN AND ROSSI!

———— ☆ ————

By Marty Allen
Actor/Comedian

I split up the very successful act of Marty Allen and Steve Rossi, after playing with my partner in every major nightclub and appearing on every television show—forty appearances with Ed Sullivan, including the first show with the Beatles when they arrived in America! Why? I wanted to diversify my talents, which included acting. I was called in to audition for a lead role in "The Big Valley." The executive producers had seen me in Las Vegas. The producer looked at my Don King hairstyle and asked me if I would cut my hair. I said, "I'd shave it and sleep with the donkey in the show if I got the part!" On the set, Linda Evans dazzled me with her kindness and beauty. But the real thrill was Barbara Stanwyck telling me to pursue more acting. "You're a helluva good actor, Marty. And you're doing a great job on this show!" I must say it was my first time out of the box and it was a great thrill.

In case *The National Enquirer* wants to know, I did sleep with the donkey!

SALLY STRUTHERS PLAYS FACE

By Dennis Doty
Producer

In the late 1960s I was the programming executive at ABC handling variety shows like "The Hollywood Palace" and "The Lawrence Welk Show"—when variety used to be a business. One day one of my colleagues buzzed me on the intercom and said, "I have a young girl in my office I'd like you to meet." I said, "Is this a worthwhile thing?" He said, "Yes, she's really unique." He brought her over and said, "Go ahead and do for Dennis what you did for me in my office." She said, "I can play my face." She proceeded to slap her face and move her lips and it sounded like a percussion section playing several songs. It was extraordinary. I'd never seen anything so unique. I asked what else she did and she said, "I can sing, act, everything." At the time we were doing "The Summer Brothers Smothers Show," so we decided to talk to the producers and told them we'd met this girl who was so perky and cute and plays her face . . . we thought she'd be good as a regular on the show. Her name was Sally Struthers. She did become a regular on the show and later went on to a real career starring in "All in the Family"—where she didn't have to play her face. A star was born!

DON'T MAKE ME LAUGH, JACKIE MASON

By Steve Allen
Actor/Author/Composer/Personality

On our old Sunday night NBC comedy show we held regular auditions, because I've always tried to give new and therefore unknown entertainers an opportunity to get their foot into the television door.

In one instance an unknown young comic named Jackie Mason struck me as so funny that after he had done only about sixty seconds of his proposed monologue I stood up and said, "You don't have to do anymore; you're hired."

"What's wrong?" he said, apparently not understanding my point.

"You're terrific," I said. "And if I hear the jokes now I'll be less likely to laugh at them when you're on the show."

ROBERT HAYS, BEFORE HE FLEW IN *AIRPLANE*

By Eddie Foy III
Casting Director

A very good friend of mine, Don Kennedy, said, "When you come down to San Diego, I want you to see an actor named Robert Hays. He's your kind of actor. He does comedy, Shakespeare," . . . he went on and on. So, I was down in San Diego casting "Harry-O" and had a long line of people reading for roles, including Robert Hays. He was not good, he was wonderful! I took him to Jerry Thorpe, the director/producer who also thought he was wonderful. So, Bobby Hays did about three or four "Harry-O"s.

I'm later doing a wonderful show called "The Young Pioneers." Pam Dixon, vice-president of casting at ABC, hired me to cast the pilot. She told me I had to find the young lead. At my first meeting with the producer, Ed Friendly (a marvelous producer), I told him, "I'm going to show you one man for a particular role." He said, "What?" I said, "I have only done this once before, but I believe you wrote this role for one person." I called San Diego and asked Bobby Hays to come up. He read for the part and was signed two days later. Robert Hays has since gone on to do feature films and television, *Airplane I* and *II*, "Angie," "Mr. Roberts," *Starman*, etc.

BOBCAT GOLDTHWAIT AND PEE WEE HERMAN . . . BEGINNINGS

———————— ☆ ————————

By Fern Champion
Casting Director

With each new movie I cast, the push is on to find fresh new talent. For *Police Academy*, I would literally spend night after night at the Comedy Store, looking for new talent. Mitzi Shore, the owner, called me at 11:30 P.M. one night and said, "I have Robin Williams." I said, "Robin is never going to do *Police Academy*." She said, "No, I have this wonderful new kid, you have to see him." We ran over to the Comedy Store, and on the stage was Bobcat Goldthwait—doing what Bobcat did. The first words out of his mouth were, "I lost my wife. I mean, I know where she is, but somebody else has her." So we called Paul Maslansky, introduced him to Bobcat . . . and the rest is history.

For the Cheech and Chong movies I used many members of the Groundlings Improv troop—including Paul Reubens who played this wonderful character, Pee Wee Herman. We ended up casting Paul as the character of Pee Wee Herman in his very first movie with Cheech and Chong.

TOM BERENGER, BRIAN DENNEHY, AND JFK

By Gil Cates
Producer

Johnny *We Hardly Knew Ye* was a movie about John F. Kennedy with a lot of good actors, including Burgess Meredith. Paul Rudd played JFK. I needed this buddy, a young guy who had returned from the service and was going to work on John F. Kennedy's congressional campaign. I hired this young man who I had seen on stage, so I knew he was a wonderful actor. But I didn't realize how much the camera liked him until we shot the first scene he was in and I looked through the camera and saw him. It was an over the shoulder shot over Paul Rudd's face to this kid's face and he looked wonderful—with these great blue eyes. And I said, "You're going to be a star. You remind me of Paul Newman." It turned out to be a very, very prescient moment. The actor was Tom Berenger and he did pretty well. Also in that same movie was a young actor named Brian Dennehy. He played a union gang foreman. He was also terrific!

AN AUDIENCE WITH HARRY COHN

By Constance Towers
Musical Actress

While singing at my church in New York City, a man approached me and asked if I could put together a forty-five-minute supper club act. I was attending dramatic school at the time and said "Sure, I can do that!" So I did. With the help of a musical person, I put the material together and—wearing a borrowed French designer gown—opened at the Maisonette of the St. Regis Hotel. The head of casting and talent for Columbia Pictures, Max Arno, was there for the first show. He was very impressed with my show and made arrangements for me to go to Hollywood to meet the head of Columbia Pictures, a man named Harry Cohn. So, after my three-week engagement, I headed for Hollywood. I had been instructed to bring the French gown—I borrowed it once again.

The morning of the day I was to meet Mr. Cohn in Hollywood, I was given a makeup artist and a hair stylist and was instructed to wear the French gown. Mr. Arno specified he wanted me to look "exactly" as he had seen me at the St. Regis. The dress was tight fitting, and required little, if anything, underneath. As I walked into the inner sanctum of Harry Cohn's vast office, my beautiful dress got caught in the doorframe. As I continued to walk, I could hear something rip. Trouper that I was, I knew the interview must go on, though I had no idea how bad the damage was to my dress.

When I approached Harry Cohn he said, "Towers, sit down." (He referred to everyone by their last name.) I said, "No thank you, sir, what I have to say I can say standing up." He asked me some questions and, head held high, I answered. After a short interview, Cohn turned to Max and said, "Arno, we don't have to test this girl, she's smart, sign her up!" As I slowly backed out of the office, I heard Max Arno ask, "Why do you think she is smart?" Harry Cohn replied, "Did you see how she responded to me? She looked me in the eye, she didn't sit down in my presence, and she knew enough not to turn her back on me!"

So there I was with a four-year contract and no screen test—head held high, I walked tall, and a dozen people watched my backside as I left the building.

HARRY HAMLIN REMEMBERS A PROMISE

———— ☆ ————

By Melissa Skoff
Casting Director

The "discovery" story closest to my heart happened way back when I was an assistant at Warner Bros. casting. I was working with Dianne Crittenden, who was away on a much-deserved, long overdue holiday. One morning I received a call from her old friend, Stanley Donen, who was about to direct a film called *Movie, Movie.* Stanley needed a favor. I offered to help. He needed an actor to test with several young ingenues for the lead in his film. He promised to pay the reader twenty-five dollars, and he would shoot an angle on him to give him a piece of film, but I was to emphasize to the actor that he was not in any way, shape, or form being considered for any role in the film.

I jumped in and told Stanley that I had the answer to his problem. A new young actor had just landed in L.A., fresh out of A.C.T. in San Francisco. He was unquestionably talented and we had extremely high hopes for him. I said, "His name is Harry Hamlin, and I'm sure he'd be thrilled to help you out. He hasn't done anything yet, in fact he's not even in the Screen Actors Guild. Let me send him over." Stanley thanked me and I called Harry.

The next day I received an ecstatic call from Stanley thanking me for Harry. He was exactly what the film needed, and he ended up with the young male lead opposite George C. Scott. Harry was so excited, he told me some day he would buy me a horse! But that's far from the end of the story. The really neat part comes next.

It's now about six years later. I was working at my office at Warner Bros. where I now had an independent casting deal. Out of the blue, I received a call from Harry. Harry was now working pretty steadily, though this was before he was hired on "L.A. Law." He was calling to fulfill the promise he'd made to me the day I helped get him started. I am a serious equestrian, and my dream was to one day own a dappled gray thoroughbred hunter.

I was delighted to hear from him. Although we had remained friends, we hadn't spoken in years. Harry, with a smile in his voice, said that although he wasn't rich and famous yet, he was now in a position to buy me the horse! Needless to say, I was flabbergasted. As my heart skipped a beat, I said, "No, Harry, you're not buying me the horse. But the fact that you called and wanted to means more than I can ever say." He didn't want to take "no" for an answer. He emphatically told me that he was indeed buying me the horse. It was a promise he made and intended to keep. But I declined the offer. And I was deeply touched.

The next time I bumped into Harry was in a sushi bar one night about five years after that. We saw each other across the room, and rushed to give each other a big hug. Instantly, Harry whispered in my ear, "You know, I still owe you a dappled gray hunter. Let me get one for you now." I had major goose bumps. Again I declined, already owning two horses. But I will always cherish Harry's intention. And we're still great friends. I think we have a lifelong bond. And that maybe happens once in about a billion times. So, Harry, when you win the Oscar, then you can buy me the horse and we'll call him Oscar!

"When you're right for the part, you're right for the part, unless someone thinks you're not.
And your entire future in the business may depend on who that person might be."

—Jennie Louise Frankel

Before They Were Stars

They've waited tables, shined shoes, delivered pizza, taught tennis, typed scripts, hammered nails . . . and won Academy Awards.

WE KNEW THEM WHEN

☆

By Gary Owens
Hall of Fame Broadcaster and Actor

In Hollywood, no one just starts out being a star. Among the great luminaries of "Laugh-In," here are a few beginnings: before Lily Tomlin got into television, she was a waitress at a Howard Johnson's restaurant in Detroit. Ruth Buzzi worked at Ontra Cafeteria on Vine Street in Hollywood. Among her customers were the world-famous philosophers Will and Ariel Durant. Other beginnings . . . Henry Gibson was a roommate of actor Jon Voight while working in New York—Henry would sleep in the bathtub and Jon would sleep on the sofa of the small one-room apartment (because Jon is six feet three inches and Henry is not)! Arte Johnson worked at Carroll and Company, the men's clothing store in Beverly Hills. Harry Nilsson, the great singer and composer, was a computer operator at a bank in the San Fernando Valley, as was the Unknown Comic, Murray Langston.

Steve Martin was working at the Magic Store at Disneyland when I first met him. I first met Sylvester Stallone at Travellini's restaurant, where he was parking cars after coming to the West Coast from New York. David Hasselhoff was parking autos at Gene Autry's Hotel Continental in L.A.

Everybody must get his start somewhere. And in Hollywood most performers, while they grow with their craft, need outside income. While toiling in radio, TV, and journalism, I also worked all night at a talcum powder ranch in Barstow and as a grizzly bear named Heimlicher at the Los Angeles Zoo.

HARRISON FORD, A STAR
WAITING TO SHINE

By Jeremy Kagan
Producer/Director/Writer

When casting the movie *Heroes*, we were looking for a friend for the character that Henry Winkler was playing, who was crossing the country looking for his old buddies, a group of guys who had been together in Vietnam. We were fortunate to get Sally Field to play the female lead. So this third lead was not as important to the studio.

One actor comes in and he's very sullen and shy . . . noncommunicative, but there's something honest and touching about him. He's very masculine without being overly aggressive, very appealing. He was very good. I brought him in for two more readings and he wasn't as good these times—the common problem of second readings. Now that there's a chance to get the part the actor gets anxious. Despite this I decided to go with him. His name was Harrison Ford.

Harrison Ford had been an actor for years and had not clicked. He was paying bills as a fine carpenter. He was seriously doubting whether a career would actually happen for him in town. He had already done *Star Wars* but it hadn't been released yet and he had no idea of its potential. I had enormous admiration for George Lucas from *American Graffiti* and I just knew he was a great filmmaker and that whatever he did was going to be successful.

I remember, there was this big scene in *Heroes*, where Harrison Ford's character was supposed to race a car he built, but he's too afraid to do it. So Henry Winkler's character races the car instead. We were filming in the town of Petaluma, California, and people were asked to come on down and watch the filming so we could have a crowd in the stands. Henry Winkler was the "Fonz" at the time and about two thousand kids showed up. It rained that day and everybody was soaking wet. I said to Henry Winkler and Sally Field, "Because of the rain, we won't be shooting, but why don't you guys thank the crowd for coming." Both Henry and Sally spoke to the kids. Huddled in the corner, soaking wet, was Harrison. I looked at him and said, "You know, some day, that crowd's going to be for you." And he shook his head and said, "Not me, it isn't going to happen to me."

Star Wars went on to become one of the biggest grossing movies of its time. And Harrison Ford went on to become a superstar.

ROBIN WILLIAMS—
FOUR FOR THE PRICE OF ONE

———— ☆ ————

By Michael Economou
Producer

In 1978 I was associate producer on a two-hour movie called *Top Secret*, starring Bill Cosby. During post production it became necessary, as usual, to do some looping (or dubbing, as it is commonly known) of extra lines for some minor Italian actors. The night before the looping session I had gone to an improvisation show somewhere in Hollywood (I believe it was called Off the Wall) and was very impressed by a uniquely funny young actor. I mean, he was demonic! He had no agent, so I asked him personally to come and do some looping work. He was very thankful, and the next day he showed up promptly at the looping stage. Cosby was almost done with his lines when we came upon a scene in which Bill was talking while four Italian bad guys were arguing in the background. Since their voices were recorded very muffled, we decided to re-voice the Italians. I would take the first one, my assistant would take the second one, the producer the third, and the young actor would try his luck with the fourth. As we prepared to record, the actor suddenly said, "Why don't I do all four voices?" Patiently, I tried to explain to him about the necessity for different voices, multiple takes to be laid over each other, overlaps, etc. "Let me try it," pressed the actor.

I will never forget Bill Cosby's face as he watched the young man tear into all four Italian characters, at the same time, in one take!!! Yes, it was Robin Williams.

RICHARD GERE AND OTHER "UNKNOWNS" AUDITION

———— ☆ ————

By Barbara Claman
Casting Director

In 1975 in New York City, I was casting a movie called *Days of Heaven*, a magnificent movie that would win critical acclaim. I was hired to do the New York side of casting. Since our director, Terrence Malick, lived in Los Angeles, I was to audition the actors, read with them, and put them on tape. We did have the producers with us—they were "going for the gold."

I can remember that week filled with relatively unknown New York stage actors streaming in one by one to read and to be put on tape and hopefully to get lead roles. Here are a few of those we got on tape:

CHRISTOPHER WALKEN—SIGOURNEY WEAVER
WILLIAM HURT—BEVERLY D'ANGELO
KEVIN KLINE—MERYL STREEP
CAROL KANE—RICHARD GERE (GOT THE JOB)
JOHN LITHGOW—SAM WATERSTON
BLAIR BROWN—JOHN GLOVER
JOHN HEARD—BERNADETTE PETERS
MARY BETH HURT—MANDY PATINKIN
CHRISTINE LAHTI—JILL EIKENBERRY
DAVID DUKES . . .

Where are these *unknowns* today? I don't think there has ever been such a concentration of extraordinary talent than the mid-seventies in New York City. And I don't know if there ever will be again!

Richard Gere had been doing a lot of off Broadway and Broadway and even Shakespeare. He came in and I put him on tape and, believe me, they did not jump up and down when they first saw him. They caught the star *quality*, but they found Richard Gere's dark quality—they didn't find his light quality. Believe it or not, they wanted John Travolta. Yes, what they were trying to do was keep the lead character with a light quality, which of course John Travolta had. But he wouldn't do it . . . I had a major fight to get them to pick Richard Gere. And finally, after a lot of arguing and wrangling back and forth, they chose him—and the rest of Richard Gere's work is history. *Days of Heaven* is a magnificent film.

The Stars Who Got Away

Some blame the studio and some blame themselves. But they still tell the story, at times with a tear in their eye, about the stars who got away . . .

STEVE MARTIN'S REVENGE!

———— ☆ ————

By Bob Finkel
Producer / Director

To my mind, this up-and-coming unknown comedian was marvelous! When I caught his act, I thought he was terrific. So I took a chance and booked him on a show I was working on at the time called *Command Performance*. During rehearsals, the agency happened to see this performer rehearsing enthusiastically backstage. To my surprise and embarrassment, these fellas came to me and said, "Get rid of this guy. He's the worst thing we've ever seen. He's crazy. Who puts an arrow in his head? It's just NOT FUNNY! . . . Get rid of him!!" . . . Reluctantly, I had to let him go. . . . He ended up being, well, Steve Martin. Now, every time I see Steve, to this day, he doesn't fail to remember it . . . nicely.

"A genuine talent finds its way."

—Goethe

DUSTIN HOFFMAN
Mumbles Himself Out of
the Wrong Job

By Eddie Foy III
Casting Director

I had just been promoted from casting director to director in charge of new talent at Screen Gems. Our new vice-president in charge of production was Jackie Cooper, who one day called and said, "I'd like to send somebody down to meet with you—I've got a hunch this guy may have something."

So this young, not very attractive man came into my office. Now keep in mind we are in television, where likability is a must. I said, "Hi, I'm Eddie Foy." He said, "Hi . . . mumble, mumble, mumble." I said, "What?" He said, "Hi, how are you?" I asked, "What are you doing out here?" He said, "I came out to mumble, mumble, mumble . . ." I asked, "Well, how long are you going to be here?" "Well, I hope to leave . . . mumble, mumble, mumble." I said, "You really don't like it out here in California, do you?" He said, "Well, no I don't . . . mumble, mumble, mumble." I said, "Can you tell me a little bit about your background?" He said, "I study . . . mumble, study, mumble, study . . ." I was literally straining across the desk to hear what he was saying. I thought, *Cooper is out of his mind. First of all this man can't speak. And when he does you can't understand him.*

So I said, "Why don't you go back upstairs and see Mr. Cooper." He said, "Thank you very much." And he put his hand out and kind of shook my hand like a fish. Two minutes later, Jackie Cooper called and said, "What do you think?" And I said, "I think Dustin Hoffman is the dullest man I've ever met." We didn't sign him and here he is one of the ten great movie stars of all time.

I HOPE I DIDN'T HURT
BILL MURRAY'S CAREER

By Charlie Hauck
Writer/Producer/Author

In 1973, when I was producing a variety special on health care for public television station WQED in Pittsburgh, I decided to hire several members of the Second City improv troop in Chicago to perform in the various sketches. There were six members of the group, but I only had a budget for five. I'd seen them perform, and I made my choices based on that. The company manager pleaded with me not to leave that one poor soul behind, but I simply didn't have enough money. The performers I brought to Pittsburgh included John Candy, Andrea Martin, Betty Thomas (later on "Hill Street Blues"), and David Rasche (who became "Sledgehammer").

The young man who didn't make it? Bill Murray. I hope I didn't hurt his career.

WESLEY SNIPES

By Pat Golden
Director

Gina Belafonte asked us to see her friend from college for a leading role. He was very intense, deeply handsome, and his reading was impressive. But the producers did not want to take a chance on a first-timer in this particular role. Oops! This first-timer was Wesley Snipes.

MERYL STREEP, BEVERLY D'ANGELO, ANDREA MARCOVICCI, AND MARY BETH HURT
The Executives Stand Corrected

By Jeremy Kagan
Producer/Director/Writer

When Universal had offices in New York, there was a remarkable casting director named Eleanor Kilgallen, who was Dorothy Kilgallen's sister. Eleanor went to every single theater that was in the city, on, off, off off, and miles away from Broadway. So she knew every actor from the stage. We were casting for my first feature, *Heroes*. Henry Winkler had the lead. We were looking for the "girl" in the picture. Eleanor said, "I'm going to bring you six women who have never been in any movie before, but I think they're terrific." Now I was into new technology and I had this rather heavy video camera that was attached by a wire to a very giant box that had a reel-to-reel tape. I decided to tape these new actresses and show this to the executives at Universal Studios in Los Angeles.

Among this group of unknowns were: Meryl Streep, Beverly D'Angelo, Andrea Marcovicci, and Mary Beth Hurt. We were excited, particularly about this blonde actress, Meryl Streep. She gave a great reading, but she had a real attitude about not wanting to be in the movies. At the time, she was doing Shakespeare for Joseph Papp in Central Park.

Back at Universal, the executives viewed the tapes and said, "Forget it! None of these girls are movie stars." And they were not going to take the chance on trying an unknown. Even with Henry as their star they wanted to have another well-known female lead. Sally Field was suggested and she came in to my surprise for a casting session. At the time, her career was not as successful as it was to become in films, so she was willing to put herself in the actor-on-interview position. She gave a great reading, she got the part, and she was terrific!

I still have the reel-to-reel of Meryl Streep's first casting tape!

CAROL BURNETT DIDN'T NEED PERRY COMO!

By Bob Finkel
Producer/Director

When I was producing "The Perry Como Show," an agent called me to interview a young lady who he thought would be a major star. I never would turn down agents who were kind to me in other areas. I made an appointment with a gangly, skinny, and then not-too-good-looking—now, very handsome I think—lady. She did a piece in my office that has since become famous for her. She was Carol Burnett. I said, "Carol, it's a wonderful piece, but I don't think it's for 'The Perry Como Show' I'm sorry, maybe some other time." Looks like Carol Burnett's agent proved to be right. She did become a major star!

TRACI LORDS UNDERCOVER

By Brad Waisbren
Producer

Over the years I've earned a reputation for discovering talent. Some of the people whose careers I've been involved with have gone on to become major stars in their own right. Normally, when I am searching for new talent, I frequent comedy clubs and actors' workshops. A director asked me to find the female lead for his low-budget picture—a young actress who would work nonunion, for next to no money, partially nude. In order to work within these limited parameters, I decided to investigate actresses in the adult film industry. I immersed myself in the search, and conducted an exhaustive and careful review of numerous, revealing videotapes. A literal bevy of young, beautiful ladies, who had no qualms about exposing their basic attributes, graced my television screen from morning until night . . . well somebody had to do it.

After my intensive and tireless research it became clear that only one actress stood out from the rest. She had an attractive face and an alluring figure, with a natural acting ability and obvious comfort in front of the camera—clothed and otherwise. Perfect! We called her in.

Traci Lords came in and introduced herself as Kristy Nussman. What impressed me most about her was her cute, sweet, girl-next-door quality. She was a bit nervous and insecure, because she really wanted the part. However, her reading was quite nice. The producers gave her serious consideration, but ultimately passed. They were concerned that her porno background would have a negative impact on the production. Notwithstanding the producers' opinion, I felt she would be an excellent choice. I also felt badly for Traci, because I knew deep down she had the talent to make it in the arena of mainstream films.

The most interesting part of this experience occurred when I walked Traci out of the building. She was on her way to Las Vegas for a personal appearance at a video convention. I expressed surprise when I saw a waiting limousine and commented that her travel arrangements did not lack style. With a wink in her eye, she twirled her flowing coat over her shoulder and said, with mock vanity and a subtle smirk, "After all, I'm Traci Lords." As she drove off, I was reminded of the Norma Jean/Marilyn Monroe dichotomy. The producers had just seen Norma Jean audition, but I was watching Marilyn Monroe being whisked off to a press conference. In time, my hunch was proven correct. Traci Lords has since done quite nicely in mainstream films and television, most recently starring in "Melrose Place."

RECOGNIZING ANNETTE BENING'S MAGIC

By Pat Golden
Director

I campaigned long and hard, but ultimately was unsuccessful in casting Annette Bening in *The Handmaid's Tale*. I'd seen Ms. Bening on stage in New York in what can only be described as riveting performances. I thought that, opposite the truly gifted Faye Dunaway, she would ignite the screen. But it was not to be. Annette Bening went on to become a major star.

FAYE DUNAWAY, RICHARD CHAMBERLAIN, AND ROBERT REDFORD
Who Can Say?

by Sam Manners
Producer

When we tested Robert Redford for "Route 66," we didn't think he was right. He was totally inexperienced. We tested Richard Chamberlain and felt the same way. Who can say? Both gentlemen have done very well. Robert Redford kids me to this day. Last time I saw him at Twentieth Century-Fox he said, "Sam you didn't think I was going to do it!"

In 1965 Herbert B. Leonard and I saw an off-Broadway performance featuring a little-known actress by the name of Faye Dunaway. We decided to bring her to California and test her at my Woodland Hills home—because it was six thousand square feet, and had the electricity to handle the camera and lights. Faye was extremely attractive, very sexy, and very talented. We didn't like the way the screen test turned out—which could also have been our fault.

I did have a second chance to work with Faye Dunaway and Richard Chamberlain in "Casanova," a four-hour mini-series with the Frank Konigsberg Company, shot in Spain and Venice, Italy. Faye was of course sensational, as was Richard. On the set, we didn't talk about the test Faye did in my home over thirty years prior. . . . I don't know if Faye even remembers the screen test she shot in our master bedroom, but my wife certainly does. After the film crew packed up the lights and camera my wife made a declaration she has adhered to for over thirty years. She looked at me and said, "Never again will I allow a motion picture company to come into my house."

MARILYN MONROE
River of No Return

By Stanley Rubin
Producer

The year was 1948. With my partners, playwright Lou Lantz and director Sobey Martin, I was producing the very first series on film for national television. "Your Show Time" consisted of half-hour dramatizations of "the world's greatest short stories." The network was NBC, the sponsor was the American Tobacco Company, and the budget and schedule called for us to shoot two half-hours a week. I mention this because it put great pressure on all of us—and that pressure is the only excuse I have for what happened. . . .

One of our film editors asked me to audition a friend of his for a small role in the next production. The friend was a young actress he described as pretty, talented, and sorely in need of work.

As a favor to the editor, I met with this young lady. She was more than pretty, she was a knockout, and a charming mixture of sensuality and vulnerability. And though she came in for just a tiny role in a Robert Louis Stevenson story, I turned her down. Our schedule allowed us only two and a half days to shoot each episode. The pressure, as I mentioned, was terrific. I felt I couldn't gamble on a newcomer. Dissolve to:

Now the year was 1950. The success of a low-budget film I produced for RKO called *The Narrow Margin* earned me a bigger deal at Twentieth Century-Fox. Very soon I was working with my former partner Lou Lantz on his concept for a large-scale western to be called *The River of No Return*. The script turned out well, and *River* became one of the first productions scheduled to be shot in the new, expensive wide-screen process dubbed Cinemascope.

I was delighted when Robert Mitchum signed on to star. Now I needed a young actress to play opposite him as the saloon girl—someone both sensual and vulnerable. It was a key role. Suddenly it struck me that I knew the perfect actress. I put the idea to the then head of 20th (the redoubtable Darryl F. Zanuck), got his blessing, and the deal was made.

The young lady we signed to co-star with Mitchum in *River of No Return* was the same young lady I had turned down for a bit part in my TV series less than two years earlier. In that brief period, she had become one of the hottest actresses in Hollywood. Her name was Marilyn Monroe.

By the way, the 1948–49 television series—even without Marilyn—won the first Emmy ever awarded.

RONALD REAGAN GETS THE LAST LAUGH!

By Bob Finkel
Producer/Director

I did a fifteen-minute show some years ago called "The Orchid Awards Show"—an MCA-packaged program. And the gimmick on the show was the host would give an orchid to the performer of the week—to Dinah Shore, Vic Damone, whomever. The host for the first show was very, very bad (although he was a successful spokesman for General Electric). I called MCA and asked them if we could find somebody else and they said we could. The gentleman we let go, Ronald Reagan, went on to eventually become the president of the United States. Dissolve to:

Years later I directed a play that was brought to the Kennedy Center in Washington. President Ronald Reagan and his wife Nancy came to see the play and they gave us a reception afterward. Dissolve to:

I'm at Pierre Cossette's Super Bowl Party at Chasen's Restaurant. It's the event of the season. Every celebrity goes as Pierre's guest and we go into the kitchen and make our own hot dogs, etc. It was a marvelous afternoon.

At that time I had a beautiful Rolls Royce. All of the celebrities were coming out of the restaurant and my car is there already. Don Rickles says, "Hey, Finkel, you paid somebody to have your car here?" Banter back and forth. I get into the car and it won't turn over. It's dead. The street is backed up because I can't start my car. The workers at the hotel pull up with a junker and hook up the battery cables, and they're talking a blue streak. I can't get the car started.

Eventually, two men in blue suits come up to me and say, "Get this car out of here, now! The President is coming!" I'm pushing the Rolls up Beverly and Ronald Reagan pulls up to Chasen's. He looks at me and says, "Hey, Finkel, isn't this a Hollywood story? One day you're directing at the Kennedy Center, and the next day you're parking cars!"

"What actors need is a limitless horizon."

—Stanislavski

CHAPTER 2

CHUTZPAH!

☆

"I never took 'no' for an answer.
I had the stamina of a steamroller.
I'd walk into the reading with a big cigar and
I'd talk myself into getting the role.
With each play I did, the part was bigger
and the money got better!"

—JESSE WHITE
Actor, "Maytag Repairman"

Believing in Yourself

Take a good look around. Successful stars who have made it had an undying belief in themselves. And if they didn't, they had someone who had an undying belief in them. But without exception . . . somebody believed!

STALLONE'S *ROCKY* ROAD TO SUCCESS!

———— ☆ ————

By Renée Valente
Producer

I was vice-president in charge of talent at Screen Gems in Hollywood, and this tough kid from Brooklyn, New York, comes into my office, looking like a weight lifter, saying "dees, dems, and dose." He had just finished a film . . . *The Lords of Flatbush*. He sat down and said, "I want to be a star." I said, "Well, you have to decide if you want to be a leading man or a character actor. If you want to be a star you really have to go to a voice coach and lose your Brooklynese. Also work on losing that muscle-bound look. I think if you have patience and work at it—it certainly can work." What I was really saying is, "You're a kid from Brooklyn and you sound it and that's tough going in Hollywood." Can you guess who that actor was? Sylvester Stallone.

He was smart, he wrote the perfect role for himself in *Rocky*. He wouldn't allow anybody to option it unless he starred in it. And I give him all the credit in the world. He didn't have any money. He didn't know anyone in L.A. He couldn't get a job, but wouldn't sell his script unless he starred in the film. He wrote what he knew would make him a star. I think that's tremendous!

DEBRA WINGER DIDN'T STARVE

☆

By Beverly Hecht
Commercial Talent Agent

Debra Winger was only eighteen years old when she came to me. A client of mine said, "I have a friend who's an actress and I wish you'd see her." I said, "What's she like?" He said, "I think you'll like her, she has your voice and your personality." I said, "Great, I'll sign her!" He brought her around and there was something really wonderful about her. She was very straightforward and she knew what she wanted. I signed her.

When Debra got a role on "Wonder Woman," they wanted to star her in a spinoff called "Wonder Girl." Debra didn't want to tie herself up and be connected with a series. I said, "That's ridiculous! There are always options and you can get out of something if you don't like it." And she said, "I don't want to do it." So I asked, "What do you want to do?" And she said, "I want to do film." My famous words to her were, "Okay, do film and you'll starve." See how she's starving? She's one of the top actresses in the world today. . . . I was at her marriage to Timothy Hutton, where she introduced me to everyone and said, "This is my first agent." And I said, "I wish I were your last."

BURT REYNOLDS TAKES OFF

———— ☆ ————

By Renée Valente
Producer

Burt Reynolds was leaving Los Angeles. He was going to New York. He was giving up Hollywood. He had just come off of "Gunsmoke," in which he played Quint the blacksmith and couldn't get another job. He was on his way to Jupiter, Florida, to become the deputy sheriff—his father was the sheriff. Jane Oliver, who used to handle Burt, knew that I was preparing a new television pilot titled "Hawk." She called and said, "Renee, if you would just meet him—I don't think he wants to act anymore, but if you love him, it might work."

So I made a date for Burt to come to the office. ABC really wanted David Carradine to star as Hawk, a character of Indian heritage. Anyway, Burt comes up to my office to see me. He really looked like Marlon Brando, weighing about 220 pounds. He's sitting in my office and I was on a very important call. He was getting very restless and angry. I put my hand over the mouthpiece and said, "Listen, you wanted to see me! Now just relax." I get off the phone and say, "You really are an angry young man!" And we started to talk. I began to see through the pudge on his face that he could be an attractive young man. I said, "I'd love to put you on film, but you'd really have to lose some weight. You're a little pudgy. Can you hang around for a couple of weeks and lose some weight?" He said, "I would love to, but I don't have a place to stay and I don't have any money."

I called my husband and said, "I met an actor who I really think could be the star of this show, he has no money and no place to say. Can I bring him home? I just have a feeling about him?" He said, "Sure." So I took Burt home. We lived in Connecticut at the time, and I put him on a diet of Bloody Marys, steak, and tomatoes. We used to have fun playing a game, giving titles of pictures, and responding with actors who starred, etc., etc.

In the interim, Screen Gems didn't want Burt Reynolds, neither did ABC. Now I'm in trouble because I have Burt at my house losing weight, and nobody wants him. I said to Jackie Cooper, who was head of Screen Gems at the time, "Jackie, I believe in this guy. Please, please, let me do a personality test on film." Well, they didn't want to come up with the $3,000, but finally did. Burt lost about twenty-five pounds and he looked smashing.

Burt knows how important this test is going to be. I rent a stage in New York, the camera is rolling, I'm asking him questions and he's standing there with his head down. I said, "Hi, Burt, this is going to be seen by people at the network and they'd like to know a little bit about you." No response, his head is still down. I keep asking him questions. No response. I tell the cameraman, "Look, when I call 'cut', keep rolling," and he did. I walk over to a ladder in the studio and climb it, knowing he's going to wonder what in the world I was doing. From the top rung I said, "For $4 million, name two William Lundigan movies." Well, nobody could answer that question and we broke up, laughing. Then, Burt realized we were filming. At the time Tom Moore was head of ABC, and he said that Burt wasn't right for something else they were doing, I believe it was "Summer and Smoke." Gratefully, Burt looked into the camera and said, "I really wanted to do 'Summer and Smoke'—I was right for that and I'm right for this!"

Then, of course, everybody saw the test and Burt Reynolds became Hawk and the rest is history.

P.S.: Over the years, Burt has called to ask me to do projects with him, and I was always under contract to one studio or another. About two years ago he said, "C'mon, it's time, let's work together." We've done two films together: The Man Upstairs *with Katharine Hepburn and Ryan O'Neal, and* Man from Left Field, *which Burt starred in. It's awfully nice to know that the word* loyalty *is still alive and well . . . sometimes.*

PHYLLIS DILLER—
THE ILL WIND THAT BLEW STARDOM!

By Phyllis Diller
Comedienne

I never had the classic problem with a casting couch that beautiful young things have because, when I started in the business, I was into forty and ugly. So I never had the casting couch problem. And by the time I got my face all prettied up, I was really too old.

In the beginning, when I was completely unknown, times were very difficult. I was truly a homeless person. You don't have to be on the bottom rung of society to be homeless. Our home had been sold and we were simply living out of a bag in New York in a rotten place that cost sixty dollars a week—and that included the roaches. I was booked by one of the large agencies into the Fontainebleu Hotel in Miami. It was during the days when they had just the top people, Frank Sinatra, Dean Martin, and Jerry Lewis! My happiness was short-lived when, after the first show, I was fired by the owner of the hotel. He didn't see the second show. By then I had all the bugs worked out and I was sensational! However, rather than work one week as I was originally booked, I worked just two shows and went back to New York.

Now here is the ill wind that blew some good. Jack Paar had just discovered me and thought I was simply sensational. The fact that I was in New York and available—Jack Paar had me on "The Tonight Show" constantly. The shows were so great they became reruns. And that is what made my name finally worth money! Ha ha ha! . . . And what happened to the man who fired me? That old (BLEEP), he's dead now! And I plan to outlive anyone who has done me wrong! Ha, ha, ha!

JOHN TRAVOLTA
WELCOMES BACK KOTTER

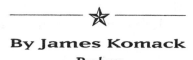

By James Komack
Producer

John Travolta was the third understudy in *Grease*. He came in to read for the part of Barberino in "Welcome Back Kotter." It was very dark in the room at the time and he said, "I'd like to read." I said, "You don't have to read, you've got the part." He said, "Why?" I said, "You're a terrific actor. I can see by looking at you." He had a charisma about himself. I asked if there was anyone in his family that had something to do with acting? He said, "Yes, my mother is a teacher." He kept following me around wanting to audition. I kept saying, "You don't have to audition, you've got the part."

AUDITIONING FOR LAURENCE OLIVIER

By Michael York
Actor

Peter Sellers immortalized the sadness and the savagery of that barbaric ritual known as "the audition" with his aging, forgetful actor, Warrington Minge, and his pathetic inquiry to the uncaring room of inquisitors, "Was it all right, apart from the dries?" I must confess that Minge's dusty ghost haunts the shadows of every audition room that I have attended. Fortunately there have not been too many of them although the peremptory cry of "Next!" will still occasionally awaken me from a bad dream.

I auditioned for Laurence Olivier with a Shakespeare speech, and I inwardly quaked at the temerity of using the same language in front of a man who had made so much of Shakespeare his own.

To this day, I have a souvenir of my most memorable audition. It is a much-thumbed edition of *Hamlet*. One page, in particular, is mottled with little brown spots—ancient blood stains! I had been trying out for the newly formed Youth Theater of Great Britain at that tough and tender age of sixteen. I was concentrating so hard on Hamlet's admirable advice to the players that they should "speak the speech trippingly on the tongue," that I bit nervously into my lower lip and sprayed the results onto my trembling text. "And all for nothing? For Hecuba?" For all that, and more . . . I especially cherish my incarnadined *Hamlet* because that particular audition was successful. Indeed, it opened the door to a long and passionate apprenticeship as one of the "abstracts and brief chronicles of the time," that continues even as I write.

OTTO PREMINGER, DISMISSED!

By Alan Rachins
Actor

Because my father knew some theater owners in Boston, particularly from his gin rummy playing, he arranged a meeting for me with Otto Preminger in New York. I had no credits, so obviously Otto Preminger was doing this as a favor. When the day of the meeting arrived, I walked into Mr. Preminger's huge office. And there he was, sitting behind this great marble desk. We had a very brief conversation, during which he asked me why I wanted to become an actor. I mumbled a few things and he then said, "Very nice to meet you," and was reaching for the phone. He was now on the phone as I was still standing there. I was dismissed and had to turn and walk ignominiously out of the office.

PATTY DUKE FLIES

——————— ☆ ———————

By Arthur Axelman
Producer

When actress Patty Duke signed with William Morris in the summer of 1990, it was a return to where she began her career nearly thirty years earlier as a child star. I was senior vice-president and had put together the autobiographical two-hour movie "Call Me Anna" for ABC, and my client, director Gil Cates.

Cates served as marriage broker between actress and agent during the making of the biopic. Patty and I both believed that, working together, we could facilitate her escape from the world of episodic television and she could once again front major television movies as she had so often done throughout the 1970s and early 1980s and—with the enthusiasm of a powerful agency—stir up her own series. She gave me only one cautionary note: "I don't fly and I don't read."

A few weeks into her new affiliation, a casting breakdown reveals the role of the bride's mother in the Twentieth Century-Fox theatrical adaptation of Craig Lucas' Broadway hit *Prelude to a Kiss* starring Alec Baldwin. Meg Ryan had been cast to play the bride. A call to producer Michael Gruskoff elicits his interest in Duke and desire to meet her. The meeting is a hit and the call comes from the director and casting exec who ask for "Ms. Duke to fly into New York to read." Fly and read?! The Saturday before the scheduled Sunday morning flight is a grueling multi-hour agent-to-client marathon. Duke's bottom line is, "How could I possibly spend five miserable hours without a cigarette?" I invent the notion that MGM Grand's airline allows smoking and arranges for her flight to be switched to MGM Grand. Still Duke is reluctant at this point in her life to go to such lengths for rejection. However, she agrees to make the trip and to read as a favor to me.

As she wanders down the gray Manhattan streets, searching for the address of the lower East Side building, script in hand, finding the number, opening the door, walking into the elevator, young actresses joining her, knowing looks, to her script, to her face, to each other, whispering "Even Patty Duke has to audition . . ." It doesn't help.

She reads. They are kind but very cool. Cold. Icy. Expressionless. It was all for nothing. At least I had set up a "get-to-know-your-new-agents" session with the New York staff. Maybe that will make the trek to New York valuable after all. She sits at a conference room table on the 32nd floor of the agency where she hadn't been since she was sixteen years old. Plays are being discussed, upcoming new Broadway plays, and an agent mentions the perfect role in a show that will open in April. Everyone agrees that Duke is ideal for the role. Everyone except for the newly arrived agent, who interrupts to say, "She can't do that play!" Duke only hears rejection. "Why? Too old, too short, what's the negative this time?!" "In April you'll be starting *Prelude to a Kiss*—you got the job!"

And that is how Patty Duke got her first feature in twenty-six years.

MAYTAG REPAIRMAN

By Jesse White
Actor

After looking at over one hundred actors for the part of a lonely washing machine repairman—with a basset hound look—it boiled down to my dear friend Phil Silvers and me. God was smiling on me that day. It was only for one shot. I did the one and it was successful. They asked, "Would you like to do two more?" I said, "Of course." I ended up doing it for twenty-five years; my contract just ran out. It's one of those things an actor gets once in a lifetime. . . . People say I've been lucky. I say I was in the right place at the right time. It's been a glorious ride—and, I might add, a financial pleasure.

Out on a Limb

Sometimes, to get the sweetest fruit, you have to go out on a limb . . .

ED ASNER'S DOUBLE WHAMMY

☆

By Edward Asner
Actor/Producer

My career was in a slump when I went to see Paul Mazursky and Larry Tucker for the role of Peter Seller's brother in the film *I Love You, Alice B. Toklas.* The first time I went to see them, Larry seemed eager to sign me. Paul seemed reticent. The second meeting was uncomfortable. I began to feel the role slipping from under me. The third meeting felt like a disaster. I wasn't even sure of Larry anymore. It was obvious they weren't keen to sign me.

Meanwhile, I was in the process of selling my house and buying a new, larger one. I moved into the second house, yet couldn't sell the first one. Months went by. On the last day of closing escrow on our new home, I made the trip to my agent to borrow $10,000. En route I passed a house where a film crew was in the process of shooting what at first looked like Albert Paulson and Woody Allen. When I got closer, it was Herb Edelman and Peter Sellers. I realized it was a double whammy, seeing that scene being shot while going to borrow $10,000. I would not have needed to borrow the money had I made the part. Fortunately, two years later, Mary Tyler Moore walked into my life.

ROBERT REDFORD
PUTS IT ALL ON THE LINE

By Warren Lyons
Entertainer / Producer / Teacher

In 1961 I was working as assistant casting director for New York theater producer David Merrick on six productions that were planned for the 1961–62 season. One of the plays we were doing was Norman Krasna's comedy *Sunday in New York*, which Garson Kanin was to direct at the Cort Theater on West Street. The actor in whom Kanin, Krasna, and Merrick were most interested for the leading role of Mike Mitchell was a California newcomer named Robert Redford.

After his audition for the role, I remember vividly Redford saying that he had paid for his flight from Los Angeles by selling a parcel of land he owned because he urgently wanted this role in a now-forgotten comedy. It turned out to be his first substantial chance to be seen on Broadway. His career advanced and his investment paid off!

WHEN DRESSING AS A WOMAN
Always Wear Sensible Shoes

By Glenn Shadix
Actor

I am a character actor, originally from Alabama. I came to Los Angeles in 1977, after college and a year of waiting tables in New York City. My goal was to be in the movies and, to that end, I began a ritual of working in Equity waiver *showcase* theater, hoping to attract the attention of an agent who could turn me into the sort of marketable commodity that Hollywood could accept. I played heroes and villains and clowns and demons and rednecks and fops . . . but nobody was buying. Then, in 1985, I worked with a director from New York on a Gertrude Stein play called *Dr. Faustus Lights the Lights* for the West Coast arm of the Ensemble Studio Theater. We made Miss Stein herself a central character and it was then decided I would play the part. I had long been fascinated by the life and art of Gertrude Stein and her years in Paris with her lover Alice B. Toklas. Together, in the 1920s, they created at their salon at 27 Rue de Fleur a unique gathering of artists and writers that included Picasso, Hemingway, and F. Scott Fitzgerald. Miss Stein was a large, somewhat masculine woman who had piercing blue eyes, crew cut hair, and always wore sensible shoes. In the Paris of the 1920s she was something to behold.

I was thrilled with the opportunity to portray such a dynamic and exotic personality . . . Somewhat less thrilled was my agent at the time. "What do you mean you're playing a dead lesbian writer? I've been trying to sell you as a character man." He was convinced that this was a huge mistake and that I was just doing a nonproductive exercise in local theater. Well, my love for the project and this wonderful character overruled my agent's misgivings and I decided to cut my hair, don the dress, and live with the consequences.

As it turns out, the play was quite successful. There were great reviews and we played to packed houses. I won an *L.A. Weekly* Award for my performance as Miss Stein. And among the audience one evening was the young director Tim Burton, who was about to begin work on his second feature *Beetle Juice*. Several months after our play closed, my agent got a call and I met with Tim Burton. I was cast as Otto, the psychic interior designer. I have since appeared in over a dozen movies, including *Heathers, Demolition Man, Love Affair,* and as the voice of the mayor of Halloween Land in Tim Burton's *Nightmare Before Christmas*.

There are many ways to break into this business and my only advice to those willing to try is, follow your instincts, damn the torpedoes . . . and when dressing as a woman, always wear sensible shoes!

PATRICK SWAYZE IN *GHOST*

By Jane Jenkins, Janet Hirshenson, Michael Hirshenson
Casting Directors, The Casting Company

Some actors are blessed with a combination of qualities. Patrick Swayze is just such an actor. He is handsome, has a great body, is rough yet vulnerable, and capable of expressing his feelings. He is also an excellent dancer. We cast him in *Skatetown, U.S.A., The Outsiders, Grandview, U.S.A.,* and *Red Dawn.* Then *Dirty Dancing* came along—which we had nothing to do with—and Patrick became a big star.

When we were casting the multi-award-winning *Ghost*, the producers had already offered the part to several gentlemen like Harrison Ford and Mel Gibson, who were either not available or not interested in the part. Patrick Swayze's agent, who is an old friend of ours, wanted to get Patrick on the film—so much so that Patrick asked if he could personally read for Jerry Zucker. We were at first concerned because this could put the director in an awkward position of having to personally turn him down. However, Jerry agreed to let Patrick come in and audition. The reading was extraordinary! By the final page, some in the room had tears in their eyes. Jerry decided Patrick was "perfect" for the part, and we were given an immediate go-ahead to cast him.

McLEAN STEVENSON—DIES FOR THE PART!

By George Sunga
Producer

Tom Smothers and I were producing "The Summer Brothers Smothers Show" when I received a phone call from a McLean

Stevenson . . . someone I did not know. He pitched one liners over the phone and said he really wanted to write for the show even though his background was as a performer. I was impressed by McLean's personality, enthusiasm, and obvious talent so I went to Tom Smothers and told him, "I'd like to take a chance on this guy." Tom asked that we bring McLean into the office to audition his material. So on the appointed day Tom, Mason Williams, and a few of the writers came to meet McLean and also to be the audience. Mac immediately went into his jokes, but Tom Smothers didn't break a smile or show any warmth at all. Now McLean is beginning to show flop sweat . . . no one is laughing at his material. Mac makes up his mind to play with the attitude that he was laying the biggest egg in front of the toughest audience ever. Finally, McLean ran out of courage and material. He bowed to no applause and retreated to the back of the room. I am feeling very bad for Mac and his failed audition, when Tom Smothers, now smiling, turned to me and said, "OK George, hire him!" Tom had set up the writers to not laugh at McLean no matter how funny the material. McLean's greatest contribution to the show, however, was as a performer.

RON HOWARD—POSTSCRIPT

By Rance Howard
Actor

I've been an actor for many years. When I was in New York, our oldest son, Ron Howard (we called him Ronny at that time) was three years old. I was making the rounds going from casting office to casting office. In the course of doing this there was this one kindly gentleman named Dudley Wilkinson, who was a casting director at MGM. He would sit down and allow you to do a scene in order to acquaint himself with your talent or your potential. One day I went to see him and his office was packed with boys between seven and ten years of age, it was pandemonium in there. The receptionist told me I couldn't possibly see Mr. Wilkinson today because he was very busy seeing these children. "May I leave a note for him?" I asked. "Surely," the secretary answered. And so, I started writing the note. I wrote, "Dear Mr. Wilkinson, Stopped by to see you, noticed you're very busy. I'll come in another day." And I signed it Rance Howard. And then, just tongue in cheek, I said, "P.S., I have a son who is a very fine actor." Then I left.

The next day I got a call from Mr. Wilkinson saying, "Bring your son up, I'd like to meet him." So I got Ron dressed up and we went up to Mr. Wilkinson's office. I said, "This is my son Ronny." (And here's Ronny, this cute little three-year-old kid, with freckles, a lot of red hair.) Mr. Wilkinson said, "Well, he's very cute, but what can he do?" Now it just so happens I had been doing *Mr. Roberts* in summer stock and Ron— through watching rehearsals and some performances—had learned Ensign Pulver's lines. So we did this little scene from *Mr. Roberts* and Mr. Wilkinson almost fell out of his seat. He gave me a little two-page scene. I took it home and Ron and I rehearsed and went up the next day and did the scene. "That's wonderful," Mr. Wilkinson said, "I want the director Anatole Litvak to test him." The end result was that Ron Howard got the part as the son of Anne Jackson and E. G. Marshall in a movie called *The Journey*. I was given a part in the movie as a Russian soldier and our family spent ten weeks filming in Vienna, Austria. My son Ron Howard went on to become a very well-noted actor/producer/director.

HENRY GIBSON'S HEART ATTACK FOR GEORGE SCHLATTER

By Gary Owens
Hall of Fame Broadcaster and Actor

Speaking of unusual casting occurrences, Henry Gibson (who used to hold a little flower on the show—now he's become a major motion picture star) was hired for "Laugh In" in a most unusual way . . . George Schlatter was on the telephone, and he had two different phones, one on each ear. "Hello, New York. Hello, Chicago. All right, I'll be right back with you." Henry comes in and he's got this little flower bit that he wants to do on "Laugh In." And he's been sitting there for an hour and George has not said hello to him yet. Henry finally stands up right next to George's desk and pretends to have a heart attack. He falls flat on the floor, and George says, "Just a minute." He walks over and sees Henry there and says, "Are you all right?" Henry says, "Yeah, but this was the only way I could get your attention." George Schlatter hired Henry Gibson.

TENNESSEE WILLIAMS' PERFORMANCE!

By Karen Kondazian
Actress

At the Actors Studio, I did a scene from Tennessee Williams' play *The Rose Tattoo* for Lee Strasberg. He said, "Do this darling, you've got to do this part someday. You were made for it." So, I decided to sculpt my own career and produce it myself. Fellini's set designer did our sets. I won the L.A. Drama Critics Circle Award for Best Actress. A friend of mine, Paul Ryan, who was hosting a cable network show at the time asked, "What birthday present would you like?" I said, "Tennessee Williams to come and see the play." Magically, the next thing I knew, Tennessee Williams was right in the middle of the audience! We had a very special night. Richard Brooks, who directed the film versions of *Cat on a Hot Tin Roof* and *Sweet Bird of Youth*, came that evening and met Williams for the first time. After the play, Tennessee Williams came up on stage, kissed me, and said words any actress would take to her grave, "You'll always be a part of my heart." He told me later that I could have the rights to any of his plays. So, taking the money I earned from *The Rose Tattoo*, I produced and starred in *Sweet Bird of Youth*. We auditioned three hundred actors and chose a young man named Ed Harris for the role of Chance Wayne. Just before Williams died, he gave me the West Coast premiere rights to one of his last plays called *Vieux Carre*. I suddenly realized how amazing it was to have a vision and to make it happen.

I guess the bottom line is, by taking a chance to produce my plays, it taught me what Helen Keller believed . . . Life is either a daring adventure or nothing at all.

MICHAEL WINSLOW, THE BIRDS AND THE BEES

By Fern Champion
Casting Director

There are many *Police Academy* stories. One of my favorites is about Michael Winslow. I first heard him from my ground floor office on the Paramount lot. There were these sounds of birds and dogs—but I didn't see anybody. All of a sudden this adorable fellow comes through my window. It was Michael Winslow! So we called Paul Maslansky and said, "We don't know what you can do with him, but he just came through our window. He could be a bird, he could be a plane, a sports announcer, Muhammad Ali, anybody." Paul knew exactly what to do with him. Michael became the Human Machine we have all come to know and love in *Police Academy*.

THE PERFORMANCE OF A LIFETIME

———— ☆ ————

By Steve Bluestein
Actor

It was about 1978. I was married at the time and was in the process of getting a divorce. I had a nine-month-old son and had just learned I wasn't his biological father. The courts had sided with my ex-wife so I lost my house, my income, my family, and, most importantly, my son. Needless to say, I was an emotional wreck and, had been crying for days.

As fate would have it, I got a call from my agent. I had an interview at Twentieth Century-Fox for a very important role. I was a babbling idiot at the time but I needed the work. I said to myself, "OK, you're an actor. Even though you're depressed, go in there and act. ACT NORMAL." I met with the casting director and acted the whole time I was there. On the inside I was suicidal but on the outside I *acted* the part of a sane man. I *acted* a glib conversation. I *acted* as if I were happy. I *acted* charming. I *acted* as if I had no problems at all. The casting director was impressed. "You get 'A' in 'office,'" was his only remark. He then told my agent, "The kid can't act." If he only knew . . . he was witnessing the performance of a lifetime.

"Quite frankly, looking at a .38 caliber makes it easy to look scared and acting dead is not so difficult.
It was absolutely terrifying. The acting challenge came when I had to act cool afterward."

—Marty Ratigan

Thinking on Your Feet

Faster than a speeding ticket, more powerful than Steven Spielberg, able to leap from casting session to casting session in a single bound. . . . These actors survive and get the part by thinking on their feet!

CLIFF'S AUDITION FOR "CHEERS"

———————— ☆ ————————

By John Ratzenberger
Actor/Director/Producer

I had lived and worked in London for ten years before I was hired to come to Los Angeles to do some writing. The casting process is different in London, you don't have to do any cold reads. The casting people pretty much know your work and they assume if you're in their office you know what you're doing. Whereas in Los Angeles, you have so many people getting off buses and trains, you have to have a more stringent *filtering* process with what's known as *cold readings*. Consequently, I was writing a late night television show for CBS entitled "Nero," it was a takeoff on "I Claudius," when I got a call. There was some casting going on for a new show called "Cheers." My agent thought it would be a good idea if I went down. I met with the casting director Steve Kolzak, who explained that the show was being done by the same people who did "Taxi." I had never seen "Taxi" because I had lived out of the country for the entire 1970s, and this went to my advantage, because I didn't know to be nervous.

When they gave me the sides, I read them badly, which is something I've always done. I've never been good at cold readings. But what I did do well was improvised comedy. My partner and I toured Europe for almost six years doing improvised comedy. Our show was called *Sal's Meat Market*. So, back to "Cheers." They said, "Thank you, we have your number." It was, "Don't let the door hit you in the butt on your way out." So, I was on my way out, I had one foot out of the door and one still in, and for some reason I turned around and said, "Do you have a bar know-it-all?" They said, "What do you mean, a bar know-it-all?" I said, "Well, the type of guy who sits in a bar, who's the fount of all knowledge. My experience is that every bar has one of these guys. There's never two of these individuals in the same place because they cancel each other out. It's like two ends of a battery short circuiting each other. Consequently, there's always one in every bar." They said, "We hadn't thought about it." I then started improvising, telling them the type of wood used in their desk, the kind of fabric their clothing was made out of, everything I could think of. Basically, I just wanted to get out of there with my dignity. I'd already put in a good ten years in London, doing a lot of stage and about twenty-two films. I really didn't want to walk out of the office with them thinking I was a schmo. I didn't want to tell them I'd never done a cold reading, I just wanted to make them laugh and then leave. I said, "Thank you" and left. A few days later I got a call saying they wanted to try this character out for seven or eight shows. The agent said, "You might as well take it, these shows never last more than seven episodes. You'll have some pocket change to take back to London with you." The show lasted eleven years. The character of Cliff from "Cheers" is now part of the American fabric.

"*If 100 percent of the experts in Hollywood said I had no talent and should give up, all 100 percent would be wrong!*"

—Marilyn Monroe

FRED ASTAIRE GETS TELE-PROMPTED

By Bob Finkel
Producer/Director

I wanted Fred Astaire to host an Emmy Awards show at NBC, but I was unable to interest him in doing it. I finally put a crawl machine on his lawn and greeted Fred as he came out of his home. The crawl read:

> "DEAR FRED, PLEASE RECONSIDER DOING THE EMMY AWARDS SHOW. YOU WILL NOT HAVE TO WORRY ABOUT MEMORIZING A THING, IT WILL ALL BE ON A MACHINE LIKE THIS, AND IT WILL BE VERY COMFORTABLE FOR YOU AND IT WILL BE A WONDERFUL MOMENT AND I KNOW YOU WILL ENJOY IT."

And Fred Astaire agreed to do the show!

BILL MURRAY—DO NOT DISTURB

By Joe Hart
Actor/Producer/Multi-auditioner

I was living in New York and had earned some Broadway credits, done some stand-up, even Shakespeare, but I was dying to do a feature film. It had been awhile since my last acting gig and the frustration was eating away at me. I had this crazy actress girlfriend at the time who had gotten an interview with Bill Murray who was casting his movie, *The Razor's Edge*. She suggested I come early and see if I could get in. I said, "Great idea, Bill Murray's wacky, I'm wacky, we'll hit it off and the rest will be history."

Once I arrive at the offices, I ask the receptionist for Bill Murray's office, and she directs me down the hall to another office. Well, I knock on the door, but there's no response, so I hit it again, and nothing. Finally, I try to open the door and boom, it opens. I stick my head in, and wow, what luck, no one there . . . Not two minutes later Bill Murray comes blasting through the door and says, "Hi, sorry to keep you waiting, I'll be with you in a minute," and goes into the main office. I was transfixed, like a deer caught in a car's headlights, I could not move. Was that really Bill Murray who just came in here? Wow, he thinks I'm supposed to be here. Those actresses are going to be here any minute, what do I do? I seize the moment, grab a pen and a piece of paper, and write DO NOT DISTURB, DO NOT KNOCK, I WILL COME OUT AND GET YOU, BM, and I stick it to the outside door, just as Bill hollers from within his office, "Come on in!"

This is it, I blow out whatever wind I have left and go into the mouth of the lion. Bill is clearing his desk and apologizing for the general disarray. . . . The phone rings, Bill picks it up and starts to discuss a job offer and goes off for a few minutes. . . . While I'm assessing the situation, Bill Murray is immersed in conversation and lives up to his reputation by walking over and stepping on top of the coffee table that lies in his path. Once he hangs up, he asks, "Who are you?" See he's scheduled to interview girls—and here I am . . . I didn't have a clue what to say. I give him my picture and resume. Bill finally says, "Look, I realize you're trying hard, and I wish you luck, but there is nothing for you in *The Razor's Edge*. You're not crazy—a bit borderline—but you've got a lot of heart. Anyway, I'm supposed to be meeting all these women today . . . I don't know where they are, but I'll walk you out." Which he did.

And as he opened the door to the hall about a dozen beautiful women turned and faced us. I kept moving and blew past the girls. Just before I turned the corner I looked back as Bill Murray tears the sign from the door, reads it, and shoots a look at me that says, "Ohhh, that was good!"

Casting Capers

Casting directors are often *unsung heroes*. Diplomats extraordinaire, they can appease the agent, buffer the client, and will fight for the actors they believe in . . .

PERFECT CASTING AT BOB NEWHART'S WEDDING!

———— ☆ ————

By Don Mankiewicz
Producer

This actually happened! A very famous character actor's daughter was getting married to Bob Newhart. It was a very pleasant, magnificent ceremony. The moment when his daughter came down the aisle on his arm, a casting director turned to a nearby agent and said, "Look who they got for the father!"

WOODY ALLEN KNOWS WHAT HE WANTS

———— ☆ ————

By Marvin Paige
Casting Director

I've done two movies with Woody Allen, *Take the Money and Run* and *Everything You Always Wanted to Know about Sex*. I've always respected Woody's approach to casting. Woody would say, "I don't know a lot of actors, but I know what I want when I see it." It was my job to find those *right actors*. Woody often didn't want the complete film script to be available when we were casting, so he'd sit with me and tell me what he was looking for. Woody, with all his comedy and humor, is very serious minded about his work. While filming he would take his relaxing breaks by playing music.

THERE'S A CASTING DIRECTOR IN MY SOUP!

By Richard Devin
Actor

An old joke goes: "If you're in a restaurant in New York or Los Angeles and you want to get a waiter's attention, just stand up and yell … "Actor! Oh, actor!" As an actor (and an occasional waiter) I never thought much of the joke. That is until I met a certain casting director. . . .

Like most actors, I do whatever I can to further my career; I read the trades, I submit to directors and producers, I network, and I attend those "pay-to-meet-a-casting-director-cold-reading workshops." Sometimes, I must admit, I actually do get an audition or two out of the meetings. But in most cases the casting director goes off with my hard-earned money and my picture and resumé, never to be heard from again.

I was looking forward to attending a particular cold reading workshop of a fairly well-known casting director (we'll call him "Jon"). The brochure listed "many new projects" that he was casting. I made my way to the studio early and took a seat right up front where I wouldn't be missed. Jon, the casting director, also arrived early. He started a very friendly conversation which soon turned to what actors must do to support themselves. I explained how I was temporarily working as a waiter in a local restaurant. Jon said that he admired how ambitious I was.

I told him that being a waiter was actually a great job; short hours, cash at the end of the shift, flexibility, and how a friend of mine was making fantastic money at a new restaurant—the kind where the waiters are really waiters. As I spoke, I thought to myself about the great connection I was making with this guy. I felt positive that I would get auditions out of this.

The time came for my partner and I to do our scene. I was so relaxed and confident that I fell right into it. My partner was great. We simply couldn't have been better. Even the other actors in the workshop cheered us. This was a perfect cold reading encounter. I had made friends with the casting director, he loved my picture and resumé, my partner and I gave a great reading, what more could I ask?

My agent and I were meeting for lunch about three weeks later. I was taking him to that new restaurant where my friend worked. It was trendy and very "in" and I could get a discount. My agent was impressed by the restaurant. Its garden feel with trees and latticework and little fountains made it very comfortable. We were shown to a table in a great power spot—not too close to the kitchen and not too far from the front door. Right where we could see and be seen. I asked my agent if he had heard anything from Jon.

"Not a word. After several, 'thank you, please keep my client in mind' notes, Jon still hasn't called." The day after the workshop Jon's office had given my agent a very nice follow-up call. Trying to take my mind off of it I turned to the menu. When I looked up, as if by magic there Jon was heading right for our table! This was great! This was perfect! Bringing my agent to this restaurant was going to pay off. I was just about to stand to shake Jon's hand when he spoke. "Hi," he said. "My name is Jon and I'll be your waiter."

"Wait!" I yelled. "Aren't you casting?"

"Not anymore . . . oh, no," he said, recognizing me. "You know? You were right! I make very good money as a waiter. May I tell you about today's specials?"

I turned to my agent who was trying to hide his smirk in a napkin. "Great!" I said. "I just paid thirty-five dollars to audition for a waiter."

Jon broke into laughter, nearly doubling over.

"Laugh now," I said. "You won't when you see your tip!"

So, the next time you're in a restaurant in New York or Los Angeles, and you want to get a waiter's attention, try standing up and yelling, "Casting director! Oh, casting director!"

SOME GREAT CASTING DIRECTORS

By John Ritter
Actor

Some of the wonderful, creative people I've met are in casting. Lee and Lynn Stallmaster, Ruben Cannon, Pam Dixon, all wonderful people. It's really great to meet a casting person who understands the problem of actors and gives something to them, plays with them when they're reading. You can sort of sense when somebody is interested in you, it's like getting a *green light*.

As a young actor you get so many *red lights*. Ethel Winant said to me one day, "I see something like a young Jack Lemmon in you." And that changed me, she helped me believe in myself. And so, through all of this, you can be infected—in a bad way—or affected—in a positive way, where you can really feel your ambition.

KEN MARS GETS CAST—SIGHT UNSEEN!

By Leonard Stern
Writer/Producer

I seldom lunched with Ethel Winant without her bemoaning the fate of casting directors whose judgment, she felt, was respected but never completely trusted by producers and directors. I rarely reached my second spoonful of soup without Ethel citing endless examples of casting directors forced to back their first choice with at least two or three other suggestions. Ethel's damaged feelings were firmly etched in my mind when we met to discuss the casting of Harry the fireman, a co-starring role in "He and She," starring Paula Prentiss and Dick Benjamin.

I told Ethel we needed a performer of avuncular intelligence, bearish warmth, and when required, feisty responses, just as I had written the description in my script. "And," I added casually, "the part is yours to cast." Ethel didn't comment. A week later she called and recommended Kenny Mars. "He's the perfect actor for the part," she said, "You couldn't do any better." "Okay," I said, "have him come over, but tell him right now that he has the part." Ethel was thrown. "Don't you want to see him first?" "Ethel," I said, "I told you last week Harry the fireman was your choice. You said that I can't do any better than Kenny Mars. I believe you. I trust you. Kenny Mars has the part. You have been telling me for years that producers don't listen to casting directors and now you're not listening to me." "Alright," said Ethel, resigned. "I'll send Kenny, but just in case let me send over one other actor."

RAGTIME

By Pat Golden
Director

R*agtime* was a wonderful picture. Milos Forman directed. Dino de Laurentiis produced and James Cagney starred. It was one of my first. I made no money, and hardly got any credit, but what a great cast we had! It was a first film for the likes of Debbie Allen, Howard Rollins, Sam Jackson, Jeff Daniels; and it was Elizabeth McGovern's second film.

NYC VERSUS L.A. CASTING AGENTS

By Pat Cronin
Actor

This story is about the essential difference between New York and Los Angeles, especially in casting. No one in Los Angeles wants to offend you . . . on the outside chance you actually might make it. In New York, they just say, "What the hell are you doing here?" when you walk in. In L.A. they say, "Oh, you're so wonderful! And if you had been here last week, you would have been starring with Tom Cruise! But we just missed you. And I'm sure . . . next week . . ." This is true, especially with agents. They're always saying to you, "You're going to be a star and as soon as our subagent comes back from Australia, I know we'll be able to sign you." But alas, that subagent never makes it.

Nobody will offend you in Los Angeles. So, when you first get to L.A. you believe these people. You actually believe you're well on your way to stardom, when, in point of fact, they're talking that way to the waitress at the local diner, on the outside chance that she may be a network executive next week. And she very well may be! Another possibility, the network executive may very well be waiting tables next week.

TURNED ON FOR NOTHING!

By Jane Brody
Casting Director

I was having people come in and do monologues. This young man came in and had a whole suitcase full of props. And one of the things that he brought in was an electric typewriter. He couldn't hook it up because he didn't have an extension cord that would reach for his blocking. I said, "Why don't you use it without the power and I can imagine." And he said, "No, no, no! I have to hook it up!" Well, all right. So, I asked my assistant to look for an extension cord. He couldn't find one. So I said to my assistant, "Curt, why don't you go to Walgreens and get an extension cord." So he came back with the extension cord. In the meantime this actor was putting on a costume and setting up the set, with papers on the floor. And he finally got the extension cord and he plugged it in and he had five minutes of warm-up. And he put some paper in the typewriter and sat down at the typewriter and it was finally time for him to do his thing. So, what he did was—the typewriter was on—he angrily pulled the paper out of the typewriter, wadded it up into a ball, and threw it into the corner. That's all he ever did!

MADNESS, MAYHEM . . . CHILD CASTING

───────────── ☆ ─────────────

By Dee Miller and Kimberly Nammoto
Casting Directors

Whenever we have a casting going on, our offices usually look like a robbery took place by the time the last person leaves. But when we have a casting that involves children . . . you can imagine what our place looks like. Parents not only bring the child who is auditioning to the casting, but their other children, sometimes family members, friends, etc. There is of course a talent bathroom that is unbelievable after castings. Dirty diapers all over the place. Clogged toilet bowls, clogged with heaven knows what, toilet paper everywhere, well . . . at the end of each day, we slowly open the door with our noses held.

Once, someone obviously sat on the sink, and after an extremely long day of casting, we went back there and there was a sound of running water. Water everywhere—no one said anything all day—for fear of being blamed, I'm sure.

Another time, there was a casting for kids and these mothers are usually loaded to the max with other people's kids as well as their own, in their mini-vans, fresh from bribing the kids to be good with McDonald's and on the go to yet another casting. One mother, in her haste not to miss out on another casting session for yet another one of her children someplace else, couldn't wait for her husband to get out of the bathroom and proceeded to drive away like a bat out of hell as he chased the van with a baby in his arms, to no avail. So they waited and waited. They were still there when we closed and we half-expected them to be there when we opened the next day.

DON'T CHANGE A THING

by Edmund Gaynes
Producer/Actor/Casting Director

A good New York actor came in to audition for a film I was casting. He was very upset that he didn't have "enough time" to study the script. People have different ideas of what a cold reading is. When I was an actor I never saw those words before I read them. Today actors think a cold reading is only having the script for an hour ahead of time. This particular actor felt shortchanged because he only had the script for forty-five minutes. In spite of this he gave a brilliant reading! The director and I thought, *This guy's got the job! No question.* But we had to bring him back for the producer. So we gave him the script over the weekend—now he has no excuses. Monday, when he came back for the producer, he was terrible.

What happens is, actors think about it, study it, they go to their acting teachers and they screw it all up. And it makes the casting director look like an idiot. Because now I have to say, "Gee, he was good the first time." It is unbelievable how many actors do that to themselves. They think they're working on their material, and they think themselves right out of what they had. The reason we call them back in the first place is because they were good. So why would they want to go and do something totally different?

Another tip for actors. If you get a callback, wear something the same or very similar. You don't want to look drastically different. You'd be amazed how many people come in unrecognizable. Women will come in with their hair totally different. You call them back because you like what you saw that day. You don't want them to reinvent themselves. It's a common dilemma. It's scary how many people have had jobs and have thought themselves right out of it—rehearsed themselves right out of it. All they had to do was go in and do the same thing again and they would have had the job. But they were too smart for that. They had to improve it.

IVORY COAST CASTING

By Tom Spalding
Producer/Director

A few years ago I produced a film in the Ivory Coast, West Africa. It was a true story of a West African from the early 1900s. I wanted to cast an African-American actor as the leader of this important African movement but was persuaded by the executive producer to try casting a man from a village near Bouake, Ivory Coast.

Arriving at this little village of about fifteen little mud and stick huts with thatched roofs, I was introduced to the tedium surrounding the native protocol. We sat on a bench by the dirt road next to the village while the elders of the community sat on a bench on the other side of the road. After about twenty minutes, they decided to talk and after another twenty minutes of negotiating and lots of clock watching, our guide said we could proceed.

A group of about ten men were lined up in the village square waiting for us. The people are a handsome tribe and much of the attire was in beautiful blue and white handwoven cloth. We interviewed several villagers with mostly discouraging results. I was aghast. Not one of the group from this little African village had ever even seen a movie! One man looked the part and seemed to have a grasp of what we were doing, so we finally decided to go with him. He also had the bearing of a leader—which was a must for the part. Still, I must say that I was quite worried . . . as I was also the director!

The casting session was just about to begin when a delegation of the village council came up with a live goat. Our interpreter told me that the chief was giving me a goat . . . and that I could either take it with me, or let them cook it and we would all share in a goat stew. I said thanks . . . let's share the goat. Later, the whole group came back with a large cauldron of goat stew and pounded yams, known as duo, which we all shared, much to the amazement and pleasure of the chief and his council. Lots of goat hairs . . . but quite good.

The first day of shooting arrived and we drove in Land Rovers out to the edge of a large lake in the middle of nowhere along with our crew and a truckload of equipment. While the crew got set up I spoke to this "actor" through my local translator . . . since I had not learned Boyle and the actor knew no English. I explained that it was time to put on the costume for the part. The actor nodded his head and with a big smile told us that he was ready.

The man had arrived with a large bundle on a stick and without another word, he set off for the bushes with his bundle. A few minutes later, he emerged from the bushes all dressed in his costume. For all the world, our actor looked like a fugitive from a children's advent play . . . long bathrobe-like costume, complete with what appeared to be an industrial mop where his beard should be. He was so pleased with himself that I actually had the camera set up and shot some film of him in his costume. It was hilarious but poignant. No one laughed.

Then we carefully explained that we had another costume and beard to try, a long white robe with matching turban and a bright red sash, along with a tall staff which Waddi Harris always carried . . . the signature attire of the real personage from the 1900s. We then had the beard, which we had brought from New York, applied by the makeup person and went ahead with the shoot.

This man we cast became the historical personage he was to be. He knew the stories about Harris who we know as The Firebrand—and his powerful performance was most amazing and surprised all of us. He was absolutely great in the part! You never know in this business!

A RANSOM TOO HIGH
Casting Disney's *Wonders of China*

By Jeff Blyth
Director

In 1981 I was making a film for Disney in China for the opening of EPCOT Center. It was to be a far-reaching film that covered all regions of the country and I felt it important that it not just be beautiful exotic scenery and masses of people. I wanted Western audiences to feel they'd met at least one Chinese person.

I chose Li Po, a famous poet of the Tang Dynasty, to be our guide and on-camera narrator. This might seem like the equivalent of using Shakespeare to narrate a film on present day England, but I deliberately chose a historic figure so that the words he spoke would not seem to some conservative members of the audience like the official party line. Remember, this was not long after China had opened to the United States.

On my last survey trip before we began photography, I requested that our Chinese partners (China Co-Film) arrange to have a dozen actors meet me in Beijing so I might have a simple casting session. I trusted them to be able to pick out some good actors because the leader of this group, a man named Shih Kuan, was himself a former film actor back in the 1940s. Shih Kuan had been the chief negotiator when representatives of the Disney Studios had come to Beijing hoping to get permission to make the first U.S.-Chinese co-production. He was a hard negotiator who never spoke to us without a translator, but I had since discovered Shih Kuan was quite fluent in English and was really a very courtly gentleman when he wasn't negotiating. I appealed to him personally to help us in the casting process.

When I returned to Beijing after a month of location surveys, I was welcomed with the usual Chinese banquet, and that night there was someone at the table I did not recognize as part of our production team. Mr. Du was a dour individual who sat silently in the corner smoking his bitter cigarettes. To my great surprise, Shih Kuan introduced Mr. Du as the man chosen to play Li Po. After a long and awkward silence, I realized there was no point in protesting because China Co-Film had already offered him the role, without any consultation with me or anyone else on the project. A done deal, as we say.

It turned out Mr. Du was a respected actor of some reputation and he seemed willing and eager to play the part. We did wardrobe and makeup tests with him and he loosened up considerably. When we took pictures of him as Li Po, we all joked about how he'd ended up looking a lot like Shih Kuan.

Our production was about to begin the first two months of photography in the fall of 1981 and arrangements were in place for Mr. Du to join us for one week at the start and then again for another two weeks in the spring, several months later. However, three days before we were to start shooting, Mr. Du announced that he now had an agent and wished to be paid for all of the intervening time between shoots, even though he was free to take other jobs. What he was asking for would amount to tens of thousand of American dollars. Of course Mr. Du, like all Chinese workers, was used to getting wages of around thirty-five to forty-five dollars a month, whether he worked or not. Suddenly he had stars and dollar signs in his eyes and was prepared to ransom our production.

I went to see Shih Kuan personally. I came down pretty hard on him in his office and let him know we felt we were being blackmailed. This was a man we never cast in the role and we weren't going to tolerate this kind of behavior. I told him he had two choices: I could get on a plane that afternoon for Hong Kong, where I knew there were many fine actors and I would have a proper casting session. Shih Kuan knew this would mean a delay of at least a week and could see all of his months of preparations beginning to unravel. Nervously, he asked me what the second choice might be.

I said we could begin as planned, with no changes to the schedule or budget—if he would play the part of Li Po.

Shih Kuan refused, of course, saying it was impossible with his many responsibilities. I tried appealing to his past film achievements but he said he'd retired from acting. I think I eventually won him over when I reminded him he already looked like Li Po.

Shih Kuan ended up playing the part in *Wonders of China* and doing a wonderful job. For the many millions who continue to see the film, he will always be Li Po, but I'm sure there were some Disney people back in the States who were shocked when they first saw their negotiating adversary up there on the screen, speaking English.

"Everyone has talent.
What is rare is the courage to follow the talent
to the dark place where it leads."

—Erica Jong

CHAPTER 3

THE RIGHT STUFF!

✮

"When you audition a lot of people
for a major part in a movie,
you begin to hear a
safe, middle-of-the-road reading,
over and over again.
What we look for as the casting people
is somebody who is going to come in
and do something different.
Or, as the director says, 'Surprise me!'
And sometimes you meet somebody
who does surprise you!"

**—JANE JENKINS, JANET HIRSHENSON,
MICHAEL HIRSHENSON
Casting Directors**

Tenacity

"Aggressive, pushy, relentless, ambitious, insistent, resilient, high-pressure, tenacious, forceful, coercive . . . but I got the part." An actor's life.

MEG RYAN MEETS ROB REINER

☆

By Jane Jenkins, Janet Hirshenson, Michael Hirshenson
Casting Directors, The Casting Company

In this industry, tenacity is key . . . tenacity on the part of the actor to *hang in there*, and tenacity on the part of the casting directors to repeatedly bring that same *gifted* actor or actress in for readings. Every so often, a fresh new talent will come through our doors, and we find ourselves compelled to bring him in again and again to read for various projects—until he hits.

We first met Meg Ryan in New York when we were casting *The Sure Thing*. She came in and she was absolutely adorable. Everybody loved her, including the director, Rob Reiner—who eventually decided someone else was "more right" for the part.

Several readings for several other projects followed and we ended up casting Meg in two feature films: *Armed and Dangerous* and *The Presidio*. She was now a working actress, but stardom was not imminent. . . .

When Harry Met Sally provided us with an opportunity to once again bring Meg in to read for Rob Reiner. This time Meg was the one who was "more right" for the part. It's the perfect example of how one gets catapulted into stardom—after tenaciously persevering. Meg Ryan was no more talented when she finally did *When Harry Met Sally* than when she first walked through our doors. From the very beginning, she was someone we just knew the public would adore.

ANDY GARCIA WOULDN'T TAKE "NO" FOR AN ANSWER

———— ☆ ————

By Dee Miller
Casting Director

Whenever Andy Garcia is asked what his first film role was, he mentions *The Mean Season*. However, there were two films in which he appeared prior to that. The first was a film entitled *Blue Skies Again*, starring Harry Hamlin and Mimi Rogers.

The preliminary casting for *Blue Skies Again* had been completed and actors' callback readings were scheduled. There had been massive tryouts on the baseball field as well as readings to test acting abilities. Callback people had been decided upon and the day of callbacks with the director, Richard Michaels, was presently in progress. This guy showed up at our office and insisted on being seen. The receptionist told him, "I'm sorry, we are only seeing the people that have already auditioned and have been selected for a callback. It's impossible for you to be seen." This man would not take no for an answer and he would not leave. As I came out of the studio to bring in the next actor, I noticed this person had been sitting in the reception room for a very long time. When I asked the receptionist who he was and why he was still here, the answer was, "He insists upon being seen." I, as the casting director for this film, said, "I'm sorry, this is for people with appointments only." He still would not leave. About an hour later, with the studio door open, the director happened to ask, "What's his story?" I explained the situation and the director replied, "Anyone with that perseverance deserves a shot." As a result, he was cast in a speaking part as one of the ball players. His character name was Kenny Lagomarsino. His real name happens to be Andy Garcia, and the rest, as they say, is history.

LISTEN TO YOUR HEART

By Barbara Eden
Actress

When I moved to Los Angeles, I lived with my aunt and uncle in San Marino. It's light years away from Hollywood—physically and mentally. I didn't know how to drive, because in San Francisco we lived in the city where there was wonderful transportation. And so, when I had a meeting with the head of casting at Warner Bros., my uncle drove me.

I went in with my very proper dress, looking very San Francisco. My hair was natural blonde—it wasn't blonde blonde—just ash blonde. I sat down and this man started telling me what "THEY" wanted and needed in Hollywood. He said, "You know, you're a very pretty girl, but you're not pretty enough. You're not sexy. They want sex in this town." And then he showed me a picture of his daughter and said, "This is what they want—big tits!"

In this day and age, that word means nothing. But at that time, I was so shocked. First of all, that he would show me a picture of his daughter and point out her physical . . . you know. And then to say the word. I was shocked. I couldn't listen. He said, "You're a nice girl, from a nice family. Go home, marry the boy back home. Stay out of this town, you don't want to touch this town."

I went out to the car and told my uncle. He almost walked in, he was so angry at the man for using that language with me. I went back to San Marino and cried a lot. Then I thought, *He didn't hear me sing, he didn't hear me read.* And I thought, *Well, I don't have to be a sex symbol. Not every actor in this town is a sex symbol. I can be a character actress.*

Three months later I moved to Los Angeles and was attending classes. One day, I was walking on the Warner Bros. lot and I heard, "Hey you! You with the pink pants! What's your name?" It was the head of casting I had the interview with! He didn't recognize me. He said, "We're going to give you a screen test."

I didn't get cast. But I got something very important out of it. I learned to not listen to what people say . . . just listen to yourself.

A MATTER OF FOLLOWING THROUGH

──────── ☆ ────────

By Harry Lewis
Actor/Restaurateur

Timing is everything in life. If you're at a certain place at a certain time, good things can happen. There was a picture called *Pendulum* with George Peppard and Jean Seberg. The way I was cast in this picture was very interesting. My wife, Marilyn, and I owned the Hamburger Hamlet chain. I was in the Hollywood Boulevard restaurant one afternoon—as I was always around at all of the restaurants—when somebody hailed me. He said, "Harry!" I said, "Yes?" He said, "I'm Billy Gordon." I said, "Of course." Billy was a talent scout at Columbia Pictures. He said, "I have an idea. We're doing a picture called *Pendulum*, and there is a part for a lookalike to George Peppard. I think you look very much like George Peppard. I would like you to come to the studio and meet the director and the producer and the casting director." I said, "Okay."

So I went to the studio and walked into his office. There was the director, the producer, and the casting director. I sat down and they started talking to me about the picture and the part and the whole thing—explaining the character and how they see it and the story line and all that. And they said, "Well, we'll be in touch." All actors know that's the kiss of death. So I left and said to myself, *I'll never hear from them*. And I didn't.

One week went by, I didn't hear. Two weeks went by, I didn't hear. I read in the paper they were going to start production pretty soon on the film. So I thought, *Well, I'll call the casting director and ask him about it. If he says, "We've got somebody else," then they've got somebody else.* It wouldn't be the first time (it would be about the 180th time!). So I called him and said, "Hi, it's Harry Lewis. I'm calling to find out about the film. Have you fellas made up your minds? Do you want me—don't want me? What is the story?" He said, "Of course we want you! You're supposed to be in wardrobe tomorrow morning!" I said, "Well, it's nice of somebody to say it!" He said, "My goodness, you were chosen the day you came in! What's the problem here?" I said, "Well, I haven't heard from anybody." He said, "You should have. Please report to wardrobe tomorrow. The picture starts next week." Which it did! And that's how I was cast in that picture!

DOUBLE NEW YEAR

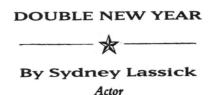

By Sydney Lassick
Actor

I remember my friend and agent, Mr. Len Kaplan, who must be credited for making some of my hopes and dreams about being in the movies come true. Len has since passed away, but he told me that he had submitted me for the role of Cheswick when they were casting the award-winning film, *One Flew Over the Cuckoo's Nest*. It was thought I was too *ethnic* to be considered for the part and Len quipped, "You mean there aren't any Jewish crazies?" The point must have been well taken and an appointment was made for me to audition and meet with the director. I won the part and am still overwhelmed by it. I often feel it was more like winning the California State Lottery. Moreover, it seems I was blessed with a Double New Year because it was on the Jewish New Year (Yom Kippur, 1974–75) that Len called with the happy news that a contract came through for me to start work on the picture in the New Year, January 1975!

ABE LINCOLN RETURNS TO
FORD'S THEATER

─────────── ☆ ───────────

By Gene Griessman
Actor

I am a little bit different from an actor who must wait for an opportunity to appear in somebody else's play or movie. In my case I have written and produced my own one-man play called *Lincoln Live*. I therefore look for opportunities to perform the play. In order to make this happen, I do what John Huston once told me, "Position yourself for lucky breaks to occur."

As a part of my visualization exercise, I visualize lucky breaks and write down my dreams and goals on three-by-five-inch cards. And every morning I visualize those dreams and goals happening. One of those goals I wrote down: I WILL PERFORM ABRAHAM LINCOLN IN FORD'S THEATER IN 1994. I didn't tell anybody.

I am a member of the National Speakers Association, so I performed the Gettysburg Address at our local chapter. A prominent visiting speaker by the name of Terry Paulson was told of my play, *Lincoln Live*, and came up to me and said, "You know we're having our national convention in Washington in 1994, wouldn't it be interesting if you performed *Lincoln Live* in Ford's Theater?" Between meeting him and subsequently meeting Pat Stanek, who works for the National Park Service, I performed *Lincoln Live* on the stage of Ford's Theater on the anniversary of Lincoln's assassination, April 15, 1994. As a result of that appearance, I performed it again August 1 at the Lincoln Memorial in front of all of the National Speakers Association.

Everybody gets little breaks here and there. You build on those and that takes you to the next break. . . .

Integrity

To know what you have to do, to honor your principles, to have pure, uncompromised integrity. It actually works . . . for some.

GOING TO BAT FOR DIONNE WARWICK

☆

By Steve Binder
Director/Producer

I was directing "The Danny Kaye Show" on CBS and we had booked many music acts for the entire season. One of the executives at CBS asked me to unbook Dionne Warwick because he had a friend who was managing another artist and he wanted me to book that artist instead. This is when Dionne was just breaking through. We had worked on a show called "Hullabaloo" together in New York. This executive called me into his office and said, "What's the big deal? I mean, we'll pay her and there won't be any problem." I said, "Because I've made the commitment and I think it's really not the right thing to do." I remember this vividly because he said, "Oh, you're one of those guys who'd rather be right than president." I honored my commitment, she did the show.

As it happened, the executive at CBS held it against me. A few years later an artist who had a new series on CBS called and asked if I would direct. I said, "Yes." Then the artist's manager called back to say, "We can't get it through this executive at CBS, because he doesn't want you to do the show."

PRIDE IN MY WORK . . . AND HERITAGE

——————— ☆ ———————

By Richard Yniguez
Actor

In the early seventies, I was up for a film, *Red Sky at Morning*, starring Richard Thomas. The book was a popular best-seller and Universal had high hopes for this World War II melodrama. Mr. Hal Wallis was the executive producer on the project, and I was very impressed that I would be meeting him. I was so impressed, in fact, I took the time to read the book, since being a Latino actor it was unlikely I would be given a script.

The day arrived for my interview with Mr. Wallis and the director, James Goldstone. I had studied the sides and was ready for anything. William Batliner and Bob LaSanka were the casting executives who ushered us into the waiting room just outside Mr. Wallis' office in the "black tower" of Universal Studios. The anticipation prior to any meeting of this magnitude is always nerve wrenching, but you try to use that energy in any way you can. The meeting was a pleasant one and after all was said and done, it came down to three of us. Finally, it was decided that the two Latino roles that were being cast would be played by one of the other Latino actors and myself. As we left the office and walked into the elevator, I told the third actor, who had not gotten the role, "You're not out of the picture yet." Mr. Batliner and Mr. LaSanka both asked me what I meant. I said, "Until I read the script, I will not accept the work." This was very bold; it was common in those days to accept work without seeing a script. I realized that I was taking a big chance.

A script arrived at my home a few days later. I had a line of dialogue which I found very difficult to say. In the early seventies profanity in films was just creeping in. But this dialogue was the strongest I had ever encountered in a major studio film. It was in Spanish and referred to doing something sexual to the mother of the main character (*Ching a tu madre*, which means BLANK your mother). It was extremely derogatory and, in Latin America, people were killed over these few words.

I decided I could not do this dialogue and expressed my feeling to Mr. LaSanka. He in turn relayed the message to Mr. Wallis. A few days later I was summoned to Mr. Wallis' office. He expressed his regrets that I would not do the film because of the dialogue, but his hands were tied. He also mentioned that if it were up to him, he would do away with that portion of the dialogue. During our discussion the director walked in and emphatically stipulated that the dialogue stays in because that's how the people in the script spoke. With that I thanked Mr. Wallis and excused myself from the room.

As I was making my way out of the studio, I heard my name being called from a distance. I turned and recognized one of the studio's talent scouts. I smiled and said hello. He in turn raised his hand and gave me the finger. He then said, "Hey, Richard. There goes your career!" Dumbfounded, I turned away and left the studio. It would be eight years before Universal gave me another chance.

It was a hard lesson to learn and a decision I don't regret making. But because of it, I can look in the mirror with pride. It's always difficult to turn down a job, but I've done well for myself in spite of that incident. And I still take time to consider the kind of work I will accept.

DO YOU EVER FOOL AROUND ON LOCATION?

By Grace Zabriskie
Actress

It was the early 1980s. We were actually sitting together on a couch, this director and I—or at least on two couches; he on one, I on another at a right angle to his. But we were making our shortest-distance-between-two-points electric glow with our 1960s vibes. He was producing his vibes more effortlessly than I, but then I think he'd been doing this all day for days, while I was madly trying to reconstruct mine for the occasion.

We'd been revealing our deepest—or at least most determinedly idiosyncratic—souls for an hour or so, he fending off worried intrusions from assistants and the casting director, when, right on the heels of a charming dissertation on his wife and children, his devotion to them, etc., he asks The Question: "Do you ever fool around on location?" (It was to be a fabulous location. I wanted the role. I felt he'd already given me the role; we were now merely getting to know one another in preparation for the most stimulating collaboration either of us had ever experienced.)

My brain short-circuited. My god, he's . . . is he . . . he's not asking me if I'll go to bed with him, is he? No. Impossible. Adores wife and children. Just said so. Next. Um . . . he wants to weed out potential troublemakers in cast and crew—asks everyone this question . . . Yeah, right.

Oh! Of course; character! It's a character thing. I must not have read the script carefully enough . . . my character must . . . she doesn't. Next. He, ah, isn't going to base any casting decisions on my answer. Just idly curious. I'm making too much of it. Oh no, if I were brighter I could figure this out.

What should I say? . . . The truth—that it was none of his damned business—didn't seem to be a productive option. After all, wasn't this essentially the kind of question that any actor worth his salt understands instantly for what it is, weighs various considerations, and then answers accordingly?

Question: "Do you ski?" (ride horses, knit, play piano, speak Swahili, etc.)

Various considerations: How fast can I learn to do this?

Answer, "Yes, blah, blah, blah," period, end of story.

Point being, you usually have a pretty good idea of what the right answer is, and this time I didn't have a clue. Because even though I knew I could probably get away with "Not really, well, a couple of times maybe," and then cinch it with some semi-impassioned reference to the importance of discretion—I was afraid to risk it. If he were trying to pre-schedule his dalliances, then what if he chose to set our appointment early in the two-week rehearsal period, say, when a refusal could get me fired, or—equally horrible to contemplate—shot around—or edited out?

If I said "yes" and he cast me, I'd never know whether he'd have cast me if I'd said "no." I could have lived with that fine, but even if his "follow-up," once on location, consisted of no more than a murmured, "My door will be unlocked tonight after 9:30," I'd have a harder time laughing it off.

If I said, "yes," and he didn't cast me, I'd feel like a major idiot of course.

The worst scenario was if I said "no," and he didn't cast me. Because then I'd never know for sure why. And the best, by far, was if I said "no," and he cast me anyway. Wow. That was worth going for. . . I said "no." I said, "I've never fooled around on location—don't think it's a good idea from what I've seen."

He seemed to love my answer. Talked about his wife and kids some more. We laughed. I think he offered me a glass of wine, and I believe I accepted.

A week later I learned that someone else had been offered the role.

I saw the film eventually. There was very little left of the character I'd read for. But I'll never know. Damn him. I'll never know.

PHILADELPHIA CUT

By Ralph Archbold
Actor

It would be my big break. I knew that the movie was going to win awards. How could a movie starring two of the hottest actors around, Tom Hanks and Denzel Washington, fail? Not only that, it was directed by Jonathan Demme and was billed as the first major motion picture about AIDS. A sure thing.

During the making of the film, Jonathan Demme lived in my neighborhood in historic Philadelphia and decided he should make Benjamin Franklin part of the film. I was offered a bit as Franklin, a part I had been playing professionally for over twenty years. I could do this in my sleep. It would be a national showcase and expand my career to movies. What a break!

Then the bad news came. It had to be shot on the following Thursday, squeezed into an already packed shooting schedule. I had out-of-town performances scheduled on that day, and there was no way to reschedule on such short notice. I spent a day wrangling with the ethics of my situation before declining the role. They found a good character actor to do "my part."

I knew when the film came out and I had to watch someone else play Franklin it would be heartbreaking. But I went to the premiere anyway. Through the whole film I waited . . . it never came. The scene ended up on the cutting room floor.

I'm glad I honored my commitment but I would love to have been a part of the film *Philadelphia*. Even on the cutting room floor.

BILL COSBY AND "I SPY"

By Sheldon Leonard
Producer

Back in the early sixties I saw a young man doing a club act on "The Jack Paar Show." At the time I was casting the two leads for a series that came to be called "I Spy." I knew I needed an athletic, attractive actor with a sense of humor. And there I was looking at an athletic, attractive actor with a sense of humor—only he happened to be Black.

At the time the television medium had never used a Black actor in a leading role. They used them in supporting roles as character actors, but television was very reluctant to take a chance of offending Southern stations by using Black actors in the same context as Caucasian actors. Bill Cosby looked like what I wanted and although NBC had the authority to okay the principal casting for an upcoming series, I decided to go to New York to persuade the president of NBC, a man by the name of Bob Kintner.

I went up to Bob Kintner's office with Grant Tinker and we did the usual preliminaries, the small talk. Then Mr. Kintner said, "How are you doing on the casting for the series, 'I Spy'?" I said, "Well, we have Robert Culp set." I then told him I had seen an actor on television the other day. He's perfect . . . and he's Black. And he said, "Well? Why don't you sign him?" And this we did. We signed Bill Cosby and this opened the door for all the Black actors who had been shut out of the medium for so many years.

HARRY BELAFONTE
AND PETULA CLARK
MAKE HISTORY

———— ☆ ————

By Steve Binder
Director/Producer

When I pitched the concept of the first Petula Clark special on NBC I was given the green light to develop the show. So I called up Harry Belafonte, whom I did not know, and asked him if he was interested in doing any television guest appearances. He begged off saying he wasn't doing any. I told him what the concept was and that Petula Clark was quite well known in England for her acting and that she was a child star. He said, "Well, let me think about it and I'll let you know." He called back the next day, "I've been thinking about this and it sounds interesting," he said. "Providing we can work out a deal, yes, I will come on board."

There was a problem with the sponsor because, I was told, off the record, Harry Belafonte was Black and Petula Clark was not. On the record, they said that Harry Belafonte wasn't a *big* enough star. We got into a hassle over this and the bottom line is that I flew to see the sponsor and we took several meetings. I stood firm on the fact that I didn't want any other guest stars, we'd go with Belafonte and Petula Clark.

We eventually went into production and everything was going really terrific. Everybody was very happy and Harry and Petula were getting along great. We got to this one segment where, while we were taping an anti-war song Petula had written called "The Paths of Glory," and, in an emotional moment of the song, she put her hand on Belafonte's forearm . . . and all hell broke lose! The next thing I know, I'm getting calls from *Time* and *Newsweek*, and it's a big international deal. Basically, it was the first time a Black and White person had touched on national, network television. And to make a long story short, I got a phone call from NBC in the control room saying, "Whatever you're doing—whatever is going on—we're behind you 100 percent." The show aired as it was shot, touching and everything. This is one of the most interesting casting stories of my life. The show was basically responsible for breaking the *color line* in prime time television.

"*If at first you don't succeed . . .*
you're simply not vicious enough to play the game!"

—John Ford Coley

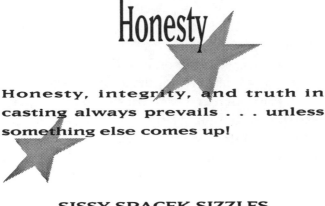

Honesty

Honesty, integrity, and truth in casting always prevails . . . unless something else comes up!

SISSY SPACEK SIZZLES

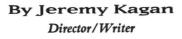

By Jeremy Kagan
Director/Writer

In 1975 I wrote and directed a piece for ABC television that was a re-creation of the life of a woman who joined a political movement in the 1960s known as The Weather Underground. It was a powerful family story and I was looking for my ideal actress. I'd written the part of a girl who had come from the upper crust aristocracy of Pennsylvania. I had been seeing every actress in town between the ages of twenty and thirty, and I couldn't find her. Finally an actor friend of mine said to me, "You know you ought to see this girl, she's done one movie, she's young, but she's really pretty good, her name is Sissy Spacek."

At first I resisted. I'd seen her movie and she was very Southern. But I finally decided to meet her. Every now and then, in the casting process, you encounter someone who is so alive, that she sizzles in front of you. She knows who she is and she likes who she is. This is very rare. Now in came such a person. She just swept me away with her intensity, her intelligence, her passion; and she did have the thickest accent from east Texas you could imagine! So, what do you do? I'm thinking, *What's more important? The actress who has the quality to give me the being I want to create, or somebody who happens to have the right sound in her voice?* The solution? I rewrote the part! No longer did the character come from Philadelphia, now she came from the Southwest. Since it is the human being that makes us identify with characters presented on the screen, the writer and the director have to appreciate this and adapt to that reality . . . or they could lose what might be magic.

GO GET 'EM KIMO SABE!

By Buddy Powell
Actor

The message on my answering machine was from my commercial agent. She said something about Cavalry men and Indians needed for a kid's breakfast cereal. After relaying the time and place of the audition, the recording ended with, "Go get 'em Kimo Sabe." Commercial actors are used to getting strange calls to go to strange places to do strange things. Hey, it's advertising!

I dug through my makeup box, found some red liquid in a bottle and smeared it on my face, just to the neckline. I greased my blonde hair back with Brylcreem, threw on a flannel shirt and jeans, and headed off to the interview. On the way, I hit a toy shop and bought an Indian headband with a neon pink feather stuck in the back.

After parking the car, I took a quick look in the rearview mirror. I saw my greasy head and sunburned face. The headband and feather haloed. With my eight-by-ten photo in hand, I walked into the ad agency waiting room. The room was packed with Indians. Real Indians. Authentic, burly, war-painted, vicious-looking American Indians. They wore animal skins and feathered headdresses. They looked at me. I looked at them. I grinned . . . I shivered . . . I left.

CHARLES DURNING THE "CABBY"

————— ☆ —————

By Jack Carter
Actor/Comedian

I once went up to Charles Durning and said, "Mr. Durning, I am such a fan of yours." And he said, "Don't you remember me? If it wasn't for you I wouldn't be in show business!" I said, "What are you talking about?" He said, "When you were casting in Fort Lee, New Jersey, for *A Hatful of Rain* and Robert Ludlum owned the theater, a playhouse, you cast me in the part of a cab driver." He said, "If I didn't get the part that day, I'd still be driving a cab today!"

What happened is, he walked in and said, "I drove my own cab over here. I'm a cabby now and I want to be an actor." We read him for the part of the cab driver and he did a great job. The playwright Michael Gazzo said, "He's perfect." I said, "You've got the part." Almost everybody in that play became a star—except for the lead . . . he disappeared.

TONY CURTIS, PRETTY BOY

————— ☆ —————

By Steve Allen
Actor/Author/Composer/Personality

This is the story of how I, rather than Tony Curtis, happened to be cast in the lead role in *The Benny Goodman Story*.

The director, producer, and Universal Studios executives had narrowed their casting list down to two, Tony Curtis and myself. Benny Goodman himself naturally had casting approval—and he decided that I would be hired. "Tony is a pretty-boy," he said. "I'm not, and Steve Allen isn't either. Also, he's a jazz musician himself so he'll seem more natural doing this sort of thing." Which means that there can be some profit even in not being handsome.

THE SWITCH

───────── ☆ ─────────

By Jayne Meadows
Actress

One day, while I was under contract to MGM, the head of the casting department phoned to say that the brilliant director, Gregory La Cava, wanted to meet me immediately. He planned to feature me in his next movie, opposite Gene Kelly.

Mr. La Cava was reportedly a fan from my appearances in the Raymond Chandler classic, *Lady in the Lake* (with Robert Montgomery) and *Undercurrent* (with Katharine Hepburn). I was doubly thrilled since Gene Kelly was a dear friend from my days on the Broadway stage. I said, "Great. How soon can I get the script?" The casting director answered "Oh, Mr. La Cava doesn't work from a script." "Nonsense. How do you make a movie without a script?" "La Cava can and does," the casting director replied. "You must go, Jayne; he wants to meet you, study you, and tailor the role to your personality. He's a famous *star-maker*."

Well, I was a dedicated Broadway actress and a character actress to boot—to whom "the play's the thing." But if a studio contract player turned down a part, in those days, the offender was immediately put on suspension, which meant no salary. I had my sister (Audrey Meadows) to support as well as myself . . . Suddenly I got a brainstorm. My sister was desperate to break into show biz. "Audrey," I said "La Cava's never met me. He's only seen me on the screen. You go and pretend you're Jayne Meadows." "What if he catches me?" "Oh, just laugh it off. Tell him I was swimming in the ocean, it was rough, I was knocked down by a big wave and I have a terrible concussion. Tell him I think you'll be perfect for the movie."

In those days Audrey didn't look anything like me, but that didn't deter us. So off she went, accompanied by my agent. According to him, Audrey played the scene exactly as rehearsed, but Mr. La Cava took one look at her and said, "Who are you?" When she got to the big-wave-knocking-me-down bit, he asked, "Is Jayne afraid of working with me?"

At that my agent burst out laughing and the jig was up. Unfortunately, Audrey didn't get the part.

A year later I was the ingenue in the last of the Thin Man movies, MGM's *Song of the Thin Man*, with William Powell and Myrna Loy. I told this story to Myrna, who said, "You fool, Jayne. He made me a star, and he could have done the same for you." However, the picture, *Living in a Big Way* (still seen on TV), was Mr. La Cava's last and was not a success.

So at least I didn't pass up a blockbuster.

INNOVATIVE AND CREATIVE CASTING!

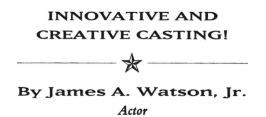

By James A. Watson, Jr.
Actor

Believe it or not!" This has happened to me four times. In baseball there is the relief pitcher—in acting there is me. . . . Four times I read for various television shows and won the runner-up spot. Each of those times the casting director called two days before the taping to explain that the original actor had been released. Could I, would I, assume the role? I did, naturally . . . for a hefty salary hike . . . naturally. (My work improved as well. Despite my search for inner peace, I must do well under pressure.)

An amusing memory of one of these assignments was a call directly from a producer who had not met me but was aware of my "relief status." As a Black actor, I am always trying to erase the color line in casting. I had been rejected by the casting director because the part of the attorney wasn't a "Black role." I had made such a stink trying to get in for the part that the producers were familiar with my name. When the actor had to be replaced, the producer called me at home in a panic. He hired me on the phone due to my reputation as an actor and my assurance that I would come through for him in the part. When I showed up on the set ready to work, his teeth nearly fell out when he saw my *complexion*. Too embarrassed to say anything under a time restraint—I worked. To everyone's delight it turned out well and the network later praised the producers for "innovative and creative casting!!" Go figure.

*"I'm now at the age where
I've got to prove that
I'm just as good as
I never was."*

—Rex Harrison

Gratitude

When favors, opportunities, and breaks are given, a new plateau is reached—a fifth dimension . . . when gratitude is involved.

JOEL BROOKS—HEARTFELT GRATITUDE

☆

By George Sunga
Producer

A very touching and meaningful moment in my life occurred when I was producing a situation comedy called "Three's Company." A very talented actor by the name of Joel Brooks read for our casting director, David Graham. David was so impressed with Joel's audition that he came to my office and asked if I would hear him. I did and was favorably impressed. Back in my office, I told David Graham to hire him. David left to tell Joel Brooks he had been hired. Moments later, David returned to my office and led me to the room where the audition had been held. There I found Joel Brooks, on the floor . . . crying. It seems that Joel had just moved from NYC and this was his first West Coast audition . . . and his first job. Joel was crying tears of joy.

"Nothing succeeds like success."

—Oscar Wilde

KEVIN COSTNER, BEFORE HE DANCED WITH WOLVES

By Jane Jenkins, Janet Hirshenson, Michael Hirshenson
Casting Directors, The Casting Company

Someone we knew sent Kevin Costner over to us when he was first starting out as an actor and asked us to help him get his Screen Actors Guild card. A SAG card is *a rite of passage* to a new actor. We cast Kevin as an extra in three feature films: *Frances*, starring Jessica Lange . . . Ron Howard's film, *Night Shift* . . . and probably the most fun for Kevin while working as an extra had to be on *Table for Five*, because the film was shot on a cruise ship! We're still using the barbecue Kevin gave us as a gift for that trip to the Mediterranean!

JASON HERVEY'S "WONDER" YEARS

By Beverly Hecht
Agent

I represented Jason Hervey from "The Wonder Years" for eleven years. He came in when he was about four years old. Jason was a character looking kid. When I first saw him I thought I couldn't do anything with him. But he did a cute thing in my office. He put his little elbows on my desk and looked up at a picture on my wall of a girl wearing something sheer and he looked back at me and looked up at the picture and back at me and said, "Now that's gross." I thought, *Wait a minute, I've got something here.*

So, I shoved him down everybody's throat. I said, "You've got to see this child. He's incredible. He's smart, has this really cute personality." Because in those days they only wanted beautiful, adorable blonde-haired, blue-eyed children. And Jason was very character. (These days, they use all kinds of children— big ears, nerdy looking, all ethnic, very real-looking children.) And even though he was not what they were looking for, he got over two hundred commercials. He had many many movie and television credits, including "Diff'rent Strokes" and two Disney series. Then he got "The Wonder Years." At this point, his mother decided he should have a bigger agency. To date, I haven't heard anything about Jason Hervey professionally, or seen him on any shows. However, it wasn't Jason's decision to leave me, he was only fifteen at the time. I do wish him all the success in the world. He is an immense talent and has a terrific personality. As far as I'm concerned, professionally speaking, those years with me were Jason Hervey's *wonder* years.

CLIFF ROBERTSON AS JFK

By Malvin Wald
Writer/Producer

An *Answer*, my 1962 JFK documentary with Kirk Douglas, had an immediate payoff for me in 1963. After the assassination of the president on November 22, I was approached by Official Films to help write and produce a one-hour biographical documentary. As a narrator, the idea of Cliff Robertson, who had played Lieutenant Kennedy in *PT 109*, appealed to me.

His friend, Dan Barton, brought Cliff to our production office, where he read the script and then hesitated about committing himself. Not able to stand the suspense, I blurted out that we could only afford to pay Screen Actors Guild minimum scale, because we were low-budget.

Cliff looked at me in anger. "Are you saying that you want to pay me scale?" I nodded.

He glared at me and said, "Let me tell you something. After I played JFK in *PT 109*, I was summoned to the White House. When I entered the Oval Office, I said, 'How are you Mr. President?' Kennedy held out his hand and said, 'Cut that Mr. President crap, Cliff, just call me Jack.' " Cliff Robertson stared grimly at me. "I had the greatest day of my life with the president and you have the nerve to offer me money to narrate his life story. Hell, I should pay you for the honor."

I insisted on paying Cliff and he promptly endorsed his paycheck over to the Motion Picture Relief Fund. Every November 22nd, somewhere in the world, our film, called *John F. Kennedy*, is played, either on commercial TV, cable, or in schools on videotape. It has become part of our history and the casting of Cliff Robertson helped the film gain its immortality.

I LOVE LUCY

By Barbara Eden
Actress

I once did a screen test at Fox, and there was a time period when I was waiting to find out if they were going to pick up the option, which would put me under contract. Meanwhile, I appeared on one of the last "I Love Lucy" shows. Lucille Ball was so good to me. She was the most wonderful, wonderful woman. I guess she liked me and wanted to put me under contract. I told her about the Fox situation and, while I was doing the show with her, I received a phone call from Fox telling me they picked up the option. Lucy was very supportive and very kind to me. I had a dress on that she didn't think was pretty enough. Lucy sat in her dressing room and put buckles on it so it would be prettier. There aren't a lot of actresses who will do that. She was supportive and just plain good to me. I was very lucky.

MICKEY GILLEY'S
LONG-STEMMED ROSES

By Melissa Skoff
Casting Director

I first met country music star Mickey Gilley when I was casting "The Dukes of Hazzard" series at Warner Bros. and put him in a guest cameo role playing himself. We became great friends instantly, and I came to know Gilley as a fun-loving, easygoing man with a deep desire to act. Like so many music stars I know, acting carries with it a mystique, and is something most intend to explore. So, needless to say, Gilley was ecstatic when he was offered a real acting role on "The Fall Guy" series. I was delighted when he called me and asked if I would coach him for the part. I was thrilled to do it, especially since Gilley would sit in on my cold reading class whenever he was in L.A. and I would coach him privately whenever we could find the time. Working with Gilley always meant a great time and a lot of laughs.

Gilley was scheduled to begin shooting on a Monday. The Sunday before, he flew to L.A. on his little Beechcraft airplane from Atlantic City where he'd been performing. I was told to meet with him and the rest of the gang at the hotel at around 5:00 for dinner first, and that I'd get a call when they checked in.

Well, when we finally sat down to eat, it was more like 9:00 that evening. This in itself was not such a huge problem, except that "The Fall Guy" script gave Gilley an amazing amount of dialogue, and the bulk of it was scheduled for first thing Monday morning! I was horrified. Remember, of course, that this man had never acted professionally in his life!

I put on my best poker face and politely asked, "Gilley, have you begun learning your lines yet?" My heart stopped beating when he replied, "There's no cue cards???" These words hit me like a brick. "Not to worry," I lied. And reluctantly added, "Trust me." At this moment in time, I was in a panic. Gilley, who was already blurry-eyed from flying his turboprop plane the length of the country only moments before, was barely awake. And it was my job to save the day. Oh, boy.

It was well after 10:00 when we left the dinner table and Gilley and I marched up to his suite, where I was to prepare him for the day he'd dreamt of his entire life. By the time we exited the elevator, he was ready to say good night. He kept chanting aloud to himself, "How can I possibly learn all these lines?" I schmoozed him into believing he could—which seemed to be the only alternative. I promised I wouldn't leave until he knew all his lines, and was comfortable with them. In truth, I was thinking of leaping from the eleventh floor . . . This was to become a crash course in acting, memorization, and how to hit marks. And the clock now read 10:45 P.M.

We repeated his lines over and over, as I tried to give him some feeling for the subtext of the scenes. But Gilley would have a huge speech, and Lee Majors line would be, "uh, huh." Then Gilley would have a monologue and Majors would reply, "Okay." The clock now read midnight. My Cinderella was in serious danger of becoming a pumpkin as I watched his lids grow heavier and heavier. So I kept pounding poor Gilley, visualizing myself as some sort of whip-cracking dominatrix beating him into memorizing his lines. And guess what? He did it! He was a champ. When I left close to 1:00 A.M., I felt somewhat secure that he would pull through. By the way, his set call was 6:00 A.M.

I anxiously rooted for Gilley in my mind all day as I sat at my desk at Warner Bros., hoping for a phone call to tell me what a great time he was having. But the phone didn't ring. Instead, a dozen of the reddest, biggest, longest-stemmed roses I've ever seen arrived on my desk with a cheerful note from Gilley. He was, indeed, having the time of his life.

Despite our nervousness the night before, we laughed. Maybe out of anguish, or out of desperation, but it was fun. Really fun. And it's still one of my favorite memories. And one of Gilley's, too. Helping him was a special moment for me. Gilley was like a kid who just won a giant trophy. One that he captured against all odds.

TOM DREESEN AND TIM REID
Salt and Pepper

By Sig Sakowicz
Radio/TV Personality

As an over-fifty-year on-air radio veteran and TV personality, I have had the pleasure of interviewing many *up-and-coming* stars, including: Ben Vereen, Joel Grey, Steve Martin, Wayne Newton, Jackie Vernon, and several hundred more! Occasionally an act will really capture my attention, and I will do whatever I can to help him or her or them.

Tom Dreesen and Tim Reid were knocking around in Chicago performing an act called Tim and Tom (the Salt and Pepper Act) and couldn't get arrested. I thought they were great! So I had them on my WGN radio show several times to help them out. Then when the International Polka Association was having a convention in Chicago and asked me to emcee, I asked Tom and Tim to come over and do their schtick at the banquet dinner. I told them, "If you guys do well here, some day you'll be big stars!" And that's exactly what happened. They performed, got standing ovations, and the rest is history. Tom and Tim said, "We'll never forget you for what you did for us!"

Tim went on to star in "WKRP in Cincinnati," and Tom became Sinatra's opening act. Both are TV stars.

P.S. Years later Tom was working in Las Vegas. I knocked on his dressing room door and said, "Tom, it's Sig Sakowicz!" He said, "Sig who? Who are you?" He said it in a kidding way. And then he said, "Of course I remember. We'll never forget you for your help and belief in us."

LARRY STORCH GETS "KISSES"

By Mitch Matovich
Producer

Larry Storch is a personal friend of Les Baxter who, in addition to being a long-time personal friend of mine, was writing some songs for a film I was producing titled *I Don't Buy Kisses Anymore*. One day Les had a problem with transportation and Larry offered to drive him to the production office. After Larry was introduced around and had asked questions about the production, he saw how proud everyone was to be associated with the film, and he became very enthused about *I Don't Buy Kisses Anymore* and said, "If you give me a part in this film, I'll agree to work for scale." We felt very fortunate that Larry wanted to work on the project, so we modified a part specifically for him.

THE FOURTH WIFE OF LAURENCE OLIVIER

By Dorothy James
Actress

The interesting thing about this experience is it was an example of the kindness of friends. Three friends of mine, including Gore Vidal and Toni Ermini, actually spoke with director Terence Young about me, recommending me for the part of Jean MacArthur, wife to General Douglas MacArthur, to be played by Laurence Olivier in the movie *Inchon!* When I met the director for the very first time at the L'ermitage Hotel in Beverly Hills, he laughed and said, "I've been getting phone calls about you all day!" And that was our meeting! During that meeting, Laurence Olivier was on the phone and I had the opportunity to speak with him! It was extraordinary to get the job! Everyone asks me, "How did you ever get the job?!"

For an actress, as you can imagine, it was an experience of a lifetime. Especially since I was a middle-aged actress, not a kid, and this was a dream come true. The movie was shot in Korea and Italy. And Laurence Olivier died a couple of years later.

I learned more about acting in those six months of filming with him than I had learned in thirty years before that. He was the consummate artist. He knew everything about acting and staging. There was nobody like him! I still have the wedding ring he put on my finger in the film!

His real wives were Jill Esmond, Vivien Leigh, and Joan Plowright. And I've been told I had the distinction of being his only American wife—on screen!

IT MAKES IT ALL WORTHWHILE

By Linda Day
Director

There was a woman who loved being around the business. She was an older woman. She really wasn't an actress, she was more of a background person. Because of her age and her weight, nobody was hiring her. And she couldn't keep up with her medical bills. So I started giving her little parts. Anytime I could put her in a show as an extra, or particularly for one line, I would. And every year, whenever she gets a residual check, she sends me some wine. I've kept in touch with her for over fifteen years now. She was so thankful. She moved to Florida and sees the reruns every so often and when she receives little checks in the mail, she gets so excited. It's just nice to be able to do something like that for people. Especially people who are fighting to get their medical benefits. To do something nice, to help somebody, it makes it all worthwhile.

AARON SPELLING'S BIG BREAK

———————— ☆ ————————

By Bernard Weitzman
Studio Executive

In 1954 I started at Desilu Productions as director of business affairs, working for Lucille Ball and Desi Arnaz, who owned the company. It was my job to negotiate deals for all creative elements on any program produced by Desilu. These elements included actors, writers, directors, and producers, and the deals involved negotiating with all major agents from MCA, William Morris, and others. During this period we did many great shows with young and inexperienced talent. This was the time of risk and chance and discovering new talent and concepts. It was at Desilu that I had the opportunity to give Aaron Spelling one of his first jobs as an actor long before he thought of becoming a writer and producer. Aaron wasn't the handsome leading man type, but definitely could become a very interesting character performer. He was a young, hungry actor from Dallas, who was fortunate to find an experienced agent who believed in him. Jack Weiner was his name. A wonderful, sympathetic, and caring man who did not personify what the world thinks of as a Hollywood agent. I respected and admired Jack for his integrity and dedication to his clients.

Jack told me his client really needed work and would appreciate anything we could do to get him a role so he could receive a screen credit and enough money to pay his bills. Because of Jack Weiner I went out of my way to find work for this young actor he represented. Our casting department found him a day player job on a series called, "The Walter Winchell Files," which paid three hundred dollars for the one day. Jack was grateful, but whatever happened to the struggling young actor, Aaron Spelling? He went on to become one of the most successful television producers in the history of Hollywood!

Groomed

They were taught how to walk, how to talk, how to do their hair and their makeup—and in the old days who to date and who to marry! They were groomed for stardom by *the powers that be.*

SUZANNE SOMERS WORKS OUT!

─────── ☆ ───────

By George Sunga
Producer

The final "Three's Company" pilot starred John Ritter, Joyce DeWitt, Norman Fell, and Audrey Lindley. The pilot was videotaped in November 1976. As funny as we thought this pilot was, it was not picked up by ABC. However, Fred Silverman, then head of programming at ABC, suggested to Don Nicholl, Mickey Ross, and Bernie West (NRW), who were the producers, that they should consider a young actress named Suzanne Somers for the role of Chrissy. They should bring her in, work with her . . . she may be the blonde they want for the show.

The only audition material on Suzanne was a hippie party scene from an episode of "Starsky and Hutch" which gave no indication as to Suzanne's performance ability. So the producers, NRW, contacted an interested Suzanne Somers. Mickey Ross rehearsed with her in his office and developed the nuances and attitudes of the Chrissy character. Mickey then rehearsed Suzanne with John Ritter and Joyce DeWitt . . . developing team spirit along the way. Soon NRW, John Ritter, Joyce DeWitt, and Suzanne Somers were off to show Fred Silverman the results of the recasting. It was more like a stage play than television as the cast performed *live* in Fred's office. At the finish, there was no doubt that "Three's Company" had found their Chrissy. At a time when ABC's spring schedule was set, Fred Silverman committed to six episodes of "Three's Company" and the series ran for eight seasons!

FROM MODEL TO STARLET

By Trudy Marshall
Actress

I was a photographic model in New York and came to Los Angeles to do some publicity for *Look* magazine with all the celebrities. Darryl Zanuck wanted to test me out here, but Earl Tyson, the magazine's editor, wouldn't allow it until I got back to New York. When I went back to New York I was called in to test. I did a scene, and back then you weren't allowed to be in the same bed with a man, or say anything. I was wearing a strapless dress and they had a real close-up of me looking smack into the camera saying, "I will not go to bed with you." And I heard that Zanuck said, "Sign her! She's got *bedroom* eyes." They called me in to sign my contract, I didn't have an agent. They offered me $75 a week. I told them, "I can't possibly sign this." They asked why. I told them I was making $200 to $250 a week as a photographic model in New York, why should I go out there for $75? So they asked me, "How much do you want?" And I told them, "I want $250 a week." So they said, "Sign."

GOOD-BYE METRO,
HELLO REPUBLIC STUDIOS
A Drop in Pay

———— ★ ————

By Anne Jeffreys
Actress

This happened after I did *I Married an Angel* at Metro, where they were considering putting me under contract. My screen test was supposed to take place around the same time Carole Lombard died. She was killed in a plane crash and everything at Metro shut down for two weeks. Everybody was walking around crying and lamenting.

My agent was upset with the woman who was arranging my screen test because she said I was limited and could only play "sweet young things" and "Southern girls." My agent said "She's an actress and she can sing . . . she can do anything!" He then took me by the hand and said, "I'll bet you a hundred dollars that I can get you another contract by noon." He grabbed me by the arm and dragged me out of the studio. We rode over hill, over dale. I said, "Where are we going?" He said, "Never mind, we're going to get your contract this afternoon."

We arrived at what turned out to be Republic Studios and my agent took me up to meet Manny Goldstein, who was the head of the studio. I remember going into Goldstein's office and my agent saying, "Take a look at her. See what she's got, she can sing, she can act. Do you want her? I have to know right now!"

Manny looked at me and said, "Yes, but how do I know she can sing?" I was sent over to see the head of the music department. We went over two or three songs. I was then told to return to see Manny, who said, "Well, you're under contract." I was stunned, I said to my agent, "Who am I under contract to?" He said, "Republic Studios." And I asked, "What happened to Metro?" He said, "To heck with Metro, we don't need them."

When I went to the pay window to collect my paycheck I looked at it and said, "There must be some mistake." I was told, "No, this is what we have down as your salary." I looked at the check and called my agent and said, "Listen, something is wrong here. I was making $350 a week at Metro and here I'm making $75 a week. Is that a mistake?" And he said, "No."

I had come down in pay, but in those days, for a contract player, it was still good money. From there, I went to RKO and started at $750 a week. So, I guess you could say I earned my way up the ladder.

REGRETS

By Jean Thorpe (a.k.a. Meg Randall)
Actress

At eighteen, I was under contract to Universal, and had just completed the role of William Bendix's daughter, Babs, in the movie version of *The Life of Riley*, and was beginning a new one titled *Ma and Pa Kettle* the following week. The head of the studio, Mr. William Goetz, announced that he was casting a dramatic 'A' movie with the female lead to be played by a serious, accomplished actress—so, you can bet your sweat socks that I figured I was just the party to fill the bill.

It took four days to get an appointment with Mr. Goetz, which gave me time to purloin the script, and to plan every word and gesture—even that I would stand instead of sit. I left nothing to chance. I rehearsed the upcoming interview mentally, repeatedly. I bought a bright purple sheath-dress and a pair of black ankle-strap shoes. And to this very day when I pass Universal Studios on quiet evenings when the moon is high and full, and dogs are baying mournfully in the hills beyond, I still remember—and shiver.

The following Monday arrived. After waiting over an hour in the outer office, his very pleasant secretary informed me, "He'll see you now." (pause) "Try to be brief." I combed my hair, again. My hand was shaking and my confidence was falling away. Just then a gentleman who looked suspiciously like Cary Grant came swinging in from outside, saying, "Is he in?" Polly nodded—he went in. I sat there wondering, *Who does this guy think he is?* Okay, it gave me time to rehearse my part—again.

Finally the one who looked, talked, and walked like Cary Grant came swinging out of the office and smiled—my brain turned to mush. The buzzer rang, a male voice says, "I'm going to lunch now." Miss Perfect said, "Miss Randall is still waiting." "Oh?" (pause) "Send her in."

They must have oiled the door hinges that day, because when I lightly touched the door it flew open and I propelled myself like a bullet into that room, while the mahogany door slammed against the polished paneling with a whap! And a startled man stared with his mouth slightly ajar. "Hello," he said. "Uh," I said. "Yes?" he said, puzzled. I didn't know where to look or what else to say, so I said, "Uh," again. The script I rehearsed in my mind a thousand times went out the window. And until my last breath flies, I will still wonder why I did the following: I turned in one full circle, panicked, and blurted out, "Sir? Can you please tell me what time my *Ma and Pa Kettle* call is for tomorrow?"

THE PREDICTION

By Trudy Marshall
Actress

I was in thirty-six films and had the pleasure of starring with Laurel and Hardy. I was the only girl who ever did comedy routines with them. We did a few scenes and the first scene I did in one take. So, for the rest of the film, they nicknamed me "One-Take Marshall." At

Fox I was pegged as a young Irene Dunne. I starred with Johnny Weissmuller in the first *Jungle Jim* movie. There were five of us who were being groomed, including Jeanne Crain and June Haver. We were publicized as "The Five Stars of Tomorrow." And then I had the audacity to *get married*. I was supposed to star with Fred MacMurray in *Where Do We Go from Here*, but because I was married, they took me out and put in someone else. When I asked why, I was told, "You get married, you have babies." They had been grooming me for four years, this was going to be my big break. I really don't mind. If I hadn't gotten married, my daughters, son, and two grandsons wouldn't have been born. So, I guess they were right, I did get married and have children—I love them all.

MY TWO YEARS WITH HOWARD HUGHES

By Patte Dee
Actress

It was 1955, and my girlfriend Sue Kelly and I were in Santa Barbara doing a Cole of California swimsuit promotion at a department store. I was surprised to receive a message that I was to return to Hollywood immediately. It seemed a motion picture studio wanted to sign me to a contract. Now, this was the era in show business where every other man gave you his business card and said, "I'm a 'talent scout,' call me and I'll make you a star!" In the three years I had been modeling, I had been approached by at least one of these characters dozens of times. The business cards always ended up in the trash can. I had no interest in pursuing a motion picture career, I wanted an education.

What was different about this man is that he was so persistent. He eventually sent a limousine to pick me up and drive me to the Paul Hesse Studios on Sunset Boulevard. It looked totally dark and closed when we drove up and Walter Kane, the man who had been calling so insistently on the phone, asked me to follow him to the office down the hall. It was here I was introduced to Howard Hughes.

Mr. Hughes had a couple of days growth of beard, no tie, an open-collared white shirt, and tennis shoes. He wore his hearing aid in his breast pocket and was constantly adjusting the volume. In his soft and low-pitched voice, he asked me why I was not interested in a motion picture career. I gave him my standard answer of how I did not believe that I had the desire or the qualities needed to pursue this career. His argument was "Who knows better, you or me, about who is qualified?" I had to acquiesce on that question. And we struck a compromise to settle the issue on a professional basis. I would do some more "test photo shots," be interviewed by five drama coaches, and the decisions and evaluations by these people would be the deciding factor. I felt that this was a safe bet on my part, because no professional person was ever going to recommend me for the silver screen! I have freckles all over my face!

So off I went! When we arrived at the photographer's studio, I realized that I had already shot some test shots with this photographer a few weeks before, and at that time I did not realize who or what they were for. Now I knew! After the photo shoot, I was whisked back to Mr. Hughes for another surprise; he made arrangements for me to be interviewed by five drama coaches the next day. Well, it is now 1:30 A.M. and I thought I was going back to Santa Barbara for my job the next day, but Mr. Hughes had made arrangements for another model to replace me while I was at the photographer's.

The next day I met with five drama coaches. One lady was outstanding. Her name was Florence Cunningham, a Vassar graduate and a former Smith College professor. I met with Mr. Hughes that evening, and he said that the reports from all five drama coaches were excellent and that I had great potential and my photographs were great . . . Mr. Hughes offered me a seven-year contract. I responded that I was only interested if I could study with Miss

Cunningham and get the equivalent of a college education, and that I was not interested in the drama part. He agreed to this idea.

Before too long I found myself living in a lovely brand-new three-bedroom home on Sunset Plaza Drive in Hollywood with a live-in housekeeper, a full-time limousine and driver, no groceries to buy, and starting my classes with Miss Cunningham. If I saw a film in a public theater, there were four rows in the back of the theater roped off for me and my driver. On the housekeeper's night off, the driver would suggest five restaurants to choose from. Every six months, my driver and housekeeper were changed, and I later learned the reason was that they got "too friendly" with me, and Mr. Hughes wanted the arrangement to be very businesslike. All of my meetings with Mr. Hughes were usually late at night at RKO pictures. He was a total gentleman, at least with me, and never came close to being a "womanizer," which is something my mother had warned me about.

This arrangement lasted two years, at which time I decided to move on. Hollywood was a small town, and word got around fast. I found that my past connection with Howard Hughes was something that no one in Hollywood wanted to deal with. This didn't bother me, however, since I never had that *driving acting ambition*—something needed to succeed in this business. So I used my new education and talent and went on to other scenes.

PAUL HEINREID 'GETS THE GIRL' IN CASABLANCA

By Armand Deutsch
Writer

Billy Wilder, an unassailable authority on the subject, is convinced that the way film actors decide on the roles they will or will not play is an unending series of puzzles within puzzles. His favorite example concerns the distinguished actor Paul Henried, who appeared in some twenty-five films. In 1941 Henried's agent brought him a script of *Casablanca*. Henried said forcefully, "I don't even want to read it. I'm tired of playing second leads. Tell me only one thing. Do I get the girl?" "You certainly do," the agent replied. Henried accepted the part.

Humphrey Bogart was, of course, the film's shining star. Once again Henried played the second lead. He did, however, get the girl—Ingrid Bergman, no less. She, incidentally, was cast after Ann Sheridan turned the part down.

"Paul's position in the history of films," concludes Wilder, eyes twinkling, "will always be secure because of his portrayal of the undercover fascist fighter in *Casablanca*. It was a wise choice on his part. I rest my case."

"*The older you are,*
the more slowly you read a contract."

—Leonard Lewis Levinson

CHAPTER 4

SIZE IS EVERYTHING!

★

"He said,
'Debbie, you really are wrong for this part.'
I said,
'How wrong am I?'
And he said,
'You're too short for the part.'
And I said,
'Well, how short is the part?' "

—DEBBIE REYNOLDS
Actress, *The Unsinkable Molly Brown*

Measuring Up

Actors may be told they are too tall, too short, too big, too small, too young, too old, too good, too late, too anything for a part—that perhaps, just perhaps, the producer planned on giving to his or her relative in the first place!

THE UNSINKABLE DEBBIE REYNOLDS

☆

By Debbie Reynolds
Actress

I very much wanted to do *The Unsinkable Molly Brown*, but they had cast Shirley MacLaine. Then there was a problem legally with her producer and Paramount, so she couldn't do it at the last minute. So, I went in and asked if I could read for the part or test for the part and they kept saying, "No, you're not right for the part." I kept going back and badgering them and waiting in the hall—bringing my lunch and sitting there—and talking to them. Finally, Chuck Walters, the director, came to my home one day. It was raining outside, I remember so well. And again I tried to plead with him to let me do the part. He said, "Debbie, you really are wrong for this part." I said, "How wrong am I?" And he said, "You're too short for the part." And I said, "Well, how short is the part?"

What happened is, the studio and the producers decided I wasn't too short for the part and I did *The Unsinkable Molly Brown*, for which I was nominated for an Academy Award. And I think I did a good job!

MICKEY ROONEY—
A TALL, THIN REDHEAD?

By Robert Easton
Actor/Dialect Coach

In 1956 I went on an interview for a wonderful part in a film called *Operation Mad Ball* at Columbia Studios. I read for the director and the writer. The part was a very tall, skinny red-haired serviceman from Tennessee. The writer had based the character on a real guy he had known in his outfit during the war. As luck would have it, I also was very tall and skinny and had red hair. I was also the right age and the writer assured me my Tennessee accent sounded uncannily like his wartime buddy.

My agent assured me I had won the part. "You're the right size and age and they love your drawl." Weeks passed and no contract was offered. Anxiously, as free-lance actors are wont to do, I called my agent. "Don't worry," he said, "You are in like Flynn." More weeks passed. I got even more anxious. So I called the agent again. He said, "Bad news. They found somebody else." Traumatized as I was, my curiosity got the better of me. "Who else," I asked, "could they have found who was young, red-headed, tall, and skinny with a Tennessee drawl?" The answer didn't surprise me. "Mickey Rooney."

As Gertrude Stein would have said: "A star is a star is a star."

PUT THROUGH THE PACES

By Robyn Whitney
Former Dancer/Choreographer

Dancers are easy to cast. They either have the skills to perform the steps or they don't. They either have rhythm or they don't. They either look the part or they don't. Simple. So most audition calls for dancers specify "tall girls who can tap dance" or "short Latin men who can do acrobatics" or "blonde women five feet three inches or under with ballet training." Very specific. I always look for tall (I'm five feet eight inches).

At one of the rare auditions where all heights, types, and hair colors of female dancers were asked to try out, it took a full six hours of intense dancing to eliminate 150 dancers down to eight finalists. Of those eight, I was by far the best trained and obviously the most experienced. As we stood panting, sweating like rain, and gasping for breath after the fiftieth repeat of the dance combination, the casting director eliminated me with the usual, "Thank you for coming." As everyone gathered up their belongings at the end of the day I was overcome with curiosity as to why I wasn't chosen. The director's curt response was, "Too tall." My retort was, "I was this tall when I walked in here six hours ago!" . . . No one likes an indecisive casting director.

A "FOX" FOR MICHAEL J. FOX

———— ☆ ————

By Laura Hill
Actress

In 1987, I was fresh out of school wondering what to do next. I had always wanted to pursue a career in acting, but the opportunities were limited in my small home town of Gadsden, Alabama. Then I experienced an epiphany straight from the mouth of newscaster Mary Hart—"Family Ties" was on a nationwide search to find a new girlfriend for Alex P. Keaton. Knowing that Michael J. Fox, though growing in stardom, had peaked at a height of five feet six inches, I was sure that "Family Ties" could use a four-foot-eleven-inch, ninety-pound Southern girl as Alex's new love interest.

I scraped together all of my money from teaching at cheerleader camps and caught the next plane to California. In my naiveté, I drove my rental car to Paramount Studios and announced to the guard that I was there to see the casting director, Allison Jones, and become Alex P. Keaton's new girlfriend. He politely informed me that, because I didn't have an appointment, I couldn't come on the lot. I refused to be shaken and eventually convinced a courier to give her a message for me. Her casting assistant came out and asked me if I had head shots, so I said "sure," and pulled my senior picture out of my wallet and told her about the local plays and commercials I had done in Alabama. After politely informing me that I needed an agent, she took my picture and gave me directions to the Screen Actors Guild. Though she was very polite, thinking about it now, I'm sure she had quite a laugh as she walked back to her office.

After knocking on more agency doors, I realized that there was a lot more to this acting business than just showing up. I've since joined SAG and AFTRA and have landed roles in film and television, including a principal role on "Home Improvement." I've also done many national commercials, including a Nissan car commercial. Thank you Michael J. Fox. I'm glad I came to Hollywood!

LONG DAY'S JOURNEY INTO NIGHT

By Dorothy James
Actress

I was fortunate enough to have starred in Eugene O'Neill's Pulitzer Prize–winning play, *Long Day's Journey into Night*. I think it's one of the finest American plays ever written. As it happens, Katharine Hepburn performed the same role of Mary Tyrone in the movie version, and, when I worked with Ms. Hepburn on a Hallmark Hall of Fame special, we both loved the play and we talked about it together on the set.

I was cast for that play the way casting usually goes. My agent arranged for me to meet the director and the producer. I read several times. One funny thing happened, regarding my audition. There were only a few people reading, and I was one of the contenders, and I felt I was perfect. I loved the role so much, I loved the play so much. And when I read for the final audition, Mr. Vincent Dowling, the leading man, got up with me, took me by the arm, and escorted me to the door. Someone later told me that the reason he was doing that was because he wanted to be sure that I was shorter than he was. There were many people who could have done the role of Mary Tyrone.

Perhaps I was cast by size . . . not by psyche! I was only five feet three inches!

JUST BIG ENOUGH

By David Stone
Actor

I drove to Santa Fe, New Mexico, to read for a part in Kevin Costner's epic western, *Wyatt Earp*. There I met the director of the film, Lawrence Kasdan. I read for the part of Larry Deger, the first marshall of Dodge City, Kansas. Marshall Deger was a giant in real life, weighing three hundred pounds. Matt Dillon, the marshall in the television series "Gunsmoke," was patterned after this man.

When I came out to the set, I was excited about playing the marshall of Dodge City opposite Kevin Costner, who of course was Wyatt Earp. Kevin Costner shook my hand and then stepped back as he said, "My gosh! This guy's going to make me look like a shrimp, and I'm six foot two!" Have you ever seen a guy try to look big and small at the same time? Well, that's me in *Wyatt Earp*.

Cattle Calls

These days in Hollywood, cattle calls are *domesticated*. And only on a rare occasion is a casting director, director, or producer injured by a wild, stampeding herd!

THE HITCHCOCK HITCH

By Marshall Barer
Writer/Lyricist

Officially known as the Open Call, more commonly the Cattle Call. (Bovine epithet refers to the full day of auditions required by Actor's Equity Association of all major productions, wherein anyone may be heard, including those who do not, as yet, carry an Equity card.) A somewhat less than exhilarating experience for Judges and Judged alike, and rarely productive, it remains a necessary adjunct to the casting process. Several theories stand out as to the origin of the term Cattle Call. Prevalent among them is the contention that it proceeds from the oft-quoted, widely resented pronouncement attributed to the late Alfred Hitchcock, to wit: "Actors are Cattle!" Earnest admirers of the great director insisted through the years that their idol had been deliberately misquoted, probably by some disgruntled passed-over actor. The matter was eventually settled on the occasion of a press conference following the conferring of Knighthood on the beloved old Master of Suspense himself. . . .

    One reporter, no doubt emboldened by Hitch's expansive mood, bluntly asked: "Is it true, sir, that you once said, 'Actors are

Cattle'?" Sir Alfred's immediate, indignant reply was: "Of course not! I would never make such a remark!" Then, after a thoughtful pause, he added, "What I probably said was, 'Actors should be *treated* like cattle!'"

OPEN AUDITIONS FOR THE STEVE ALLEN SHOW

By Leonard Stern
Writer/Producer

The Steve Allen Show," essentially a revue, was always in search of highly inventive comic performers for whom we could develop unique characters. To assure the flow of new talent, we held open auditions on Wednesdays. We had two specific requirements for all comic performers. They had to be funny and, most importantly, kissable! Among those who passed this stringent test were Don Adams, Tim Conway, Bill Dana, Gabriel Dell, Pat Harrington, Don Knotts, Jim Nabors, Louis Nye, Tom Poston, etc. Elaine May and Mike Nichols did their first television performance on "The Steve Allen Show." Their remarkable timing and unique material impressed us. They were our type of people. You kissed them immediately! (A list of the non-kissables will be supplied upon receipt of a self-addressed envelope and several thousand dollars.)

PASSWORD

By Gina Francis
Actress/Comedienne

I selected the game show "Password" because the winnings were cash, no stupid useless taxable prizes, and a lot would depend on my own intelligence. So I went to audition number one. The room was full of people who looked like they were gathered for the end of the year sale at Kmart. After filling out our paperwork, which stumped half the room, our contestant coordinator entered. She'd been rejected from the army for being too tough. For our purposes, we'll call her Mac. Mac taught us how to play the game, then gave us a chance to show what we'd learned. Well, I was a whiz. I caught on quick, was funny, helped others, and was damn cute.

Four auditions later, with fewer and fewer people each time playing the game longer and longer, I was selected to attend tapings of the show for a week. At any time I could still be eliminated. I was saddled with the same group of people, sort of like going to some strange summer camp. At this point, Mac was convinced we could play the game, but could we hold up under the pressures of lights, cameras, and a real audience? *Ha!* I thought, *Let me at 'em.*

We watched another group play for real. Surprisingly, it was exciting. We were sad when someone lost, knowing all they'd gone through to get there only to leave humiliated and empty-handed. I started to panic. What if that happened to me? At least the incredible catered food was some consolation. I should have brought a bigger purse.

Eventually, it was my group's turn. We'd already lost a couple to nerves, and one for belligerent behavior. I tried to remain optimistic. Who would be selected first from our group? Who? As long as it wasn't me. . . . *Calm down*, I told myself, as everyone wished me luck. I wasn't playing against them, so hopefully their wishes were sincere. Besides, I was an actress, I could handle it all. I hear my name. I bound out blathering like all those other game show contestants you wanna take out with a .45. Blah, blah, blah . . . Would I never shut up? Finally we play.

As the game begins, I forget every rule carefully drilled into me. We lose immediately. My only chance was that the other team against us was just as bad. We won the next round. There was hope.

Now, I'm playing with Phyllis Diller. She looked unbelievably great, but had she had one facelift too many? Miraculously we win the final round. My summer camp group goes wild. I'm having trouble breathing. Because absolutely all the players for the past week had been so terrible, the jackpot I was about to play for was now worth $25,000. $25,000! We play . . . down to the last second . . . Phyllis says, "Brush."

The clock literally moves to zero as I say, "Paint?" Pandemonium ensues as I win the wad. Phyllis, who's looking like Pamela Anderson right about now, falls to the floor as I attack Bert Convy. At this point I am one of those embarrassing, nails-on-the-blackboard contestants through and through. Only I was $17,000 richer! Uncle Sam was richer too!

THE JOHN HUSTON STORY

———— ☆ ————

By Robert Forster
Actor

This is a small part of my John Huston story. It's 1966. I came out to Los Angeles from New York . . . I'm here for two days. My agent calls me and says, "Do you know who John Huston is?" I say, "No, I don't." He says, "Well, he's a big guy in this business and he wants to meet you for *Reflections in a Golden Eye*." I read it in college—I felt literate! I read it again, quick. I jump on an airplane, I fly to New York, it's a Saturday afternoon. I go to a hotel on Madison Avenue where I'm supposed to meet this John Huston. I walk into the lobby, I look around, there are fifty guys who look like me! I thought he wanted to meet *me* for *Reflections in a Golden Eye*—how naive. I took a hike. I cooled off. After an hour or so I went back. There were fewer guys. I put myself on the bottom of the list. I wait and presently I'm called. I'm escorted up the elevator. We wait outside a room. Somebody is let out. I'm let in. I'm introduced to this tall, old guy. "What have you done?" he says. I said, "Listen, I haven't done much. I only did one Broadway play. I wasn't bad, but I don't make myself an actor. I never did a movie. I don't know how they're made. I don't know what the tricks are. But, if you hire me, I'll give you your money's worth."

John Huston says, "Ray! Ray! Would you please come in here. I'd like you to meet an ACT-TOR." I'm thinking to myself, *Who is this guy?* I just told him I wasn't an actor. He introduces me to a Ray Stark.

I turn back to the tall guy. He says, "You'll be hearing from us." I figured that was the kiss-off. The whole thing only took three minutes.

I left, went to the airport, stopped in Rochester to say hello to my father before going back to L.A. This is only two hours later. I get off the airplane, my father says, "Quick call your agent. They just made a deal!" Is that how deals are made? I had no idea!

"MOVIE TALK" PILOT
Decision by Committee

———— ☆ ————

By Diane Robison
Producer

When my partner and I were making our "Movie Talk" pilot, we had everything in place. The movie for review was set, the "high-profile" male host was on board, the guests were lined up, crew and shooting site chosen, and audience in place. One small task left . . . find an attractive co-hostess who could walk and talk at the same time. In a town with thousands of talented and beautiful women, "no problem." Reality hits.

We registered with the Breakdown Service and pored over literally hundreds of photos and resumés, narrowed it down to about twenty women, and spent two long days interviewing—making sure each talent had a complete opportunity to understand the show and her role, thereby presenting to us her finest creative abilities. In one fell swoop, the financial interest and the host shot down all our best bets. But they did agree (an experience that happened only once during the whole project) on a top model-actress. The attributes she possessed appealed to their physical nature (both appearing to have a crush on her). We gave in (like we had a lot of choice), feeling that one more battle might sink the ship. We were wrong, we should have gone to bat one more time.

Unfortunately, we helped, once again, to prove that talent sometimes plays a small part in the casting of a project in

Hollywood. Had we had the time, energy, and the experience we now possess as creative producers, things would have been different. You live and learn—that's what this process is about.

We lost the battle ... but we won the war. The financial interest drummed himself out of the business, the host nearly did very much the same. We now completely own the "Movie Talk" pilot. And like all good projects, it is once again finding its time and place in this unique world we call entertainment. Miracles can—and do—happen ... even in Hollywood.

PLAYBOY CASTING

———— ☆ ————

By Phil Savenick
Producer

I was directing a short film for the Playboy Channel and we were casting a part that included some nudity, so with much anticipation, I made an appointment with the Playboy modeling agency. They sat me in a room and several extraordinarily beautiful women paraded before me, showing me modeling portfolio photos of themselves in various stages of undress. I was way too nervous to ask any of the Playmates to take their clothes off, although a few volunteered. I would have liked to hire them all, but the tragedy of any casting session is the fact that you only get to send one person home happy. Sometimes, on a cattle call audition, hundreds of people might show up and you can only give out one job.

"A rose is a rose is a rose, unless the budget can only afford to pay for a daisy. Then makeup and wardrobe do their magic."

—Anonymous

Fitting the Part

Actors will go to extremes to get a role. One actress actually cut the seat belt out of her car to take in as a prop for an audition as a stewardess. Dangerous? Yes. Ridiculous? Yes. But, she got the part! . . . and a ticket.

JULIA ROBERTS, "MYSTIC" BEGINNINGS

☆

By Jane Jenkins, Janet Hirshenson, Michael Hirshenson
Casting Directors, The Casting Company

We were in New York casting *Mystic Pizza* when a relatively unknown Julia Roberts came in wearing a pair of baggy jeans and a big floppy shirt. We had seen a lot of young ladies in both Los Angeles and New York and it was becoming apparent that this particular part was going to be difficult to cast—there is one in every movie. When we first saw Julia, there was a quality about her that made us think she was really right for the part—even though she was blonde (the part was for a Portuguese) and she had not yet read the script in preparation. We suggested she return the next day and "start all over again."

The following day, Julia Roberts had colored her hair and returned wearing a mini skirt and a T-shirt—much more appropriate for the character. She had done her homework, focused and concentrated on what she was doing—and just nailed it. By the time the director arrived in New York we told him, "We have a young lady we think is quite terrific!" Julia landed the part and the movie was a big success.

CHRISTOPHER PLUMMER
BECOMES THE PART

By Gil Cates
Producer/Director

During the casting for *After the Fall*, we all agreed that Christopher Plummer would be terrific as Quinton, playing opposite Faye Dunaway. I met with Christopher and we talked about the part. He then asked me, "Who would you really have liked to play the role?" I thought to myself, *How courageous of him to ask this question.* After all, here we are offering him the role and he's asking who I would really like to play the part. And I said, "Well, the truth is that one of the actors I always thought would be good for this role would be George Segal." This is because the character in the play seemed to me to be Jewish, an upper-middle-class lawyer type, someone who did very well in his business but would be kind of overwhelmed to meet this woman, played by Faye Dunaway. He called me on the phone and said, "Would you be willing to invest five hundred dollars in an experiment?" I thought it was an odd request, but I was eager to have him in the production because he's a brilliant actor . . . an extraordinary man. I said, "Yes." He called the following week and said, "Dear boy, what are you doing about 6:30 this evening?" He then asked me to meet him between his matinee and evening performances at a theater where he was in a Neil Simon play.

I arrived at the theater and I knocked on his dressing room door, told his dresser I was there, and was told to wait one minute. I waited, and a voice said, "You can come in now." I walked in and there, seated behind the dressing room table, was George Segal. Or, at least, someone who I thought was George Segal. What

Christopher had done was to have a wig custom-made that actually made him look like George Segal. From our discussion and from the wig he developed this character of Quinton which he played with extraordinary results. Faye Dunaway's Maggie was sensational and received marvelous reviews as well. It was one of the best-reviewed productions I'd ever been involved with. I produced and directed it.

AUDREY MEADOWS, YOU'RE THE GREATEST!

☆

By Leonard Stern
Writer/Producer

Audrey Meadows was cast as the character of Alice Kramden the very day she was rejected as Alice Kramden. According to my sources, fellow writers on "The Jackie Gleason Show," Jackie had found Audrey physically wrong for the part. He told her agent, Val Irving, she was too young and much too pretty. When Audrey learned why she'd been turned down, she did, as Audrey usually did, the unexpected. She decided to *become* Alice. Ignoring Val's objections, she told him to get a photographer to her apartment as quickly as possible. She then plotted her wardrobe, restyled her hair, and removed all her makeup. Her pictures were developed before the end of the day. They delighted her—she looked dreadful! Sending them by messenger, she told Bullets Durgom, Jackie's manager, that under no condition was he to reveal the identity of the woman in the photos. Bullets complied. He showed them to Jackie without comment. Jackie's response was immediate. "That's more like it, pal," he told Bullets. "That's our Alice! Who is she? Where is she? Can we get her?" Grinning, Bullets told him it was the girl who had been there that morning, Audrey Meadows. Gleason got her on the phone immediately and told her she was Alice. He then added his first ever, "Baby, you're the greatest!"

MAKING AN IMPRESSION ON
MICHAEL DOUGLAS

By Joseph DiSante
Actor/ABC Executive

I had learned from inside sources that a film called *The China Syndrome* was going to be produced. I boldly walked in on Michael Douglas, dressed and acting like a news cameraman. I had just finished a stint working as a real news cameraman, so I was extremely confident. Michael admired my spirit, but told me, "This just isn't done anymore, kid." "Why not?" I asked, "I have experience as a real cameraman and I'm a real good actor!" "Fine," he exclaimed, "get your agent to set up a real appointment!" I got the real appointment, but not the part. Little did I know that Michael himself was set to do the cameraman opposite Jane Fonda's reporter.

WONDERWORKS

by Edna Harris
Actress/Comedienne

I was eleven years old and auditioned for a Wonderworks film on PBS starring Amanda Plummer, called *Gryphon*. I went in for the part of a girl, but I wasn't right for the part—because they were going with another type altogether. When I read for the director he had an idea that surprised me. He asked me to read the role of a boy. He made me put on these glasses because the boy was a preppy kid in the class. He liked my reading so much, he decided to change the role of the boy to the role of a girl. The role was far more interesting than the original part I tried out for. My friends were impressed and surprised when they saw the film because I was playing a character against type. It made me realize that nothing is etched in stone and characters can be changed—and someone can change their vision. I think taking risks is what acting is all about.

CAPTAIN AMERICA!

——————— ☆ ———————

By Kurt Schwoebel
Actor and "Star"!

Actors rarely get to experience all the trappings of being a successful actor until they become successful and it's too late. I had the experience of being a *celebrity* in one of my acting jobs and it's not all it's cracked up to be.

While hustling in New York City for acting gigs, I had the opportunity to interview at Marvel Comics to play Captain America for personal appearances. The audition I thought would be fairly easy—let them look at my body, a little small talk, and that's it. What I wasn't prepared for was to put on the costume and just walk around the office and introduce myself to everyone! Needless to say I experienced a little stage fright but also realized that this is what I would have to do out in public THE WHOLE TIME I WAS WEARING THE COSTUME . . . What a scary thought.

I was hired and soon was sent out on all kinds of promotional jobs, from theme park and comic book store openings, to charity spokesperson and corporate conventions. I quickly developed a character inside the costume and learned I had to keep it going the entire time I was in the public. It was exhausting!

I did learn a lot about the ups and downs of being in the spotlight. The good things were how to handle live interviews, how to handle on-the-fly public appearances, clear diction and posture, and finally using the power of a positive role model to affect people, especially children, in a healthy way.

The not-so-good things included being on a heightened state of alertness at all times with the costume on: Do I look right? Am I giving the right vibrations out? Do they like me? There was one instance where I was going to do an appearance at a children's hospital and I didn't have time to eat so I went into the hospital cafeteria, which was practically deserted. My initial desire was for bacon and eggs, or something unhealthy (but tasty to me the person!) but at the last minute I realized "Captain" probably would not eat that way, so I ordered a bran muffin and orange juice. Sure enough there was a reporter there witnessing my meal and he wrote an article for the local paper entitled "Even Super Heroes Get Hungry," listing exactly what I had for breakfast!! You never know. . . .

Anyway, my experience as a part-time celebrity gave me insight into the part of show biz that you don't have any control over once you get there. At least I was able to take off my costume and be anonymous and relaxed. I still want to be a success in the biz but now know of the pitfalls of being in the spotlight. Maybe I'll wear a ski mask when I go out to practice what's ahead.

BEAUTY AND THE "BEST"

By Gary Gardner
Producer/Director/Actor/Drama Teacher

Many students, who when they were in school doing frightening things at auditions for roles I didn't cast them in, are now doing major roles. Susan Egan, who is now on Broadway as Belle, the

Beauty in *Beauty and the Beast,* was nominated for a Tony. . . . During her freshman year, I was directing *A Chorus Line,* and she was good, but not *exceptional,* and so I put her in the pit as one of the singers. She was completely hidden from the audience. And the girl who played the lead in the show has twice been her understudy in professional shows. . . . So, maybe I know nothing about casting.

FROM THE LYONS DEN

By Warren Lyons
Performer

IN MEMORY OF HIS FATHER, LEONARD LYONS

This is from "The Lyons Den," a column by my father, September 3, 1947. . . .

George Cukor gave a luncheon party for Katharine Hepburn, Ethel Barrymore, Gypsy Rose Lee, and Fanny Brice. There was a thunderstorm during the luncheon, and the lights went out . . . "Suppose we suddenly were entombed here," said Miss Lee, "and stayed this way—here at this table—dressed as we are—for thousands of years. I wonder what the archeologists of the future would think, when they found us."

The guests continued this theme and added the supposition that the archeologists knew only that one was a stripteaser, one was a distinguished actress, one was a comedienne, and the fourth was a lady of social background.

They agreed that the archeologists would decide that Miss Hepburn was the stripteaser, Miss Lee the lady of social background, Miss Brice the distinguished actress, and Miss Barrymore the comedienne.

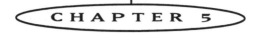
OUT OF THE BLUE!

★

"A minute later the balding little man
was back asking, 'Are you a dancer?'
My wise-ass response was,
'No. I just dress like this to stay cool.'
. . . He smiled and said, 'Hi, I'm Bob Fosse.'
It was the most embarrassing moment of my life . . .
how I became Fosse's dance assistant
for his show *Dancin'* on Broadway!"

—ROBYN WHITNEY
Former Dancer/Choreographer

Say What?!

After years of preparation and sometimes countless rejections, the *big break* will happen when you least expect it, coming off the wall, from left field, completely out of the blue . . .

BOB FOSSE, DANCIN' ON BROADWAY!

☆

By Robyn Whitney
Former Dancer/Choreographer

ONLY IN NEW YORK: When I arrived in the Big Apple I was full of hope and many years of training, but I was incredibly naive. I was at a rehearsal facility where there were large dance spaces for rent for various shows that were in preparation. While on a break from the nightclub review I was hired for, I was standing in the open doorway of the women's dressing room in my tights and leotard. I had used a pin to close the neckline of my leotard and it caused the fabric to rip, so I was sewing the hole at my cleavage closed by watching it in reverse in front of a mirror. Out of the corner of my eye I saw a short, middle-aged man peek in at me. I ignored him and he walked away. Several seconds later he reappeared and asked, "What are you doing?" I was beginning to think New York was full of creeps, so I quipped, "Sewing up this hole so guys like you don't look in." He disappeared. A minute later the balding little man was back asking, "Are you a dancer?" My wise-ass response was, "No. I just dress like this to stay cool."

Instead of being insulted, he laughed and told me he was a choreographer. He needed a dancer to help him create pieces for a concert he was working on. I was extremely skeptical. He looked more like a cab driver than any director I'd ever seen. I told him that I already had a job on a nightclub gig but that if the money was right I'd come across to his space to help him whenever I could. I said my name and extended my hand to shake his. He smiled and said, "Hi, I'm Bob Fosse." It was a good thing that he was holding my hand because my knees went right out from under me from shock. It was the most embarrassing moment of my life . . . how I *auditioned* and became Fosse's dance assistant for his show *Dancin'* on Broadway!

I DREAM OF JEANNIE

By Barbara Eden
Actress

I received a phone call one day from Sidney Sheldon. He said, "I hear you're my Jeannie." And I said, "Oh, I hope so." I knew they had tested every brunette in town and so I had lunch with him at the Beverly Hills Hotel. And I had the part!

DYLAN McDERMOTT,
IN THE LINE OF FIRE!

By Jane Jenkins, Janet Hirshenson,
Michael Hirshenson
Casting Directors, The Casting Company

Once in a great while an actor will do an outrageous audition that will stick in our minds. Dylan McDermott was fresh out of Julliard, when he came in to audition for *The Princess Bride*. He did not land the role. But we taped his audition for another film and when we were casting *In the Line of Fire* we showed the tape to Wolfgang Petersen who said, "He's perfect, cast him." So Dylan received a phone call saying, "Congratulations, you'll be starring opposite Clint Eastwood in *In the Line of Fire*." Dylan said, "When did I audition for this?" . . . We received a telegram from him saying, "Go ahead, make my career."

THE RIGHT PLACE AT THE RIGHT TIME

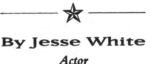

By Jesse White
Actor

I've had a lot of lucky breaks in this business—but the most important thing in my life is my family. I was blessed with two beautiful daughters and three gorgeous grandkids. I love to spoil them, and knock on wood my success has allowed me to do that.

One major turning point in my career came when I was about to call it quits in New York and head home to Akron, Ohio, with my wife. I had been in six straight Broadway flops. I'd rehearse a show for five weeks, only to see it close after three days . . . So, I'm loading up my new car (purchased for three hundred dollars from actor John Forsythe) and I'm dead set against staying. My family back home is actually waiting for me to arrive! I happened to go back into the apartment to get a carton. The phone was ringing. "Are you Jesse White?" the person asked. "Yes," I replied. "Were you in a play called, *Mrs. Kimbal Presents*?" I said, "Yes." She said, "Mr. Brock Pemberton is producing a play called *Harvey*. He and the author Mary Chase would like to meet you. Can you be here at four o'clock?"

I had a ritual when reading for a new play. I'd buy a one-dollar cigar—whether I could afford it or not. I lit that cigar and sauntered in with an air of confidence—I just knew I was going to get that role. Mary Chase saw me and laughed. "That's him!" she said. "That's Wilson the sanitarium attendant!"

And that changed my whole life. My hair stands on end when I think that a minute sooner or a minute later I would have missed that call and gone back to Ohio. I worked for four years on Broadway in that role. And that opened up radio and television for me. Here I am, sixty-four movies, seventeen Broadway shows, four different TV series, and countless commercials later. It's been a good life.

"I'VE GOT A SECRET"

By Jayne Meadows
Actress

In 1951 very few people in Los Angeles had television sets and the movie industry in particular was quite indifferent to the new medium. The coaxial cable linking the East and West Coasts had not as yet gone through. New York City was the center of the Golden Age of Television.

As a Broadway and movie actress, I had no interest in TV and didn't own a set myself. My next-door neighbors, Gloria De Haven and her husband John Payne, did, however, and they invited me to watch the Rose Parade and football game—and all we actually saw was a test pattern, all day long.

My marriage to my first husband was breaking up, so I decided to return to New York and my first love, the Broadway stage. Instead I ended up in—you guessed it—TV. I had hardly unpacked when my agent sent me on an audition for a new game show called "I've Got a Secret." All TV was live in 1952, and "Secret" was televised on Thursday nights. This was a Friday—no chance for me to see the program which had only been on for two weeks.

Mother and I decided to stroll over to the CBS Studios since we had to walk our dog anyway. I was amazed to see practically every actor in New York City trying out for the show. As I stood bewildered in the entrance, I heard a perfectly strange man call out. "You, the redhead in the doorway—what's your name?" It was the legendary producer, Mark Goodson. Fortunately, his assistant knew of my work and whispered, "That's Jayne Meadows." I was asked to sit at the panel and play the game. After about twenty minutes, Mark dismissed all the actors and said, "Miss Meadows, you are a great game player—and I think your saucy personality is very commercial. We'd like to try you out for the next three weeks. Be at the theater in an evening gown at 8:30 P.M. The show goes on the air at 9:00."

That was it; no rehearsal; there wasn't even a makeup man or hairdresser all the years I was on the show. After my debut show, Mark signed me to a seven-year contract. What he didn't know was that as a missionary's daughter born and raised in China, I had spent my childhood playing games. My teen years were spent in a tiny New England town, population 1,100. We had no theaters, no restaurants, nor bars, only a tea room in the local inn, and churches—lots of churches. A big night on the town meant going to a friend's house with my older brothers to sing or play parlor games. I knew every game ever invented.

"I've Got a Secret" became one of the highest-rated and longest-running shows in TV history, and Mark Goodson told me that my personal TVQ rating was higher than all his other panelists put together—which included "What's My Line?," "To Tell the Truth," etc. My starting salary was $165 a week. When I left the show seven years later, with fan mail second only to that of Lucille Ball according to the CBS press department, my salary had escalated to the enormous sum of $500 a week. Garry Moore, as host of "I've Got a Secret" started at $500 a week. The first year my sister Audrey (Alice Kramden on "The Honeymooners") was on "The Jackie Gleason Show," she got the same salary as I ($165), and was on the show every other week.

Unlike the astronomical salaries of today's young performers, we were all paid peanuts—but we loved our work, much of which is greatly respected today.

A COMMERCIAL THAT LED TO A LEAD

By Kenneth Mars
Actor

I have a lot of stories from the *naked city*, shaded with palms and blighted by freeways. From the time I first played a swinish Nazi in Rodgers and Hammerstein's *The Sound of Music*, through the Mel Brooks movies *The Producers* and *Young Frankenstein*, I had been frequently typecast. On one particular occasion, after having won a CLIO Award for Spokesman of the Year, for a commercial I had done for Ocean Spray cranberry juice, Ethel Winant, the casting director, called writer/producer Leonard Stern. She told him I would be right to play Harry the fireman on "He and She," starring the incredibly talented Paula Prentiss and the wonderful light farceur Dick Benjamin, who has gone on to direct, and of course the zany Jack Cassidy and Hamilton Camp. A terrific cast. Because Leonard had great trust in Ethel's discerning taste—which we all know was considerable, after all she hired me—Leonard gave the go ahead on his trust in her alone—though he had never even seen me. This kind of fast and loose casting never happens anymore. Thank you, Leonard Stern and Ethel Winant!

DESTINED FOR *KEY LARGO*

By Harry Lewis
Actor/Restaurateur

Usually, when you are cast in a film you have to read for the part—unless you're one of the top stars or they have you in mind when they write the script. Today, even the biggest actors go in and read for a part—though they're not too happy about that. With that in mind, the following is how I was cast for the part of Toots in *Key Largo*, a very big superstar picture. . . .

I was told by the casting director at Warner Bros., where I was under contract, to report to director John Huston and producer Jerry Wald. I went into their office expecting to see a group of people. To my surprise, the only people in the room were John Huston, Jerry Wald, and me! They said, "Sit down." I sat down. They said, "We're doing this film called *Key Largo*." And they listed this big superstar cast: Edward G. Robinson, Humphrey Bogart, Lauren Bacall, Claire Trevor, Lionel Barrymore. Then they said, "We want you to play the part of Toots in this film. (Toots is a baby-faced killer bodyguard who goes all the way through the film; everywhere Robinson is, Toots is with a gun protecting him). I said, "That's terrific. Do you want me to read for you now?" They said, "No, we don't want you to read at all. We want you to play the part!" I said, "Oh?!" . . . as I kind of fell between the chairs. They said, "We start rehearsals next Monday. We rehearse for two weeks, and then we start to shoot the film." I said, "That's wonderful!" So we all looked at each other and I said, "Well, thank you!" And they said, "Well that's fine. We're very happy to have you." I said, "Is that all?" They said, "That's all, just report Monday for rehearsal," which I did. And we made the film. And that is how I was cast in *Key Largo*. It's extraordinary. Things seldom happen like that!

WATERWORLD BREAK

By Henry Kapono
Actor/Singer/Songwriter

I was at my home in Honolulu, working on songs for my latest album, when I received a call, out of the blue, to come and read for the part of a drifter in Kevin Costner's movie *Waterworld*. The part was small, but I thought, *Why not? I'll just stop by on my way to a singing gig in Waikiki.* When I walked in I saw many people I knew who had been acting for years, all dressed like drifters. I was wearing my performing clothes and felt overdressed. The producers seemed to like the reading I gave. They then asked me to read for the part of the gate man. They seemed to like that reading as well. I was in a rush to get to work, so I thanked them and said good-bye. I thought, *Well I gave it a shot.* I then forgot about it. About four days later, they called to tell me I got the part. It turned out to be a principal role! I ended up having six weeks of work—and a second career!

THE WRONG JOE

By Joseph DiSante
Actor/ABC Executive

This is perhaps the ugliest thing that ever happened to me. I was sitting in my apartment watching my baby daughter play with her toys—she was quite young. I had not worked in a long time. Sitting there watching her play, I kept thinking, *Why in the hell did I even choose this profession? How am I going to be able to give this little girl a decent life?* It was the worst feeling in the world.

Out of nowhere, the phone rang, and there is a casting director on the other end. His first name was Tony. I can't remember his last name. He immediately starts talking to me about a role in a film that was called *Johnny Got His Gun*, written by Dalton Trumbo. And he says, "Is this Joe DiSante?" I said, "Yes, yes it is!" He starts discussing the role of a doctor who treats the lead character in the story. He is discussing the role with me based on the premise that I already had the role. "We want you to start this Monday. I'll be sending the script over to you . . ." and so forth. I was beside myself! I couldn't believe it! One minute I'm ready to jump out the window, and the next minute the phone rings, and I am being offered this very plum role! *This is incredible*, I thought. Charlie Chaplin was right when he wrote in his autobiography, "In show business, your life can change in a minute!"

I started asking this Tony some questions about the role. He was very polite, very wonderful, he started answering all my questions. And as we're talking, I distinctly get the feeling, ever so slowly, that we were discussing a much, much older role. "Excuse me," I said, "how old is this doctor?" He said, "Oh, he's in his early sixties." I immediately knew he had the wrong Joe. Finally, he said, "Well, what do you think, Joe, it's a wonderful role for you," etc. I answered, "I think you have reached the wrong Joe. I think you're calling for Joe DiSantis!" "Yes, Joe DiSantis," he said. I said, "I'm not Joe DiSantis. I know who you want, he's the older character actor. I'm Joe DiSante!" Tony was dead silent. He did not say a word. I said, "I know Joe . . . you've got the wrong Joe." And finally, you know what he did? He flat hung up. Slammed the phone in my ear without even an "I'm sorry," nothing . . . he just hung up. Never said another word. I stood there looking at the phone for a second or so and then I just went back to watching my daughter play with her toys, thinking, *Why in the heck did I ever choose this profession!?!*

TOPPER

By Anne Jeffreys
Actress

My husband Robert Sterling and I had an act with which we toured the most popular nightclubs. We opened at the Chase in St. Louis, then we played the Empire Room at the Waldorf in New York, the Palmer House in Chicago, and the Broadmore in

Colorado Springs. Finally, we were at the Sands in Las Vegas for six weeks. While we were there, we received a call from our agent saying, "Annie, I've got a TV version of the original movie *Topper.* Would you and Robert be interested in doing it?" And I said, "Oh, would I, would I!" I had been a big fan of the *Topper* movies. "I'll send you the script," he said.

They sent us the script and we both loved it. You didn't read in those days. If you were an established actor, ordinarily you didn't have to audition or read. We closed at the Sands, then played the Coconut Grove in Los Angeles. While we played the Coconut Grove at night, we shot the pilot during the day. And when we closed our engagement in Los Angeles, we went to the Fairmont in San Francisco. While we were performing there, the agent called and said, "It's sold! Cancel the rest of your tour! It's the quickest selling pilot we've ever produced! Come right back! Let's go to work!" We've been very lucky that way.

"It never fails,
everybody who really makes it
does it by busting his or her behind."

—Alan Arkin

Awkward Moments

One of the most frustrating situations, inherent in *the biz*, is when, despite the best-laid plans, you mess up. And upon reflection you search, think, and ponder, finding absolutely nobody to blame . . . but yourself.

YOU'RE IN GOOD HANDS WITH RANCE HOWARD

———— ☆ ————

By John Thomas Lenox
Producer/Director

There are a couple of people whom I consider to be my *good luck charms*. If I am in town, I will not do a film without Pat Cronin and Rance Howard (father of Ron Howard, actor/director). When we were doing *The Long Hot Summer* mini-series in Louisiana, Rance was perfect for one of the roles—so we cast him as a local farmer. He was, once again, my good luck charm, because we got an Emmy nomination for that one.

This is another wonderful Rance Howard casting story. Rance does a lot of commercials. This requires going to lots of interviews. He's very good about figuring out what people are looking for, and that's what he'll deliver when he goes into the casting session. He was called in for a State Farm Insurance Company commercial audition. He gave what he called a "rocko, socko, wonderful audition!" Everyone in the room raved about how *right* he was for the spot. He just knew he had this commercial in his pocket.

Rance was thrilled. It was time to go and celebrate. He walked to the door, and turned around to face all the executives, producers, and agency people. Then, he cupped his hands and said, "You're in good hands." He turned around and walked out. Closing the door, he realized that this was the signature of Allstate, not State Farm.... He lost the job.

TOO LATE

☆

By John Ratzenberger
Actor/Director/Producer

I was casting for a project. The brother of a well-known actor came in to read and sauntered in forty-five minutes late. I'm a real stickler for punctuality and he was acting like he was going out on the patio to have a lemonade. He plopped down on the chair and said, "Hey man, how's it going?" I said, "Fine. I don't know if you knew this, but you were supposed to be here forty-five minutes ago." He laughed it off and said, "Yeah, crazy, isn't that something!" He acted like it didn't mean anything. I thought, *Is this going to happen on the set if we hire him? Will he keep a hundred people waiting on the set if he gets the job?* So, basically, he was the best person to read for the part, but we decided not to give it to him.

As an actor, I would always show up an hour early for any casting session. First of all, I'd make sure I have the building and the place right. Then I'd go have some coffee and relax. Often, some young actors lose jobs because they come into the office huffing and puffing. They only have ten minutes to *strut their stuff*. But the first five minutes sometimes is taken up with the huffing and puffing and the traffic and how they almost didn't make it. And so they waste a lot of time talking about things they shouldn't be talking about. But if you get there an hour early, know where the building is, get the address right, then you can relax, walk in like you own the place and do the best job you can. I still do this for business meetings: I show up an hour early and make sure I know where I am, relax, have a cup of coffee, and read the paper.

THE CLOSE CALL

By Billy DaMota
Casting Director

There are a number of things I could write about . . . interesting . . . sexy . . . profound. This is the story I chose. I call it The Close Call.

A number of years ago, I was lucky enough to work with Dennis Hopper on a film called *Colors*. I was a big fan of his work as both an actor and director, and it was a thrill for me to be involved with him on his "comeback" directorial project, which was set to star two other favorites, Sean Penn and Robert Duvall.

The casting process was grueling. Three months and thousands of interviews. We had over one hundred roles to cast and Dennis wanted to cast real gang members in a number of the roles. We spent a great deal of time in East L.A., South-Central, San Pedro, and Venice, and many a time we would find ourselves in a deserted parking lot, after midnight, taking Polaroids, and *hangin' with the home boys*. Now I grew up in a pretty tough neighborhood in San Francisco and I've seen the street close up, but this was quite an experience even for me. On occasion, the police would come by and break up our little rendezvous, but we were a little naive and never encountered any serious problems. Until . . .

Back at Lion's Gate Studios (a facility in West L.A. where we did our casting), we set up some additional sessions with real gang members. But this is where our naiveté became potentially dangerous. You see, at that point we didn't really understand that you couldn't put rival gangs together, and that's just what we had planned. We had scheduled, through leaders of both the Crips and the Bloods, two rival gangs from South-Central L.A., to see members of their gangs respectively for supporting roles in the film. The problem was that we had scheduled them (lots of them) to arrive at nearly the same moment!

As it turned out, and quite fortunately for us, a member of CRASH, the LAPD gang control unit, was at the studio and realized what we were doing. He quickly made us aware of our faux pas and, for the next few hours, we madly called every member of the Crips to ask them nicely to come by the next day. Needless to say, everyone working at the studio was aware of our predicament— some left for home, other thrill seekers stuck around on pins and needles ... and amidst all the drama, Dennis was in his glory, but we had a producer who was about to have a cardiac.

As we hung up on the last of our insane flurry of phone calls, our first appointments, about twenty carloads of Bloods, began arriving! Loud, all RED, and lots of attitude. And luckily for everyone—NO CRIPS!

Later, after all the day's interviews were over, and more than one hundred gang members, old and young, men and women, had been seen, interviewed, and Polaroided (without incident, I should add), the producer made us promise to see any other gang members away from the office ... actually, as I remember, it was more of an order.

SOUTHERN EXPOSURE

By Gina Francis
Actress

My best friend Patrick is one of the most talented people I know. But as is the case with truly talented people, they usually have many self-doubts. He is no exception. After much prodding on my part, I finally convinced him to go to this audition with me. Together we worked and worked on a scene, so he felt fairly confident. We arrived at the audition and in the waiting area I said, "There was something I wanted to tell you." "What was it? something about the scene? Think, think, what was it?" he asked. I said, "I can't remember, it must not be anything." Soon after, he's called in to read. Later, as we are both leaving the audition, I finally remember. "Oh, yeah. Your fly's open."

ENTICING CARY GRANT

By Sid Luft
Producer

I had the pleasure of trying to entice Cary Grant to play the lead role in *A Star Is Born*. Warner Bros. had approved a certain amount of money to be offered—unfortunately not a percentage of the gross of the profits. Cary had an agent at Music Corporation of America, known as MCA. Prior to getting into the nitty gritty of talking money or percentages, Cary and I became very friendly.

Cary knew I liked to go to the racetrack—as a matter of fact, I think I owned a piece of a racehorse at that time—and I remember going to the track with him. The stories of Cary being frugal were true. One time on our way to Hollywood Park Racetrack, he said, "I have to stop by my manager's office to get $100." In those days there were only eight races. He said, "I bet $10 per race and leave $20 for food and gasoline. My favorite jockey is Bill Shoemaker."

One morning, Cary called saying he wanted to go to the races. I told him, "I have a tip on the first race, a horse owned by some friends of mine." He said, "Fine." I picked up Cary at his agent's office and we arrived early. To make a long story short, I bet $200 at sixteen to one. My horse won easily, and I won nearly $4,000. Cary didn't bet because he bet Bill Shoemaker. I was elated, I had won a lot of money. Cary Grant asked how much money I'd won on the race. I told him about $3,900. I then said I was going to bet half of it on another horse called Alley Cat. The significance of my hunch was that Arthur Freed, who had produced most of Judy Garland's musicals at MGM, had made a crack to Mervin LeRoy when it was announced that Judy and I were going to do *A Star Is Born*, "Wait till those two alley cats try to make a movie." That's why I wanted to bet on this horse Alley Cat. Cary said to me, "If you bet on Alley Cat, I won't do *A Star Is Born* for you. Anyway, the race came up and the horse went off at fifty to one and I only bet $40 . . . forty dollars! When the horse won, I could have killed him! . . . And Cary Grant didn't even end up starring in the movie!

ENTER LAUGHING, EXIT WITH DIGNITY

By Alan Rachins
Actor

Early in my career I auditioned for Joyce Selznick, who is a very famous and formidable casting director in New York City. This was for a part in *Enter Laughing*, a Carl Reiner movie. As I was reading, she started shaking her head slowly side to side in a no motion, which was really demoralizing, because I had to look up and face her with each new line I had to say—only to see her head going from side to side. (If I had *entered laughing*, I certainly didn't leave that way.) These situations are something any actor has to overcome in order to maintain one's sense of dignity.

"THE MIKE DOUGLAS SHOW" AUDITION

By Ari Dane
Singer/Actor/Performer

We all have to face it sooner or later. Rejection is a part of the showbiz process. *B.C.*, that's *before comedy*, I was a young boy singer. I auditioned for "The Mike Douglas Show" in Philadelphia. It was the late fifties and I was nervous as heck. I strummed my guitar and sang, "Try to Remember a Kind of September . . ." I swear, that's as far as I got when the director of the show stood up in the back of the studio and screamed, "I HATE THAT (BLANK) SONG!!!!" and stormed out of the room . . . OK, I wasn't too crazy about it myself. The whole trick in handling rejection is not to take it personally. The best revenge is success!

THE UNKNOWN UNDERSTUDY

By Jeremiah Morris
Director/Actor/Writer, Actors Alley Theater

This took place in Pittsburgh at the Nixon Theater in the early 1950s. This actress had been an understudy all her life and had never performed. This one evening she came into the theater and was finally told, "You're going on!" She thanked the stage manager for telling her. She walked up one flight of stairs to the star's dressing room—which was hers for the evening. She opened the window, went down the fire escape, left town, and was never seen or heard from again!

Foot in Mouth

We've all been through it, at least once in our lives—it seems to come with the birth certificate! Something is said or done and, when the shock and embarrassment wear off, we quietly extract our size ten foot out of our gaping mouth.

CAROL BURNETT AND HARVEY KORMAN "KILLED" WITH IT!

☆

By Gene Perret
Writer/Producer

We were writing the pilot for a show called "That's TV." We didn't need stars because the show was the star. We hired unknowns. My partner, Bill Richmond, and I had written for five years on the "Carol Burnett Show," and we had some sketches of ours that had played well. So, we grabbed a couple of pieces of material and brought them with us "just in case."

A young girl and guy team came in to audition and didn't have any material. So we gave them a sketch Carol Burnett and Harvey Korman had performed on the show that had gone over very well. We said, "Read this over and we'll set up a little setting here, a table and chairs, and you can play the sketch." They got up to perform the sketch and it was dying. We all sat patiently and when they were done, we thanked them. The young lady came over to Bill

Richmond and I, and said, "You know, we really are better than this, but you can't do a good job when the material is so crappy."

CLINT HOWARD, AN ACTOR'S ACTOR

———— ☆ ————

By Rance Howard
Actor

Shortly before my son Ron Howard had done a pilot for "The Andy Griffith Show," our second son Clint was born. Time passed and Ron was having much success as Opie in the series. When Clint made his debut on "The Andy Griffith Show," he played a character called Leon. Clint was very much in demand in the business and he was doing a lot of anthology shows and some commercials. Clint is a terrific actor, really solid. As a child, he came closer to being a pure method actor than anyone I've ever seen. He was just brutally honest: always was, always has been.

Now Clint is about three and a half years old. I took him up to audition for a Bayer aspirin commercial. He quickly learned the dialogue, we went in, and he did the scene about this little boy who loved Bayer aspirin. The agency people, the clients, and the production people were all enthralled. They thought, *This is our kid.* Shortly before we left, Clint looked up at one guy and said, "Mister, have you ever tried St. Joseph's aspirin? They're a lot better." And everybody kind of looked at each other . . . they looked around the room and I said, "Uh oh." And so we left and he didn't get the job.

"I'm not sure acting is a thing for a grown man."

—Steve McQueen

AN AUDIENCE WITH
PRINCE CHARLES AND LADY DIANA

By Patrick Macnee
Actor

In the 1960s I starred as John Steed in the television show "The Avengers." As a result of that show, and Albert R. "Cubby" Broccoli taking an interest in me, I had the pleasure of being involved in a most wonderful casting experience. It began as follows. . . . I was featured in a "Magnum P.I." and Cubby's daughter, Barbara Broccoli, was in Hawaii with a friend and told her father, "Don't you think Pat Macnee would be good as the part of the jockey?" Cubby Broccoli said, "Don't you think he's a bit large to play the role of a jockey?" And Barbara replied, "Don't you think you could change the character?" And he did, he changed the character to a racehorse trainer. Oddly enough, my father himself was a famous racehorse trainer named Shrimp Macnee. Because of this change in the character, I was given this very lovely part in this film called *A View to a Kill*, which was Roger Moore's last James Bond film. In fact, all my leading ladies, Joanna Lumley, Diana Rigg, and Honor Blackman, have, of course, been featured in James Bond films. When this came to me in 1984, I was delighted to do it.

I had no particular contract with the producer. My part, although small, turned out to be significant and I starred alongside the others in the movie. As a result, in 1985 I attended the Royal Command Film Performance, in London, which was attended by Prince Charles and Lady Diana. This took place at the Odeon Cinema in Leicester Square. It was a very smart and wonderful occasion, covered by the media. I was in the middle of the receiving line, between Tanya Roberts, a very beautiful lady who played the lead in the film, and Grace Jones, who I think a lot of people know as being a *volcanic* and talented singer. Before the film began, we had to stand and wait to be introduced to the

Prince and Princess. They were starting to come along the line and were being introduced by Cubby Broccoli's stepson, Michael Wilson. As they got toward us, the ladies on either side of me were chatting away about some startling, exciting subjects and I said, "Look, the royal couple is coming." They didn't know or particularly care, and they didn't seem to have the same sort of reverence that I, coming from the United Kingdom, had for the monarchy. Anyway, I got them to stand beside me like two little soldiers and Princess Diana came first and made sweet remarks to all of us. Then came Prince Charles, whose knowledge is encyclopedic. He dazzled me with his knowledge of my father and some of the horses he had trained, in particular one called Rivalry. I was glowing with pride. Then Michael Wilson took him on to Tanya Roberts who was on my left. I heard, quite clearly, this royal person suddenly turn to Tanya Roberts, "And my dear, did you get this job on the casting couch?" I was stunned! Poor Tanya didn't know where to look, she sort of rocked on her heels. I found it gorgeously funny, very charmingly done, quite mad, and absolutely out of context.

"*Good judgment comes from experience.*

And experience?

Well, that comes from

bad judgment."

—Anonymous

MY INTERVIEW WITH
GEORGE ABBOTT

————— ☆ —————

By Jayne Meadows
Actress

While still in high school, I spent my summers in stock companies in Connecticut and Millbrook, New York. In the latter company, Celeste Holm was the leading lady and the leading man was the brilliant Montgomery Clift. I played everything from comedy ingenues to an Italian peasant girl in *They Knew What They Wanted* (which would later become the hit musical *Most Happy Fella*); a middle-aged, cockney nurse in the classic drama *Night Must Fall*; and a Russian princess in Noel Coward's *Tonight at 8:30*.

At sixteen years of age, I felt perfectly capable of taking on Broadway and was chomping at the bit to graduate. As soon as I did, and armed only with my mother, the confidence of a teenager, and a letter of introduction to George Abbott given me by a member of my father's congregation, I made a beeline for the Great White Way.

Unfortunately, my kind patron couldn't remember Mr. Abbott's office address, but she assured us that he was the most successful writer/producer/director on Broadway and that his office would certainly be listed in the phone book. Mother and I did as instructed, and though several G. Abbott's were listed in the Manhattan book, we picked the one at One Broadway since we knew that Broadway was the theater district.

We took the bus all the way down to the Battery and went up to Mr. Abbott's office. When I opened the door and saw about fifty secretaries all typing away I thought, *Wow, this man really is a big producer.* My legs were shaking so that my mother, who looked and talked like actress Billie Burke, stepped up to the manager's desk and sweetly asked, "Is Mr. Abbott in?"

The manager said, "And who wants to see him?"

"My daughter Jayne. She's an actress." And with the gesture of a magician's assistant she presented me to the bewildered gentleman who answered, "I'm sorry but you have the wrong George Abbott. This is the George Abbott Coal Company."

I met the real Mr. Abbott, incidentally, for the first time in the mid-1980s, when he was in his mid-nineties. Even then he was irresistibly handsome. Had I not been happily married to Steve, I could have fallen madly in love with this genius.

ROBERT DE NIRO AND TONY RANDALL
The King of Comedy

by Camille Harris
Producer

I was representing Tony Randall through Diamond Artists when we received a call for Tony to do a cameo in a film starring Robert De Niro and Jerry Lewis, directed by Martin Scorsese, titled *The King of Comedy*. The deal was worked out, Tony shot the cameo, and went on to do his series "Love, Sidney" on NBC. When they called for Tony to do an additional scene, he was busy with his series and it was difficult for him to arrange the time. I kept receiving phone calls from a Bob De Niro, and I must admit that it was an unwanted distraction that became an annoyance, because we were so occupied with the new series. Bob De Niro and I kept missing each other. Finally, they tracked him down in the editing room and I assumed that he was an editor—I somehow didn't make the connection that Bob De Niro was indeed Robert De Niro. However, Tony did. And when he realized that Robert De Niro was personally asking him to do this as a favor, of course he complied. As fate would have it, the additional scene ended up on the cutting room floor.

WILLIAM HOLDEN DIED COOL

———— ✯ ————

By Mark Edwards
Newscaster

In the sometimes wonderful, at times entertaining, but often unpredictable realm of live radio broadcasting, unaccountable things often happen. Here's the way an audition for a news radio job went for me, on one of those unforgettable days.

After a brief period of going through the routine of editing and arranging, I began my live five-minute audition with a standard assembly of international, national, state, and local news. I wrapped up the newscast with the story of the tragic, sudden death of the world-famous actor, William Holden. And here is how the last line of that whole obituary went: "Moviegoers from around the world will miss William Holden. He was sixty-four degrees!" . . . You got it. I had inadvertently jumped ahead in my mind to the weather part of the newscast.

"If at first you don't succeed,

try, try again.

Then quit.

There's no use being a damn fool about it."

—W. C. Fields

CHAPTER 6

DATE WITH DESTINY!

☆

"All the world's a stage,
and all the men and women merely players.
They have their exits and their entrances.
And one man in his time plays many parts."

—SHAKESPEARE
from *As You Like It*

What If?

Where would these stars be now if they hadn't been in the right place at the right time?

DAVID LETTERMAN'S BIG BREAK
One Man's Gratitude

——————— ☆ ———————

By Terrie Maxine Frankel
Writer/Producer

SCORE
DAVID LETTERMAN 10
HUSTLER CENTERFOLD 10
THE FRANKEL TWINS 0

Fifteen years ago, getting an audition for "The Tonight Show Starring Johnny Carson" was nearly impossible, particularly for up-and-coming comediennes. Yet, my sister Jennie and I did it! In the process we ended up changing the course of our lives as well as the life of our "friend," David Letterman.

Jennie and I were in Las Vegas visiting Joey Bishop, who was performing at the Riviera Hotel. (We had originally performed with Joey on a USO tour in Vietnam and had kept in touch with him over the years.) We asked Joey if he would please set up an audition for us for "The Tonight Show." (After all, we had been working on a five-minute presentation at the Comedy Store and the Improv for over a year and felt we were more than ready for the *shot.*) "No problem," said Joey. Our conversation was interrupted by a young comedian from the Comedy Store, Alan Bursky, who showed up for an interview with Joey Bishop. Joey excused himself and went off to talk with Alan. Twenty minutes later, Joey returned. We asked Joey what he was doing with Alan Bursky. He explained he needed to hire a comedian to write for him during his own upcoming two-week stint as guest host for "The Tonight Show." We told Joey that Alan was "okay," but . . . "Joey, there is a much better guy to hire—a terrific new comedian who just came to Hollywood from Indiana. His name is David Letterman." (At the time, David was introducing performers at the Comedy Store for twenty-five dollars a night.) Joey told us to have David call him at his hotel in Universal City in a few days to set up the interview. We did.

David Letterman got the job writing for Joey Bishop on "The Tonight Show" for two weeks, and called to thank us. His exact words were, "Gee, thanks, Terrie and Jennie. If there's anything I can ever do for you, just ask!" Uh, right.

Our own "Tonight Show" audition was *colorful* to say the least. Our *big break* came in a room at the NBC Television Studios in Burbank. "The Tonight Show" producer assigned to hear our audition had his legs hoisted up on a desk in front of us, with a *Hustler* magazine opened and spread out before him. He told us to begin. We bent down and whipped out our accordion and Melodica and as we started our routine . . . he thumbed through his *Hustler*.

We were brilliant as we flawlessly executed the "Mirror Image" routine Joey Bishop taught us. We blew right through our "Revolving Piano/Melodica/Liberace" bit and finished with our grand finale, an "Accordion-toting Miss America"—glissando-ing to a high C. We gave the performance of our lives. We stood there anxiously awaiting some kind of response—a "bravo," perhaps, or maybe even a smile. Instead, he turned the magazine around so we could see the rather large-breasted *Hustler* centerfold and said, "Nice, huh?" We didn't know whether to agree with him or not. There was a deafening silence before we both corroborated. He then commented on our audition. "I like the first three minutes, you'll have to work on the rest." We were dumbfounded. We thanked him, hoisted our accordion into its crushed purple velvet-lined case, packed away the Melodica, and made our way down the NBC corridor. We passed David Letterman, who waved hello as he scurried off to "The Tonight Show" set to work with Joey Bishop.

We loaded the accordion into our trunk for the last time, never to be played again. Jennie turned to me and announced she was quitting show biz to go to law school. Which she did! I ended up enrolling in the Hollywood Scriptwriting Institute and then took off for Hong Kong for a year.

As for David Letterman, well, the rest is history. We understand that as a result of his two-week stint writing for "The Tonight Show," David hooked up with Betty White and her husband Allen Ludden, who took an interest in him and helped to move his career along. To date, Jennie and I have asked David Letterman for five favors—none of which he has granted. Our last request, also denied, was for tickets to see his show.

HOW WILLIAM SHATNER WAS CAST IN "STAR TREK"

☆

By Bernard Weitzman
Studio Executive

Desilu Productions hired Gene Roddenberry, a former LAPD motorcycle cop, who decided that being a writer was a much safer profession. Roddenberry had only written a few scripts for some syndicated TV shows. Herb Solow, Desilu's production head and a former NBC television production executive, liked what Roddenberry presented and worked with him to develop a science-fiction piece for a prime time network show. Solow had a great relationship with Herb Schlosser, then head of programming for

NBC, and Solow sold the concept to the network. NBC wanted a sci-fi show because such a show had never been produced for prime time, and they decided to make a two-hour pilot.

Casting was a major concern as NBC wanted a major star for the lead role of Captain Kirk. The network and Desilu agreed on a handsome young movie star, Jeffrey Hunter. Hunter had starred or co-starred in many B and A feature films and certainly fit the part.

The pilot was produced and delivered to NBC. Much to everyone's surprise and shock, they thought the show looked good but was too slow, and they wanted much more action. NBC asked Desilu to do a second two-hour pilot. Desilu had no alternative and had to renegotiate the deals with all the performers to do the new pilot. Jeffrey Hunter said, "If NBC didn't like the first pilot, why do a second one? I'm not interested." And he walked. Now, we all had a dilemma. Who would replace Hunter on such short notice on a failed first pilot?

Fate played a major role in casting, as a young Canadian actor named William Shatner was very available and was selected to become Captain Kirk. We know the rest of the story. "Star Trek" and Captain Kirk/William Shatner are now world famous. The bounce in the couch made history again.

MARILYN MONROE'S BIG CHANCE!

by Kathleen Hughes
Actress

Back in 1949, Twentieth Century-Fox—the studio where I was under contract—was casting a picture called *A Ticket to Tomahawk*. They wanted to use four contract players to play four dancing girls. I was asked if I knew how to dance. I said, "I don't know, I've never tried." So a studio dance director took me over to a soundstage and spent from 9:00 A.M. to 6:00 P.M. trying to teach me one little time step. In those days I had two left feet. I could not pick it up. At 6:00 P.M., the dance director threw up his hands and told them I was hopeless. . . . So, guess who they got to fill in for me? Marilyn Monroe! Weeks later I sat on the stage and watched Marilyn Monroe dance the little part I had flunked out on!

The funny thing is, I had seen Marilyn the previous year at a Fox Studio Club Show for the employees. The secretaries and the mail room people were all abuzz about this young contract player who was so great. She could sing and dance and was fantastic. And the number I saw her perform was sensational! But she had just been dropped from the studio and I thought, *If any of the studio executives from Fox see this show, they're going to realize what a mistake they made. They're going to re-sign her.* Well, they didn't. But they called her back for *Tomahawk* because they knew she could dance—and then they put her in *All About Eve*—and the rest is history!

THE BEST JOB
KEVIN COSTNER NEVER GOT

By Barbara Remsen
Casting Director

Kevin Costner was working as a stage manger on Stage Five at Raleigh Studios, which is across from my casting office. The time was approximately 1984. Bill Tuidor worked at the studio and had the reputation of trying to help everyone. Bill came knocking at my door with a plea, "Barbara, you've got to help Kevin Costner get an acting job." I knew Kevin and his buddy, Jim Wilson, who was producing a low-budget independent film on the lot while I was then casting for ABC daytime soaps. Kevin didn't have a soap look but thought he should read for me just to find out if he could act at all. Then, if he was good, I could always use him on other projects besides the soaps. I had received some new audition material for an upcoming role on "One Life to Live." It was the role of Asa Buchanan's nephew. I had cast all the Buchanans and felt Kevin might be right since the role was for a western type. Before giving the audition material to Kevin, I asked if he would consider moving to New York where the show originates. His reply was, "I'll go to the moon for a steady acting job!"

Kevin had been in my office many times, including putting wood blocks under a wobbly desk. But this day he came in as an actor. Having already read forty actors for the role, I told him a little about the character and to just relax and be himself. We started to read the scene together and I went "up" on my lines, something that never happens to this old seasoned casting director. Kevin said, "Did I do something wrong?" My embarrassed reply was, "No, no, just start again at the beginning." Soap scenes are difficult at the best since they contain every emotion possible to see if the actor can handle it. As we continued to read, I heard the well-worn scene come alive. From someone I didn't know to be an actor, he became one before my eyes—absolutely natural and brilliant! He was shocked with my reaction. I immediately got on the telephone and arranged for him to meet with the New York casting people for the show. I went to great lengths to explain how I had found a very interesting actor who was not the typical soap type, and even told them that Kevin will surely arrive for the audition in jeans and a flannel shirt as he works for a living.

Normally I read with the actors whether it's in my office or for the network, but this time we called a reader to come in for Kevin. During the scene, I watched their faces and I knew the casting people just didn't see "it." Afterward they said to me, "You really think he's good?" I said, "I think he's probably one of the best actors I've ever read and he's going to be the biggest star in this town in five years." They looked at me and said, "But we don't see it." Needless to say, he did not get the role. If he had, he might have been on "One Life" . . . From then on I knew what a great actor he was and proceeded to tell everyone. He remains a dear, dear friend and sometimes when he comes to see me he says, "Remember that time they didn't want me for the soap?" To which I always reply, "Kevin, it was the best job you never got!"

ROBERT STACK IN "THE UNTOUCHABLES"

——————— ☆ ———————

By Bernard Weitzman
Studio Executive

Desilu Productions had sold a new series of programs to CBS and Westinghouse Electric called the Desilu-Westinghouse Playhouse, which would include a combination of dramatic one-hour programs and a group of one-hour comedies starring Lucille Ball and Desi Arnaz.

In his search for dramatic material, Desi Arnaz became aware of and interested in the book entitled *The Untouchables* by Eliot Ness. Desi loved the book as he grew up, and he had gone to school in Miami with Sonny Capone, Big Al's son.

We intended to produce the book as a one-hour show, but it was so exciting, Desi decided to do the show in two parts over two consecutive weeks, a TV first. It was never expected to be a series and so I acquired the series rights at no cost as no one else had thought of it as a possible series. That was a bonanza for Desilu.

Since I was then vice-president of business affairs, I would be negotiating the major talent deals. Casting of the Eliot Ness character was discussed. I brought Bob Stack to Quinn Martin's attention, which he liked. Desi and Bert Granet, the executive producer of the original two-hour movie, were thinking about Van Johnson as Ness.

Desi said to Quinn Martin and myself, "Make the deal for Van Johnson," and that was it. I actually made the deal with

Johnson's agent, but told Quinn Martin that I would make a backup offer to Bob Stack through his agent, Bill Shiffrin, who was very reluctant to do such a thing as he might lose his client. However, after reading the script and listening to our admiration for Bob Stack, Shiffrin agreed to make this very unusual arrangement which later proved to be beneficial to all concerned.

I left for the weekend with all deals concluded for the show. Rehearsal and wardrobe fittings were scheduled for the following Monday when all hell broke loose. Desi called me in Las Vegas to tell me that Mrs. Van Johnson repudiated the agents' deal, claiming a misunderstanding of the money terms. Since it was now obvious that Mr. Johnson was trying to improve the deal under duress, Desi would not be intimidated and refused to change the deal. Desi and Bert were on the phone immediately and asked if I could negotiate a deal with Bob Stack. I told them that I thought it was possible and soon confirmed this after a short call to agent Bill Shiffrin. With that call, Bob Stack forever became Eliot Ness.

"GENERAL HOSPITAL" AND MARVIN PAIGE
"Relentless"

———— ☆ ————

By Anne Jeffreys
Actress

When Marvin Paige cast me in "General Hospital," I didn't want to do it! He called me just as my husband, Robert, was going into the hospital to have a back operation. I just wanted to get him through that. Marvin called and said, "Anne, there's a part in 'General Hospital' coming up that we'd like for you to do. It's just a cameo thing." I said, "I just don't feel like doing a soap opera. Robert is going into the hospital and it's just not my bag." He said to me, "Well, it's good enough for Elizabeth Taylor to do one, for Sammy Davis to do one, and for Milton Berle to do one. It's not good enough for you?" I thought, *Oh dear*. I said, "How many would I have to do?" He said, "Well, no more than ten." I said, "Well, let me think about it."

In the meantime I went to the hospital with Robert and I was sitting there with him, not thinking about the soap opera at all, and I got a call from Marvin Paige. We were at St. John's Hospital and I don't know how Marvin found us, but he did. By Robert's bedside, he said, "What's the decision?" and I said, "No more than ten, huh?" and he said, "Probably three." I said, "Okay, if you'll get off my back, I'll do the darn thing." A couple of months later, I went into "General Hospital" and I wound up in over two hundred performances.

VIETNAM VERSUS VEGAS—
THE RIGHT CHOICE

——— ☆ ———

by Tony Diamond
Comedian/Producer/Head of BRAVO Network

At one time I was an up-and-coming comedian. I was handled by International Artists and was lucky enough to have two booking offers at the same time. One was to go to Las Vegas—which would have been a big break—the other was to go to Vietnam. The choice was mine. I chose Vietnam, and my life has not been the same since . . . The reason I chose Vietnam is I felt I had an obligation to pay back the joy I experienced while seeing a USO Show starring Dick Contino and Jamie Farr at K13 Air base in Su Won when I was stationed in Korea.

When I returned from Vietnam, it was difficult for me—my agent didn't pick up my option. At that time, it wasn't a favored thing to have gone to Vietnam. However, I knew that I was here for a purpose and one night the light went on . . . BRAVO! Which is the acronym for Brotherhood Rally of All Veterans Organizations. And what started as a once a year picnic developed into a world media organization for Veteran Affairs. We currently produce a nationally syndicated show called "Sound Off," on PBS and community cable stations around the country. We also publish a bimonthly newspaper distributed internationally called *BRAVO Veterans Outlook*. We are told it is the most respected publication in the Veteran community. What I may have lost in my show business career, I've gained in my purpose for being here.

FILMEX AUDITION FOR "L.A. LAW"

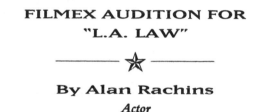

By Alan Rachins
Actor

I was looking to resurrect my acting career, but nothing was happening. My wife and I were very friendly with Henry Jaglom and his wife at the time. Her name is Patrice Townsend. We spent a lot of time together, like three or four nights a week going out to dinner. And at one point Henry, who is a very well-respected independent filmmaker, declared he was going to make a movie about a married couple and their best friends—he and his wife would be the married couple and my wife and I would be the best friends. We were very excited about this.

About a month after this idea surfaced, Patrice announced she wanted a divorce, and they soon separated and divorced. While the main point is that Henry's marriage collapsed at that time, the idea of that movie collapsed as well. So, I had my own disappointments about what had happened. And my wife and I just kind of shrugged our shoulders and said, "It was a nice idea, too bad that it went away."

About a year or two later Henry came back with the idea that he was now going to make a movie about his divorce—instead of about a happily married couple—and that we would play the couple that used to be the best friends of the couple prior to the divorce. So the movie was again on, with a different twist—he had incorporated this major change in his life into the new idea for the film.

He made this film, *Always*. It got a wonderful screening as the opening night event of FILMEX that particular year. My wife and I invited everyone we knew to this screening, including Steven Bochco, who created "L.A. LAW." And it was there that he really got a chance to see me play a part that was not exactly Douglas Brackman, but had some of Douglas Brackman in him. Really, that was my casting session for "L.A. LAW," I'm pleased to say.

GEORGE HAMILTON'S LOVE AT FIRST BITE!

By Joel Freeman
Producer

Producers sometimes go through their own casting process. George Hamilton and Bob Kaufman were executive producers on a film they had brought to financer/producer Mel Simon's company. George and Bob called and asked me to produce their new film. At the same time I got a call from Bob Relyea who worked for Mel Simon. He also asked me if I would be interested in producing the film. I said, "Well, has the deal been made with your company?" And he said, "No, not yet, but I think you can help the situation if you come on board." I decided to do the film.

I suggested we change the name from its original title, *Dracula Sucks Again*, to *Love at First Bite*. I don't have to tell you, the picture was very, very successful. George Hamilton was perfect for the role—it was one of the best things he's ever done.

IRONY IN CASTING

☆

By Michael Levine
Publicist and Author of **Guerrilla P.R.** *and* **Lessons at the Half Way Point**

Irony in casting has always been a favorite subject for me, like, for example, the movie *Reversal of Fortune*, which chronicled attorney Alan Dershowitz's celebrated defense of Claus von Bulow, played brilliantly by Jeremy Irons. To play the part of Dershowitz, the first choice was none other than Woody Allen. Not surprisingly, Allen didn't pan out, and Ron Silver inherited the role. What's the irony? Well, oddly enough, when Mia Farrow became involved in a bitter child custody case with Woody Allen, she used Alan Dershowitz as her attorney.

In addition, Norman Jewison's 1987 hit comedy/romance, *Moonstruck*, was developed by Sally Field for her own production company. In the end, Ms. Field was unhappy with the script, and decided against playing the lead role. The role was later played by Cher, who won an Academy Award for her performance.

Finally, as a publicist, I'm always interested in how people strategically position themselves for things. For example, when Steven Spielberg followed his hit *Jaws* with the 1977 science-fiction classic *Close Encounters of the Third Kind*, Spielberg gave the part to Richard Dreyfuss, after the actor had waged a heavy campaign to win the role.

Also, I love "what if's?" Would Al Pacino have been considered for his Oscar-winning role in *Scent of a Woman* if he had agreed to play Rambo? What if John Travolta had accepted *An Officer and a Gentleman* instead of the pitiful *Staying Alive*?

"Imitation is the sincerest form of television."

—Fred Allen

Long Searches for the Right Actor

With millions of dollars at stake, not to mention reputations, the *right* combination—the perfect marriage of talent—is the true *art* of the business. (The possibilities for mess ups are endless.)

THE GIRL WITH THREE NAMES, MARY TYLER MOORE

——————— ☆ ———————

By Sheldon Leonard
Producer

In my experience, casting comes in a couple of different situations. If I know who I want—for example when I know I want Don Knotts, there are no casting procedures involved. I just have my representatives look up Don Knotts and we make a deal. If you know who you want, casting is very simple. But when you go on a search—as we do mostly when we're looking for young people with no extensive background—it's more difficult, which was the case when I was casting "The Dick Van Dyke Show."

We needed a girl in her twenties to play Dick Van Dyke's wife for the show. We started interviewing with not too much success. Danny Thomas, my partner, vaguely remembered that when we were trying to replace one of the young members of "The Danny Thomas Show," we came up with a very attractive, very impressive young lady. The only problem was, she didn't look like she belonged in the Danny Thomas household. So we regretfully passed over her. Danny's suggestion was that she'd be great to film with Dick Van Dyke. And I agreed. But we couldn't remember who she was. And all Danny could remember was that she had "three names." With that clue to start with, and the fact that we remembered her only theatrical credit had been playing the spirit of a refrigerator in a commercial, and nothing but her legs were showing . . . with that information to go on, our casting director dug up a girl by the name of Mary Tyler Moore. . . . The girl with three names!

WHOOPI GOLDBERG IN *GHOST*

──────────── ☆ ────────────

By Jane Jenkins, Janet Hirshenson, Michael Hirshenson
Casting Directors, The Casting Company

For us as casting directors, the process begins with black and white markings on a page—the script. Our job is to break down the script into the various characters—talk with the director and producer, get their input—and visualize a variety of stars, ingenues, or character actors or actresses playing each of the individual parts. Every so often we will read a script and agree among ourselves that we hear the voice of only one actor or actress saying the lines of a particular part. This happened for us when we were casting the multi-award-winning feature film *Ghost*. Janet and I had read the script and met with the producers and the director and suggested Whoopi Goldberg for the part of Oda May. They said, "We've thought about her but we'd like to see who else is out there."

So we proceeded to start casting all the parts. In the course of the three months of casting, we must have met approximately 150 actresses for the part of Oda May. We saw famous actresses, unknown actresses, everybody was good from Nell Carter—who gave a particularly wonderful audition—to Tina Turner, Patti LaBelle, Alfre Woodard—you name the actress, known and unknown, she came in for the part. After some of these casting sessions, we'd turn to Jerry and ask, "Now can we hire Whoopi?"

About a month and a half into casting we actually met with Whoopi Goldberg, who said she was dying to play this part—that she thought it might be the part of her career. Jerry told us, "I really like her. But let's continue to see who's out there."

Finally, Whoopi was off shooting a movie with Sissy Spacek. By this time we had hired Patrick Swayze. So Jerry Zucker and Patrick Swayze flew off to wherever she was shooting and met with her in an executive lounge in an airport, chatted with her, and came back. Janet and I had just gone to a London premiere of a James Bond movie that we had cast. When we arrived at the hotel, there was a cable waiting. It read: SO NOW CAN WE HIRE WHOOPI GOLDBERG? . . .YES! . . . GIVE MY LOVE TO THE QUEEN, LOVE JERRY. We went berserk in the hotel lobby. Whoopi Goldberg went on to win an Academy Award for her performance in *Ghost*! And as Whoopi herself had predicted, it turned her whole career around.

THE NATIONWIDE TALENT SEARCH

———— ☆ ————

By Robert Easton
Actor/Dialect Coach

In 1961 I got cast in a film called *The Nun and the Sergeant*. For months and months prior to the filming, the producer, Eugene Frenke, had garnered enormous amounts of publicity for the film through his nationwide talent search to find just the right actress to play the nun. In city after city the newspapers announced he was looking for an unknown to play this part and whomever he finally selected would become a big star. After months and months of this well-publicized search, Mr. Frenke made his choice. By the most amazing coincidence, he chose his own wife, Anna Sten, who was certainly not unknown to the industry—nor to Mr. Frenke.

CAMERON DIAZ—
ONE IN THREE HUNDRED LADIES

By Fern Champion
Casting Director

My partner and I read close to three hundred ladies for *The Mask*, including the 'A' list of actresses and some of the world's top models. Cameron Diaz had something special when we taped her auditions, but the camera picked up more than just special. It picked up *movie star moments*, those undefinable elements that make people want to sit in a dark room and follow a character through a two-hour journey. We can break it down and say she has beauty, humor, spontaneity, innocence, and a certain flair that works perfectly for the character. But ultimately, it was our reactions as audience members that won her the role. All the men adored her and all the women wanted to be her friend.

JIM HANKS MAKES IT ON HIS OWN!

By Brad Waisbren
Producer

I was requested to cast a picture with a total of thirty-six speaking roles; a massive endeavor under normal circumstances and time constraints. However, the casting had to be completed in less than two weeks, which obviously added to the difficulty.

I decided that the discovery of a new face for the male lead would be important, and extra efforts were put in that direction. We would surround him with more established actors in supporting roles.

The lead role required a funny, talented, and likable actor, and Tom Hanks filled the bill. Tom Hanks wasn't available, however. His brother, Jim Hanks, was. I discussed with Jim his potential involvement in the film, and his audition was excellent. I was confident that we had found the lead, but he still had to read for the director and producer.

I wanted Jim to win the role on his own merits and talents, rather than riding on the wave of his brother's fame, especially since I had great faith in his abilities. We agreed that Jim would complete his audition under an assumed name, and Jim felt that it would promote his self-confidence to do so. For once, he could gain the respect of others in the industry on his own efforts, without basking in the sunlight of his brother.

Consequently, we introduced Jim as "Jim Matthews." There was some minor stir about Jim's resemblance to Tom Hanks, but it was clear that the relationship was not suspected, nor was it a factor in the determination by the producers and the director.

Jim was booked in obvious recognition of his comedic and acting skills. Our little secret remained so until after the paperwork was completed. We all enjoyed a good laugh, and Jim Hanks had his first lead role!

INGELS AND ASTIN
MEET DICKENS AND FENSTER

———— ☆ ————

By Leonard Stern
Writer/Producer

The first show I created on my own was "I'm Dickens, He's Fenster." I had written the part of Arch Fenster for Marty Ingels, a talented clown I had met at a Steve Allen audition. A futile three-month search for an actor capable of playing Harry Dickens, a thirty-year-old engaging paranoid who made ambivalence into an art form, led me to consider renaming the show "I'm Fenster, He's Fenster." That implausibility might have become a reality if Ethel Winant, a one-of-a-kind casting director who had the ability to recognize gifted actors long before they became established, hadn't entered my life. In a John Houseman production of Jon Dos Passos' *USA* at UCLA, Ethel had cast the then relatively unknown John Astin in a key role. My wife and I, having decided at the last moment to see the play, found the only seats available at opposite ends of the theater. At the first intermission, Gloria and I literally ran to each other shouting, "John Astin is Harry Dickens!" And he was! From that time on, I never missed a play at UCLA. If Ethel is learning this for the first time, I take this opportunity to thank her for casting my shows, without pay, for the better part of two years!

MAE WEST AND GEORGE RAFT— FULL CIRCLE

By Marvin Paige
Casting Director

Mae West's first film was a 1932 movie called *Night After Night*. George Raft was the star of the film for Paramount Pictures. Having seen Mae on stage, I recommended her for a key role in that film, which had originally been slated for Texas Guinan. Mae, with her inimitable style and double entendres, became a star overnight. Her subsequent film literally saved Paramount Pictures, which at that point was having financial problems. When I was hired to cast *Sextette* in 1977, Mae West's last film, I had what I thought was a brilliant idea to cast George Raft. Again, on the big screen they were magic.

DR. HAING S. NGOR AND
THE KILLING FIELDS

By Pat Golden
Director

I was engaged by producer David Puttnam and director Roland Joffe to find someone to play the role of Dith Pran in the film, *The Killing Fields*, based on *New York Times* columnist Sid Schanberg's true story. The story takes place in 1973 during the Vietnam War, and is centered around Pran and Schanberg's simultaneous, but separate, and narrow escape into Thailand, from a Cambodia inundated with Khmer Rouge, or Communist Cambodians.

Bruce Robinson had written a great page-turning screenplay, which I absorbed on the plane en route to California. Mr. Puttnam's company, Enigma, had made preliminary contacts within the Cambodian community which were then turned over to me. I began scouting the communities by attending social events and political meetings in the greater Los Angeles area, San Francisco, New York, and Washington, D.C. Subsequently, I interviewed hundreds of Cambodian people, 85 percent of whom told a similar story of the terror of escape. Inevitably, both interviewee and interviewer would hug, then part in tears.

As a college student, I'd majored in theater and anthropology. As an anti-war protester, I'd been appalled by the bombing of a neutral country. Here, years later, contained in one grand chance, was the opportunity to help set the record straight, to explore an intriguing culture and to maintain the dignity of the Cambodian people by discovering a Cambodian man to portray this universal but particularly harrowing tale of life in Cambodia at the time.

Mr. and Mrs. Prasert Hou, with whom I'd become friendly, invited me to a wedding. There I saw a man who looked interesting, so I asked if I might take a picture or two, without his glasses. He said, "Yes." I shot. As the Polaroid took on a life of its own, the image jumped out of its frame, grabbed me by the throat, and tried to strangle me. He was extremely photogenic. His name is Dr. Haing S. Ngor.

A few days later, I sat in the office on the Warner lot waiting for Dr. Ngor to show up. Before leaving the party we'd exchanged numbers. I'd called him and we'd set up an appointment. But he was a no show. I called again. Again, he was a no show. This went on several times, but I was not willing to concede, not without auditioning a subject who was so photogenic.

Finally, weeks later we met at a Cambodian Association's social room, and we read a scene from the script. He was brilliant, completely believable. Haing had never had an acting lesson in his life, but he had far more. He had been given a gift. Haing ended up winning an Oscar for Best Supporting Actor.

"I don't think anybody grows up saying,
'When I'm older, I'm going to be a casting director.'
Everybody sort of evolves into it.
You're an actor who stopped acting.
You're a producer for a while and you move into it.
You're somebody's assistant and you go out on your own . . . "

—Dennis Gallegos

Network Approval

No casting decision is set in stone, until it is blessed by the *powers that be.*

HARRISON FORD— FBI AGENT

——————— ☆ ———————

By Barbara Remsen
Casting Director

My husband, Bert Remsen, was hired for his very first casting job by John Conwell, casting supervisor for Quinn Martin's "FBI" series starring Efrem Zimbalist, Jr. John Conwell had been an actor himself and had great respect for actors and, with Quinn Martin's approval, paid them very well, not the norm for television. Bert felt Harrison Ford was a very good actor and had the perfect FBI look and demeanor and was able to use him in as many episodes as possible.

Later when I had joined Bert in casting, we were casting a movie of the week and Harrison's agent called to plug him for a co-starring role. The network felt we needed a bigger, better-known star for the role. Thanks to his agent giving me the latest credits on Harrison, I was able to plead his case by saying he had just completed a lead role in *Star Wars*, which was expected to be a mega-hit. The network's answer to this was, "We don't know what *Star Wars* is." We fought the network, Harrison got the role, and the rest is history.

There are actors who remember and actors who forget. Harrison Ford is the kind of actor who remembers. It's a wonderful feeling as a casting director, or just as a person, that you can help someone. I can open doors and give opportunities, but then the actor has to do the job.

TOM SELLECK'S
FIRST DRAMATIC ROLE

——————— ☆ ———————

By Barbara Remsen
Casting Director

I had been in the business since 1951 and was working with my husband, Bert Remsen, who was head of casting at Lorimar. We were doing a movie of the week pilot of *The Best Years of Our Lives*, with Dan Petrie directing. All actors were cast with the exception of the Dana Andrews role. We were scouring this town for every tall, good-looking guy. While Bert was upstairs with Lee Rich, into the office walked Tom Selleck. He was about twenty-five years old, tall, good looking, and thoroughly charming. I asked about his credits and he told me he was working on "The Young and the Restless." I said, "Oh, you can't tell anyone you're on a soap," because at that time, if you were young, good looking, and on soaps, it was the erroneous belief you couldn't act. Since I started in live television, I happen to think that some of the best actors in the world are on soaps. I asked Tom if he had any film on himself and he said, "Well, I did do one episode of 'Lucas Tanner.' " His tape arrived and all with the project thought he was perfect for the role. Tom was talking one on one to David Hartman on the demo and he was wonderfully natural. The network initially said no but we won out and Tom did a terrific job in his first dramatic role. He has continued to be a friend and fondly remembers our first meeting.

WAITING FOR A STAR
TO COME ON BOARD
From Barbra Streisand to
Debbie Allen

By Phil Savenick
Producer

There is a rather short list of performers the networks accept for television specials. We used to say they were only interested in Tom, Tom, or Tom (Cruise, Selleck, or Hanks). Casting often becomes a long and exasperating process, and the studios had to pay a whole staff to sit around and wait in the interim. A Disney executive explained the problem to me. A few years ago, the studio had to keep a crew on for months while they waited for Barbra Streisand to agree to sing the big finale for "Mickey Mouse's 60th Birthday." After two months of waiting, she turned them down and they tried to get Paul McCartney. After a month of not hearing back from Paul, it became the Elton John song. Then for another month it was the Billy Joel song. I finally turned to the Disney executive and said, "I remember seeing that show and none of this rings a bell." He said, "Oh, that's because we ended up casting Cheech Marin and Debbie Allen."

"When you try to match a guy and a gal actor

you look for charisma."

—Marvin Paige

"I LOVE LUCY"—CASTING WRITERS

By Bernard Weitzman
Studio Executive

In comedy, the most difficult talent to cast is writers. When you think of the early days of television, the shows had a few good writers per show who provided scripts for the entire broadcast season, usually consisting of thirty-nine shows. Shows such as "Your Show of Shows," "I Love Lucy," "The Dick Van Dyke Show," and "Burns and Allen" developed many young writers, and paired with former radio writers, they created the half-hour television format that still exists today. Some of the writers that actually worked on each show and delivered a weekly script were Mel Brooks, Neil Simon, Woody Allen, Larry Gelbart, Mel Tolkin, Norman Lear, Leonard Stern, and Carl Reiner.

When CBS was looking to develop a new show starring Lucille Ball, they assigned their contract writing team from Lucy's radio show, "My Favorite Husband," Bob Carroll, Jr., Madelyn Pugh (Davis), and the creator/writer/producer Jess Oppenheimer to develop the show for television. None of these writers had written for television before. The choice was right and "I Love Lucy" was created, probably the greatest weekly comedy series of all time.

After the great success of the series, Desilu hired two more young talented writers, Bob Schiller and Bob Weiskopf, to strengthen the writing and sustain the outstanding quality of the show, which still stands up in reruns to today's demanding audience.

Lucille Ball outlasted the writers, Desi Arnaz, and even "I Love Lucy." She was determined to come back with a new show called "The Lucy Show" without Desi. Lucy recognized that only good writing would sustain quality. Bob Carroll and Madelyn Pugh were no longer available. Lucy found another top writer named Milt Josefsberg who had worked for Jack Benny, Bob Hope, and Joey Bishop. Milt knew comedy and became the backbone of the new Lucy shows. He hired old pros to write free-lance scripts. He discovered and gave opportunities to new writers such as Garry Marshall and Jerry Belson, even guaranteeing their first script because neither Lucy or the network would risk scripts on untried, inexperienced writers. Milt's courage paid off. As we all know, Garry Marshall went on to do great things in both television and motion pictures. Gary Marshall subsequently showed his appreciation for the chance given him by hiring Milt Josefsberg to supervise many of his television shows and giving new writers a chance to write for him, as well as other top series.

THUMBS UP FOR GLEN CAMPBELL
Passing the "Ladies in the Office" Test

By George Sunga
Producer

We were preparing for "The Summer Brothers Smothers Show" and, because of Tom Smothers' foresight, and knowing we would need a hot host to sell the show, he arranged for Glen Campbell to guest star on the second season of the regular "Smothers Brothers Comedy Hour." These guest shots were used by CBS to test the appeal of Glen Campbell as a musical host and star of the proposed summer show. The most important test, however, might have been when Mike Dann, the head of programming for CBS, tested the episodes for the ladies in his office. The feedback we received was that they loved Glen's boy-next-door qualities along with his musical talents and country charm. We hoped that if Glen was good enough for the ladies in the office, Mike Dann would approve Glen for our summer show. Not only did this happen, but because of the success of the summer show, Glen earned approval for his own series, "The Glen Campbell Goodtime Hour," which premiered in January 1969 and ran for several seasons.

SONDRA LOCKE
Academy Award Nominee

By Joel Freeman
Producer

I produced a television movie at Paramount called *Weekend of Terror*, starring Lee Majors and Bob Conrad. The director, Judd Taylor, and I had suggested two people who were Academy Award nominees to play the young nuns. One of our recommendations was a young woman named Sondra Locke (*The Heart Is a Lonely Hunter, Bronco Billy*, etc.). The other actress, also an Academy Award nominee, was of equal recognition. When we made the proposal, the network head (Michael Eisner) said, "Who are they?" and insisted we go with people who had some "TVQ" rating. We ended up with Lois Nettleton and Carol Lynley. All went well. But it is interesting how movie and television casting sometimes do not cross over.

ORSON WELLES—
RISING TO THE OCCASION

By Bernard Weitzman
Studio Executive

Orson Welles' career was at a low point in Hollywood. Desi Arnaz and Lucille Ball had high regard for his talent and felt they could help him return to his former glory by developing unusual quality programs with him for television, which Orson had never done before. This would be a first if the networks would accept him. Desi felt Orson could succeed if given the proper support, and Orson accepted the challenge.

Since Orson was still very independent, and did not take to many people, Desi assigned me and a young art director, Claudio Guzman, to work with Orson. Orson loved Claudio and tolerated me. Out of an extensive list of material, most of which was unavailable, I finally obtained the rights to a John Cheever short story entitled *Fountain of Youth*. It was an interesting and unique production, using special effects that were then not customarily used in television, but Orson was a visionary and determined to do something unusual and different. That he did.

Who said Orson Welles was "finished"? He was the *old* Orson Welles of *Citizen Kane* fame and the complete artist again. On this show, Orson was the sole writer, director, producer, wrote all the original music, edited the picture, and was the host/narrator. Unfortunately, this show was his last great singular effort. What a talent, what a shame he didn't do more. The networks didn't believe he could sustain a weekly series.

I ask myself, 'Who would I want to meet?'
And I answer: 'Tennessee Williams, Laurence Olivier,
Gore Vidal, Katharine Hepburn, and on and on . . .'
And then knowing that I actually worked with these legends!
That has been the best of it!"

—Dorothy James

Matchmaking

**Love, it makes the world go 'round . . .
And love *Hollywood style* also makes
for good reading in the tabloids!**

DELTA BURKE AND GERALD McRANEY

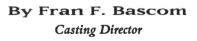

By Fran F. Bascom
Casting Director

Matchmaking has to be the last thing on a casting director's mind when it comes to putting an actor into a particular role. In fact, there are so many other things to think about that you often consider yourself lucky if the actors actually get along with each other. But every once in awhile the chemistry between the characters carries over into the lives of the actors playing the roles. And that's what happened on the set of "Designing Women" when I cast Gerald McRaney as the ex-husband of Delta Burke's Suzanne Sugarbaker.

The producers, Harry Thomason and Linda Bloodworth-Thomason, had a handful of actors in mind for the role of Dash Goff, a well-known and irascible Southern writer. But I knew the moment I read the part that it was perfect for Gerald McRaney. I had seen "Mac" (as he has always been affectionately known) in his series "Simon and Simon" and in his many stage roles. I knew that he could provide the perfect combination of cynicism and gentility to the character. I also thought that he and Delta would be convincing as a couple. I pushed hard to put Mac in the role, and Linda and Harry agreed.

Then, at the last moment, it almost didn't happen. Mac's agent called to say that his client's brother-in-law was very sick and in the hospital in Virginia. Mac felt he should be with his sister at such a difficult time. He would have to turn down the part. Normally, we would have expressed our sympathy, hired another actor, and that would have been the end of it. But after pushing so hard to get him, I was persistent. The week before that episode was to be filmed I spent hours on the phone with Mac's agent and the show's producers, determined to make it work out. Finally, after some juggling of the rehearsal schedule, we arranged a way for Mac to be with his sister when she needed him and to come back to Hollywood in time to play the part.

The attraction between Delta and Mac was apparent even at the first "read-through" of the script—when the cast simply sits at a table and reads their lines with the director and crew. There was something playful and almost flirtatious in the way they traded lines. And Linda Bloodworth-Thomason's script, which centered around the unresolved sexual attraction between Suzanne and Dash, gave them plenty of material to work with. As rehearsals progressed, the cast and crew could sense that the two (who had met only briefly before) were really hitting it off. It was clear that Mac at least was smitten, but we knew he still had to convince Delta. Everyone hoped for the best, but doubted much would come of it, since Delta had frequently expressed her complete lack of interest in being in a relationship, saying she much preferred her independence. She had even declined to try to catch the bouquet at Jean Smart's wedding, because, she insisted, she did not want to be married.

So it wasn't until the actual taping of the show that we knew for sure that romance had indeed blossomed between the two. In one of the episode's final scenes, the script called for Suzanne and Dash to kiss. Normally, a screen kiss is a pretty dull affair to watch from behind the camera. But when the time came for the kiss between Delta and Mac, it was so obviously heartfelt and real that the audience let out a collective gasp. And, when it was over, they burst into spontaneous applause. It seemed that everyone knew they had witnessed a very special moment between two people. Of course, they were right. Within a few months, Delta and Mac were married, in a beautiful and lavish ceremony, as dramatic as the way they met and fell in love.

MARY TYLER MOORE
MEETS GRANT TINKER

───────── ☆ ─────────

By Sheldon Leonard
Producer

Grant Tinker represented Benton and Bowles on behalf of the sponsor of "The Dick Van Dyke Show," Procter and Gamble. Grant was sent to California from the New York office to report on what progress we were making and what difficulties we were encountering. He arrived in California, came up to my office, and introduced himself. I took him on the set and introduced him to everyone, including Carl Reiner, Dick Van Dyke, and Mary Tyler Moore. Grant and Mary were eventually married, started their own production company, MTM, and went on to produce many, many shows, including "The Mary Tyler Moore Show" and "The Bob Newhart Show."

PAULA PRENTISS AND
RICHARD BENJAMIN

───────── ☆ ─────────

By Leonard Stern
Writer/Producer

There was a time when network executives encouraged television producers to utilize their talents and expertise fully in order to control the quality of the writing, directing, producing, and casting of their shows. Mike Dann, the vice-president in charge of programming at CBS, was such an executive. I had developed "He and She," a romantic comedy, for the network. Mike felt that Paula Prentiss was ideal for the female lead. "Get Paula," he said, "and you have a commitment."

That night, fate sat in on my weekly card game. The player on my right turned out to be Paula's agent. I sent him a script and he in turn sent it to Paula who loved it, but (and there's always a but) she wanted Richard Benjamin, her husband, to co-star. At that time, Richard had not done anything in television, film, or even off, off, off Broadway. Fortunately, he had been in a road company version of Neil Simon's *Barefoot in the Park*, which my wife Gloria had seen (fate again) in Chicago. Gloria was so impressed with his performance she made a point of calling me to say, "I've just seen your kind of actor. Remember the name Dick Benjamin." I remembered. I called Mike Dann and told him I had a commitment from Paula Prentiss and he responded gleefully, "You've got a commitment." I told him there was a hitch, a catch, a condition— Paula wanted to co-star with her husband. Without missing a beat, Mike told me to go ahead and make the deal!

Approximately one week later, wherever I went, there were messages to call Mike Dann in New York immediately! When we finally connected, Mike didn't bother to say hello. He frantically wanted to know if I had made a deal with Paula Prentiss. I told him I had. Mike then asked, somewhat nervously, "Is her husband an actor?"

THE PERFECT CASTING OF
SHARON GLESS

——————— ✭ ———————

By Barney Rosenzweig
Executive Producer

After two previous incarnations, one with Loretta Swit and the other with Meg Foster, CBS agreed to renew the television series "Cagney & Lacey" for the fall of 1982, contingent upon the recasting of Christine Cagney. Perhaps ten or twelve people crowded into the Los Angeles office of CBS chieftain Harvey Shepherd, all of them with ideas on who should play the part. The list was long. I sat there quietly. Finally, Shepherd turned to me and asked my opinion. "I only have one name to submit . . . Sharon

Gless." The then head of casting for CBS, Jean Guest, scoffed, "You can't get her." "I will get her," I said. Harvey Shepherd spoke up. "If you can get Sharon Gless, this meeting is over." "Well then," I smiled, "I'm leaving." And that's what I did.

It was not that easy. Some weeks later, a meeting was arranged with Ms. Gless at Musso and Frank's restaurant in Hollywood. It began with the statement from her that she didn't want to do the series. Having just replaced Lynn Redgrave in "House Calls," she did not want to become known as the actress who kept replacing other actresses. I sat there at lunch with my then associates, Richard Rosenbloom and Barbara Corday. Ms. Gless was accompanied by her manager, Monique James. I pointed out that she was not simply replacing another actress, that in fact this was always her part, that it was conceived for her and that each time we had previously begun preparations for the project she was not available. Ms. James acknowledged the truth of that. I went on. I did the best I could to convince her. Rosenbloom and Corday did their best as well. The meeting ended with the promise that our proposal would be given every consideration. In other words, it did not look good.

The actress and her manager made their exit into the restaurant's parking lot. The manager spoke first, "I think we should think about this, sweetpea."

"You said I wouldn't have to do it. That this was merely a courtesy meeting."

"I know, but this is a very interesting, very special project and I think you should do it."

"I don't like the guy with the beard," Gless said, meaning me.

We worked on the show together for six years. Sharon and I each received two Emmys for our work on the show and many other awards as well. In 1991, in the middle of "The Trials of Rosie O'Neill" (our second series together), I proposed and we married. Recently we have made some "Cagney & Lacey" reunion movies together as I continue to look for yet another vehicle to star this remarkable actress. We don't always agree when it comes to material so, "I don't like the guy with the beard" is still something I remind her of when she goes on about her instincts.

THE LOVERS OF THE GLOBE

———— ☆ ————

By R. Thad Taylor
Founder and President, Shakespeare Society of America

The casting couch probably started with the cave man and surely it was very popular in Grecian and Roman days. Cleopatra was no doubt so cast in her starring role. One of Shakespeare's mistresses was the Dark Lady of the Sonnets, one of drama and literature's biggest mysteries. Shakespeare certainly auditioned her on his Elizabethan casting couch. Although boys performed the female parts in the Bard's days, women were the models for the roles.

As a Shakespearean director/producer for twenty-eight years, I can relate to the latter reference points with experience and authority. It isn't necessarily the director/producer that benefits from the casting. Once proper auditions have produced the cast of a show, actors, technicians, office and box-office personnel, and virtually the whole company will pair off in one form or another. They will go to one another's apartments, party, live together, and some even get married. We've had over a dozen marriages at the Globe Playhouse and I don't know how many children were conceived there.

For myself as artistic director, casting director, talent scout, and executive producer, modesty prevents me from expounding. I have had some nice relationships because I really was instrumental in starting some careers—but there were no catches or promises other than two consenting adults—normal to the extreme. Well, that's life in almost any game involving the sexes. But beware in Hollywood, the land of the Casanovas, Don Juans, and the many self-ordained producers who say, "How would you like to be in movies?"

CHAPTER 7

MUSIC, MUSIC, MUSIC!

★

"When the historian seeks a symbol of our time,
he will find it in musical comedy,
which is our equivalent of the Roman arena."

—GILBERT GABRIEL
New York Evening Sun

Broadway

Who hasn't wanted to sing and dance in a Broadway musical? Thousands of actors have hoofed and sung their way across stages with the hopes of vaulting up to a Tony!

LETTER OF RECOMMENDATION FROM JOSEPH PAPP

By Gary Morris
Actor/Singer

My whole involvement in theater and television came about quite accidentally. In 1984 I had just won country music's Song of the Year with a song called "Wind Beneath My Wings," and my manager wanted me to go do an opera in New York City, which I had no interest in. After quite a bit of prodding and record label work, I decided I'd audition for a gentleman named Joseph Papp—I didn't know who he was at the time. It was my first real venture into the theater, other than high school and college. I went and auditioned and they gave me the role of Rodolfo in *La Boheme*.

For the audition, I came in with Wranglers and a white cowboy shirt. They had a pianist, but I brought my own piano player with me, a guy from my country music band. I sang an aria from *La Boheme*, and I watched them go from being patiently amused to, well, when I walked out, I told my manager, "I think they're going to call me on this. Now what do I do?" I did get the part and at the end of the production, Joseph Papp wrote the nicest letter. It was a "To Whom It May Concern" letter. It said, "Gary, I will do any production that you would want to do for public theater—build one around you—either a straight play or a musical—and would not hesitate to put you in any of my productions, including Shakespeare." I thought it was a very nice letter.

I sent a copy of Joseph Papp's letter to my agent at William Morris. I got a call from the Aaron Spelling folks to come read for the role of a blind singer on a television show called "The Colby's." I think I could have not uttered a word, but just on the basis of that one letter from Joseph Papp gotten the role. So, at this point, I was two for two. It's been an interesting career. If it hadn't happened this way, I don't believe I would have ever been able to even get a role because I didn't come up in the rank and file—do the necessary community theater, or study with the right acting coach. I've been truly blessed.

A CATTLE CALL FOR *HAIR*

By Robyn Whitney
Former Dancer / Choreographer

Dancers are hardcore athletes. We stretch our bodies to excruciating extremes, work out ten hours a day, starve ourselves, and sacrifice everything that resembles a normal lifestyle for the few years that we are physically able to do the thing we love. So it makes a "gypsy" very grumpy when an audition is not based on casting the best-skilled dancer for the role.

When the renegade contemporary choreographer Twyla Tharp was hired to set the dance sequences for the movie *Hair*, all the rules went out the window. It was the hottest day in the history of New York City. Four hundred top dancers were left standing on the melting pavement for a "mass" audition that began over two hours late, so tempers were flaring. Once we got inside the rehearsal hall we were looking forward to sweating for the right reasons—to show off our pirouettes, kicks, and leaps to land a part in a movie. Instead, we were directed to lie on our backs on the sticky floor and improvise "sizzling like pieces of bacon." At first we all laughed—it had to be a joke about the heat and humidity. But then it became apparent that the casting people were serious. This silly, humiliating exercise was the last thing a group of disciplined, hardened Broadway pros were going to put up with. From the back of the group came the irritated voice of a chorus queen who had heard enough; "Who do I have to (CENSORED) to get OUT of this show?" We doubled over with laughter, took our bags, and went back to our Broadway shows, leaving only the kids who just got off the busses from Iowa to "dance" for *Hair*.

COLE PORTER
AND THE METROPOLITAN OPERA

By Gary Gardner
Actor/Drama Teacher

For the past twenty-one years I've been teaching drama at UCLA. Years ago, I was called to a rehearsal studio to audition for a Cole Porter revue. I am not a *singer* singer, I am a loud, funny singer. Well, I was confused. I was in New York and I didn't realize there was a rehearsal Studio A, Studio B, and Studio C. So when the stage manager called "NEXT," I walked in, gave my sheet music to the pianist, and in my best *belt-it* manner, sung an old Cole Porter song called, "Please Don't Monkey with Broadway." And I was singing, "Please, please, I'm down on my knees, don't monkey with old Broadway." I was very good . . . or so I thought. The auditioners looked at me in horror! I walked out and saw my friend who was going to accompany me waiting for me at the entrance to another rehearsal room. I had just auditioned for the Metropolitan Opera's production of *The Desert Song!*

This was one of the most embarrassing moments in my life. Here I thought I was damned good, and realized I was auditioning for an opera, instead of a musical called *Cole Porter Revue!*

GOWER CHAMPION SAYS . . .

By Fred Curt
Dancer

Gower Champion was the greatest guy in the world. There was nobody like him, never will be. Once I went for an audition where they wanted people over forty-five years of age. I was forty-seven. Gower Champion yelled at me, "Fred, what are you doing here?" I said, "I came for the audition. You wanted people over forty-five." He said, "I know, but what are you doing here?" I said, "I'm forty-seven!" He said, "No you're not, you're thirty-five." I said, "Gower I'm forty-seven." He said, "You're not the kind of forty-five I want."

THE SEVEN YEAR ITCH

By Vanessa Brown
Actress/Journalist/Documentarian

I've done a lot of musical theater. My dancing and singing have landed me roles in feature films. But my favorite part was playing the original lead female role in *The Seven Year Itch* on Broadway, at the

Forty-Sixth Street Theater (today it is the Helen Hayes Theater). The play first came to my consciousness when Miriam Howell (who was the agent of the famous actress Margaret Sullavan) told me she would like to recommend me for the lead. I was very pleased. She wanted me to meet the producers, Courtney Burr and Elliot Nugent, which I did. I was told that Courtney Burr had seen me on a show called "Twenty Questions" while he was at a bar. Everyone in the bar was laughing at me. They thought I was funny when I answered a question on chicken livers. Luckily, the reaction of the people in the bar made a good impression on Courtney, and the rest is history.

I played six hundred performances of *The Seven Year Itch*. My first husband Robert Franklin and I made an offer to George Axelrod and Courtney Burr to buy the property. Had Axelrod not wanted to go with Billy Wilder, whom he really wanted to work with, we might have gotten to produce the picture ourselves. When Billy Wilder came into the picture and acquired the rights, they decided to go with a name female, Marilyn Monroe, and a name male, Tommy Ewell . . . therefore I was out of the picture. The film became a classic. I have no regrets. The stage experience is something I will always treasure.

AN ARTHUR PENN
CASTING STORY

——— ✦ ———

By Hillard Elkins
Producer / Personal Manager

We were producing the musical *Golden Boy* on a pre-Broadway tour and the show was in very, very deep trouble. A lot of the material had to be redone. I was lucky enough to get Bill Gibson to do the rewrite when Clifford Odets passed away.

We were also extremely lucky in getting Arthur Penn, who was a prestigious New York film, television, and theater director, though he had never done a musical before. We needed to replace one of the dancers for Arthur and I traveled from Philadelphia to the Majestic Theatre in New York. When Arthur walked in and looked at the stage there were 240 girls in leotards auditioning to replace the one dancer. Arthur, who had just directed *The Miracle Worker*—a Bill Gibson play about Helen Keller—turned to me and said, "What have I been doing casting all those blind children all my life?"

SEAN YOUNG,
A STARDUST STAR

☆

By Louise Westergaard
Producer

In 1993, Westergaard Productions produced the Broadway play *Stardust* in Los Angeles. The cast consisted of Toni Tennille and Hinton Battle (three-time Tony-Award winner). Still, we wanted another star.

I received a phone call explaining that Sean Young wanted to do our show. "Who is he?" I asked. I was informed that *she* was a major Hollywood sex symbol and starlet. Sean came in and auditioned. It was a great dream of hers to go from Hollywood to Broadway. She was fantastic. In fact, she was so exceptional that we shifted some of our songs and choreographed more numbers to give her a bigger part, so that she might light up the stage as the "star" we were looking for.

Indeed, Sean Young did her first Broadway musical in Los Angeles. Between her dancing and singing, Sean was a hit—an excellent find. The critics were satisfied and so were we!

AGNES DeMILLE, WITH A "D"

———— ☆ ————

By Fred Curt
Dancer

I was just seventeen at the time, living in New Jersey, and had only been dancing for six months when I went with some friends to an open-call audition—because I was *good luck* for them. I sat in the back up on the stage while my friends auditioned. When it was all over, this lady out in the audience called out, "The young man in the striped shirt! Can you dance?" I was the only one in a striped shirt. I said, "A little, I guess." The person asked me to do some balletic things, Jete's Tour Jetes. She yelled, "Keep your back up!" And I did. She said, "Can you do cartwheels?" I said, "One hand or no hands?" Everybody gasped. So I did them with one hand. The voice said, "Thank you." I went back and sat with my friends who were furious with me. I told them I didn't want to be thrown out. The man who I now know was the stage manager came around and called out the names of people he wanted to stay. My friends' names weren't called out, so we got up and started to leave. The man yelled, "You with the striped shirt! Can you come over here and get into this line?" I told my friends I'd be right out.

I stood in the line and they were going down a list calling out names. They came to me and this voice in the audience said, "The young man on the end. What is your name?" I said, "Fred Curt, with a 'C'." There was a "Thank you." Then I waited a moment and raised my hand. This voice said, "Yes?" I said, "Can I ask you a question?" The voice said, "Yes." I said, "What's your name?" Everybody gasped. She said, "Agnes DeMille, with a 'D'" (choreographer of *Oklahoma, Carousel*, etc.). I got my first job. It was in the national company of *Allegro*—Rodgers and Hammerstein's first big flop, but we toured for eight months. That's how I got into the business.

BREAKTHROUGH CASTING IN
ONCE UPON A MATTRESS

By Marshall Barer
Lyricist/Author

We have an opening for a princess ... and a prince ... and a king ... and a queen ... and a minstrel ... and a wizard ... and a jester ... and some knights . . . and some ladies-in-waiting." The casting of *Once Upon a Mattress*—a musical first presented in August 1958 at Tamiment, an adult camp in the Poconos famous for its resident company of professional players, writers, composers, and designers, offering an original Broadway-caliber production every week from Independence Day through Labor Day. The shows were usually "revues," but occasionally a "book-show" was given a shot, and *O.U.A.M.* was one of those. Written by three of the resident writers, Mary Rodgers, Jay Thompson, and moi, this first version, called simply *The Princess and the Pea*, was in one act and ran a little over an hour.

Auditions began in March 1959 for the off-Broadway production in New York at the prestigious Phoenix Theatre. There had been changes: new title, new producers, many new songs, an additional book writer (Dean Fuller), and most significantly, a new director! None other than GEORGE (Mister) ABBOTT!! The auditions were virtually an embarrassment of riches . . . The combination of Phoenix prestige and Abbott power proved to be a honey pot no fly could resist! We woke one morning and there they all were! Hovering . . . trying out for the part of the queen . . . they were all good! But Ms. Jane White (daughter of Walter White, founder of the NAACP) was superb! And everyone agreed that she was the one to play Aggravain. Everyone, that is, except Mr. Abbott! He exclaimed, "Out of the question!" His reason was, "A Negro queen in a white court? Are you all insane? It would throw the whole show off balance!" "But with makeup, Mr. Abbott?" "No!" he boomed, "It's not the color (actually Ms. White is not all dark) it's the features! She'd stick out like a sore thumb! Forget it!" But, I couldn't forget it. Neither could Jack Sydow, Mr. Abbott's assistant and a close friend of Jane's! We arranged to have her return with a special makeup created by the brilliant Marcus Blechman (also a good friend). What he had done was amazing, and even Mr. Abbott was convinced that she would blend perfectly. Somewhat reluctantly, he agreed to let her play the part, but only on the condition that there would be no publicity about it! (He hated PR "gimmicks.") And there never was. To this day few are aware of this important casting breakthrough, but we did get the best possible Aggravain!

"A fan club

is a group of people

who tell an actor he's not alone

in the way he feels

about himself."

—Jack Carson

Stage, Screen, Television, Tours, Etc.

From Broadway to the silver screen, to school plays, to the shower . . . there's a Frank Sinatra or Madonna in us all.

TRYING TO REMEMBER
HER FAVORITE THINGS

☆

By Gary Gardner
Actor/Drama Teacher

My favorite student story—while casting at UCLA, where I teach drama—happened when a girl came in to audition for a musical. The student decided to audition with the Rodgers and Hammerstein song, "My Favorite Things." Unfortunately, she couldn't remember the lyrics. And so her audition went like this: "Rain drops on roses and rain drops on roses. Rain drops on roses and rain drops on roses," etc. Finally I said, "My dear, if you don't remember any of your 'favorite things,' don't sing this as your audition song!"

This same student told me she also knew "Try to Remember," from *The Fantastiks*. I said, "Fine." She gave the music to the accompanist and she could not remember anything past the title of the song. Her audition went like this: "Try to remember the kind of September, try to remember, and try to remember, and try to remember." I thought it was a comedy skit this student was doing . . . but she simply could not remember lyrics.

JACQUES BREL IS ALIVE AND . . .
OH, WELL

By Ari Dane
Singer/Actor/Performer

My favorite show in the mid-sixties was *Jacques Brel Is Alive and Well and Living in Paris*. My friend, Shawn Elliot, an original cast member, suggested I audition for the upcoming road company.

I used to learn a tune in the morning and perform it in the evening, but I really wanted that part, so I took a month and Shawn coached me on four or five of the songs from the show. Not trusting my fate to any accompanist, I even learned to play them on guitar. When I stepped onto the Village Gate stage for that audition I was more than comfortable. I was ready. I was prepared. I was in control. That is until the director looked at me and said, "Sing anything you like . . . as long as it's not from the show!" OK . . . Well, so much for rehearsing!

BEAUTY AND THE BEAST AUDITION

By Phil Savenick
Producer

We were casting a singing role for an actress who could look like the cartoon heroine in *Beauty and the Beast*. After auditioning about sixty brunettes who had each dutifully learned Belle's song, in came a petite blonde in tie-dyed clothing carrying a huge guitar case. She said, "I hope you don't mind, I'd like to accompany myself and sing 'Both Sides Now.' "We all sat there with our mouths open as this little hippie, flower child warbled her Joni Mitchell song, curtsied, and left. After her, the next thirty girls sang the same song from *Beauty and the Beast*, and the truth is, we all were very grateful that the little hippie chick had broken up six hours of monotony. At least it was "something different." She must have figured, *I'm not prepared, I'm not going to get the part, but at least I'll get the attention of a room full of producers.* She sure did!

YOU! OUT!

By Linnea Quigley
Actress

I thought I could do anything. An audition where I had to play the drums—sure. A big dance number—sure. I remember walking into this dance audition. People were swirling and stepping. The lead dancer was showing people these steps: One, two, three, one, two, three, turn, kick, spin, flip. I felt sick, but I got in line. The lead dancer kept pointing at people and yelling, "Out! You out!" I still stayed in line. Well, at my turn, I think I got to one, two, then it was "Out, you!" . . . I also faked it one other time when I went for a Disney kids aerobics class for television. I had no real routine. I ended up improvising this move that looked like a dog peeing on a tree.

THE PIRATES OF PENZANCE AUDITION

by Samantha Leffel
Student/Actress

I was thirteen when I decided to audition for our annual school spring play, *The Pirates of Penzance.* Two days before the tryouts, I told my vocal teacher, Mrs. Ann Fyrr Gamble, that I would probably be more comfortable playing a guy in the play. I had told her that because of my voice range (alto) it would be much easier to sing a lower part, rather than that of the high girl's part. I ended up playing a policeman in the second act. This part appealed to me because 1) I've always been a tomboy, 2) the idea of flouncing around the stage in a hoop skirt didn't particularly interest me, and 3) I don't have a soprano voice.

Maybe the guys were intimidated by me. I don't know for sure—this is what I've been told. The good thing about this part was that nobody could recognize me.

This didn't really hurt my social life a bit. In fact, after the play, one of the crew members asked me out!

MENASHA SKULNIK

By Marshall Barer
Lyricist/Author

I'd been an adoring fan of Menasha Skulnik since the days when, in earlier years, his work was still confined to the Yiddish stage, where he had become something of a Second Avenue Legend.

Later, when the lights went out downtown, he was one of the few survivors, who along with Molly Picon, managed to "cross over" to English-language entertainment. Despite (or possibly because of) an accent you could slice with a kosher knife, there were parts for which he was "Poifect!" Particularly successful was his appearance in the starring role of a comedy about the garment district called *The Fifth Season*. It ran for two years on Broadway. Barely five feet three inches and with a face like some kind of Hasidic monkey, he exuded a transcendent charm difficult to describe . . . the quintessential Jewish character man . . uncompromisingly Jewish . . . Jackie Mason times two! Jewish with a capital Yid! My purpose in going into so much detail is simply to prepare you for the ironies in store.

Stick with me now as I enter the office of my agent, Barry Levinson, one fine morning in the spring of 1968. Barry's first words are, "Hey, do you know any Jewish character men?" "Far vuss?" I ask. "They're making a movie of *The Fifth Season*, and can't find anyone to play the lead ... The producer (who shall be nameless) is so desperate, he's sent this bulletin to all agents on both coasts!" The bulletin said: NOW HEAR THIS! We need someone like Menasha Skulnik to play the lead in *The Fifth Season* and we need him NOW!!

"So tell me," says Barry, "can you think of someone like Menasha Skulnik?" My instant response: "There is no one like Menasha Skulnik." But then I think for a moment, and add: "Except ... Menasha ... and I happen to know he's not working ... We've stayed in touch."

Happy to be the bearer of such good tidings, I get the Adorable One on the phone and start to fill him in, but he's way ahead of me: "Of course I know about that movie! I get *Variety!* Weeks already I've been wondering why they haven't called me ..." I clear that one up easily, "Obviously, because it hasn't occurred to them! So now, I'm asking: Is it mazel tov time, or what?" Menasha cheerily agrees that it's mazel tov time, and three minutes later Barry has been "put through" on the hot line, and, slipping into full agent mode, inquires, "Are you still looking for 'Someone Like Menasha Skulnik'?" "Oh, yes!" exclaims the needy executive, "Who have you got?" "Are you sitting down?" asks Barry, practically purring ... "I've got" (a long pause for dramatic effect) ... "MENASHA SKULNIK!" (An even longer pause at the other end ... then) The schmuck on the hot line delivers my punch line: "WE DIDN'T MEAN ANYONE THAT MUCH LIKE MENASHA SKULNIK."

JANET JONES AND "DANCE FEVER"

By Paul Gilbert
Producer

When I was producing "Dance Fever," Janet Jones tried out as a contestant in St. Louis. She was tall, bubbly, great personality, great expression, and a wonderful dancer. I knew she would be really successful. She made it to the finals in "Dance Fever," beating out hundreds of couples and eventually went on to play leads in the following films: *A Chorus Line, Flamingo Kid, Grease II, One from the Heart, Police Academy*, etc. Some people, when you meet them, you know they have something special.

THE TWISTERS GET ZAPPED!

———— ☆ ————

By Phil Gilbreth
Musician

It's the summer of 1980. The band I was in, The Twisters, were playing at the Whiskey A-Go-Go." Little did we know that in the audience was a director. He was filming the epic classic, *Zapped*—a comedy takeoff on *Carrie*. The film was almost finished and the big ending would soon be shot. We were playing a song we wrote called "Star Spangled Baby." The hook of the song is, "America's queen is just seventeen." Very deep. Apparently this struck the director as the perfect song for the big ending. The director asked if we would like to be in a movie? We said, "Sure we would!"

All in all it was a lot of fun. We were paid a $10,000 advance for the use of the song, $350 each for each day we worked, and $100 a day for our gear to be there (five days). The movie came out about two years later. And there I was on the big screen! I still get royalty checks to this day!

"If at first you don't succeed, you're doing about average."

—Leonard Lewis Levinson

THE BIG BREAK

————— ☆ —————

By Bob Soler
Producer/Composer

For many years my partner, Bobby Zee, and I have been producing and writing music for ourselves as well as other recording artists. When a producer, Vladimir, approached us to act as well as do the soundtrack for a major, music-filled, feature film, we were excited indeed. This was quite frankly a dream come true. We were breaking into an area we'd always wanted to explore—film. And for us to jump right into this arena with a major motion picture, acting and producing the music! Wow, how lucky could we get? When it came time to sign the contract, we happily drove to Palm Springs with our three-hundred-dollar-an-hour attorney. Music, photographs, attorney in hand, we sat down to make the deal. The film? We don't know because the contract and the title were in a foreign language. The worldwide distribution? From one side of Bulgaria to the other!

AT LAST! THE LEAD IN *GODSPELL*

————— ☆ —————

By John Downey III
Actor/Producer

Finally getting to play the Jesus role in *Godspell* was both an amazing and very spiritual experience for me. I had done the show three times before, but had never played the lead, so this was truly a turning point in my life.

I always wanted to be a soap opera actor. An internship at a daytime talk show led to a production job on the show "Attitudes," so I followed a new game plan, but always continued to dabble in acting on the side. When the show was canceled, and I could not get a job to save my life, I decided to go back to plan one and auditioned for a local production of *Godspell*.

I showed up the first night of auditions, did my thing, and figured that was that. After the audition the director took me aside and asked me if I could come by the next night for callbacks. They started talking to me about the production schedule. I was very excited to finally have the opportunity to play the Jesus role that had evaded me for eight years. I got totally into the role, grew a beard, lost thirty pounds, and enjoyed the chance to carry the weight of this special show on my shoulders.

OPEN CALL FOR RAPPERS

By Bobby Zee
Producer/Composer

My partner, Bob Soler, and I had been hired to do a commercial for a national company that manufactured running shoes. The song they had us write was a rap song and, though they liked my version of rapping the demo the best, for authenticity's sake they decided to ask me to audition several people and come up with three rappers to record the song and star in the commercial. The open audition brought us numerous people who really believed they had talent. All of them wanted the work, so much so that they were actually willing to do anything to convince us they could rap and dance. It takes special talent to be a rapper and even more special talent to dance. You have to have rhythm for one. Many of these guys were out of touch with reality. The first rapper must have been wrapping presents at Bullock's, because he had no idea whatsoever of how to rap. The second person who came in was a great dancer, but he also couldn't rap. Another auditionee had no rhythm but he could sing. Finally, after auditioning many, many people, we wound up with three rappers who could do everything. Producing this commercial gave me a whole new perspective on the casting process.

A STAR FOR THE NICHOLAS BROTHERS

By Fayard Nicholas
Dancer/Actor

I've been in films, television, and radio for sixty-four years. Everything that has to do with the entertainment business, except opera. Maybe someday my brother and I will do a tap dance to opera! We were very lucky, we had wonderful parents. They were musicians in Philadelphia and played for wonderful artists like Louis Armstrong. My brother, Harold, and I would go to the theater every day and sit as close as possible to the stars. We started professionally right away. In 1930, I was eleven years old and my brother was seven. We auditioned for the Standard Theater and only had to do one number and we were hired. That's the last audition we ever had to go to. On February 1, 1994, my brother Harold and I got a star on the Hollywood Boulevard Walk of Fame.

BEST FOOT FORWARD

by Edmund Gaynes
Producer/Actor

Best Foot Forward was a musical starring Liza Minnelli in her first stage performance, along with Christopher Walken and myself. After the show opened, over the course of several months, the actors made changes, as they often do. One day the director came to see the show and he ran backstage screaming, "Everybody! Take out all the improvements!"

MAY THE BEST MAN WIN

By Carolyn Dyer
Dance Casting Director

I was casting dancers for a job in Branson, Missouri. This one dancer had all the talent to do the job—but his attitude wasn't very good and it was decided not to hire him. People just want to see your talent and know that you're going to be pleasant to work with.

THE MUSICAL FROM HELL

By Lilly Walters
Actress

Our local community theater, a beautiful house that seats about 470 people, was doing a children's production of *Aladdin*. A guest director was brought in and I was precast in a principal part as a storyteller who carries the story on. This new director had the music director judge the kids on a scale of one to three. One meaning they cannot carry a tune, no way. Two meaning at least they had pitch. Three meaning, "Wow, great voice! Use them!" The same scale was used by the choreographer. Lastly they auditioned for the director, who looked each youngster over and had them read a few lines.

Everyone had a casting sheet with their *grades*—which they carried with them as they went around. They turned the process over to this new director as the final step.

The director called ALL of the kids back to callbacks. We thought this was unusual, but, oh well. He sat them all down in front of him, set all the sheets aside, and looked out at this crowd of expectant faces and said, "Okay, I want you and you and you . . ." I was sitting there thinking, *He's casting these kids by their looks, not by their talent! No, can't be. He must have a photographic memory. Wow! I'm impressed!* But no. He managed to cast thirty people by their looks—choosing them because they looked a little bit Arabic! Only three of the thirty kids could carry a tune. We had some kids who couldn't sing. I don't mean not sing well, I mean they could not sing at all! We had only six people who could dance at all! Eventually we had to say, "Please talk the songs." Because, when they sang, it was very painful. We had some kids who couldn't do a grapevine across the stage. We had to do a great deal of standing and swaying to the music. It was the musical from hell! To this day, I remember the show and go into a cold sweat!

"An agent is someone who believes

that an actor takes 90 percent

of his or her money."

—Anonymous

CHAPTER 8

OH, THOSE ANIMALS!

☆

"My secret is . . .
I use a lot of food, a lot of praise,
and a lot of companionship.
I reason with the animals
and make them *want* to do it."

—FRANK INN
Legendary Animal Trainer
(Benji, Lassie, and Purina Cat,
to name a few)

Film

From a sea gull named Jonathan, to
a dog named Benji . . . animals too
have television and movie heroes.
Here are but a few!

BENJI
Saved from the Pound—
Destined for Hollywood!

———— ☆ ————

By Frank Inn
Animal Trainer

After a near fatal car accident over fifty years ago—when I thought I would never walk again—a friend of mine gave me a dog to keep me company during my recovery. (My dad never allowed me to have a dog while growing up because he believed they dug up plants and flowers.) By the time I recovered from this car accident to a point where I could walk, my dog could do so many things. People would tell me they wished they could do those things with their dogs. I felt like there was something I could do that people would think well of. My secret is . . . I use a lot of food, a lot of praise, and a lot of companionship. I reason with the animals and make them *want* to do it.

Eighty percent of my animals were given to me by people who didn't want them. I got Benji from an animal shelter. One day a man called me from an animal shelter in Burbank, California, telling me I had to have this dog. The dog was ready to be gassed, so I took it home. Benji's original name was Higgins. His first call was for "The Beverly Hillbillies." The second job was to be the train-chasing dog on "Petticoat Junction." Benji was an instant hit as a film star. Benji dolls and jigsaw puzzles followed, over 150 items. The movie *For the Love of Benji* grossed $45 million. The year it was released it was the third highest grossing film, the first was *Jaws*. (*Jaws* cost several million dollars to make, *Benji* cost $500,000). Numerous Benji movies and Benji TV specials have been released over the years, as well as a Benji TV series. Yet more Benji movies and TV specials are slated for the future. To date, this little dog from the pound has been responsible for making many, many millions of dollars!

CLINT HOWARD
TAMES A GENTLE GIANT

By Rance Howard
Actor

This is a casting story about when my then six-year-old son Clint auditioned for the movie *Gentle Giant*. The story was about a relationship between a boy and a big black bear. Clint and I went out to Ivan Tors' animal compound at Africa U.S.A., where Ivan had many exotic animals for a TV series he was shooting called "Daktari." Clint was introduced to the bear and they set up the camera to do the screen test. Clint had learned the dialogue ahead of time. The scene between Clint and the bear was just getting started when the bear—who was sitting on his haunches—reached out his front paw, put it around Clint, and took him right down. Everyone was startled! My son wasn't hurt, but it interrupted the scene. He got up and tenaciously started the scene again. Clint had all the dialogue, but the bear at that time was not a real good listener. So, Clint was going on with this long soliloquy about the bear and how much he loved him. Bears, by the way, when they get impatient, swing their head from side to side—which is what the animal was doing while Clint was trying to do the scene. Clint is a terrific method actor. He has wonderful power of concentration and really gets into the scene. Clint has always been great at establishing eye contact. So he was having trouble doing this with the bear swinging back and forth. Finally, Clint reached out, took the bear by the chain collar, jerked him, then looked into his eyes and yelled, "Now, you listen to me!" And the bear calmed down. Clint continued the scene—with the bear listening intently. And that wonderful courageous act won Clint a principle role in the movie *Gentle Giant*, which was the basis for the subsequent television series "Gentle Ben"—which he also starred in.

FIRST BIG BREAK
A Star Is Born

———— ☆ ————

By Frank Inn
Animal Trainer

As a child I worked around stables for free, to be near the animals. One time I caught a runaway horse and saved somebody's life, and in return, was given a job at the studios. You made $5.00 a day at the studios back then. I worked my way up to $29.95 a week as a union member ... then I had my accident. During my recovery I trained my first dog.

Back on the job, I remember one day I was leaning on a broom watching the filming of *The Thin Man*. There was a scene where a dog was supposed to jump on a bed and crawl under the covers, then peek his head out from under the covers. This man's dog wasn't doing what he wanted it to do. I brought my dog in, picked up a cover, tossed a ball in, said "Fetch," and the dog got the ball. I did this progressively, each time starting out with the dog farther and farther away from the cover. Finally, for the shot, I had the dog running up stairs, jumping on the bed, looking under the covers—when the ball wasn't there—and peeking out from under the covers. They got the shot and my dog got the job! It was the beginning of an exciting new career for me. My next job was training the dogs on the feature film *National Velvet* with Rennie Renfro. After that I worked for Rudd Weatherwax for thirteen years on "Lassie." Countless feature films and television shows followed, including, of course, the ongoing Benji movies!

JONATHAN SEAGULL

By Gary Gero
Animal Trainer

This is how we found Jonathan seagull back in the 1970s. The director, producer, and director of photography and I were scouting locations in Monterey, California. As we were eating lunch at Fisherman's Wharf, there were seagulls sitting on the ledge outside, and people would feed them through a little crack in the window. There was one especially aggressive, beautiful, nice seagull that looked like he was the ruler of the roost there. So I opened the window and he came in and jumped on the table and became a member of our cast!

"If you count all of the time and the labor and the expenses to train animals, financially you're better off washing dishes."

—Hubert Wells

THE ARMED AND INNOCENT COCKATOO

———— ☆ ————

By Benay Karp
Animal Trainer, Benay's Bird and Animal Rentals

When I was first called for the movie *Armed and Innocent*, they were trying to cast a small bird like a cockatiel for a really big part. After reading the script, I realized that the part was really for a much larger bird like a cockatoo. So, when I went down for the casting with a cockatiel, I also brought along my sulfur-crested cockatoo Shaka. She is the same type of bird that was used on the old "Baretta" series. As soon as the director and producers met Shaka, she won them right over. And luckily so. She made all of her scary scenes much more dramatic than a little bird could have. She was amazing.

MAN O' WAR LOOKALIKE
ALMOST MAKES THE BIG SCREEN!

———— ☆ ————

By Bernard Weitzman
Executive Producer

I acquired the rights from Sam Riddle to his life story. Sam Riddle owned the famous racehorse Man O' War. And I hired W. R. Burnett, who wrote *Little Caesar* and *This Gun for Hire* to do a first draft screenplay. We decided that, along with the screenplay, we'd deliver a horse that looked like Man O' War as part of the package. So, we went to Saratoga, New York, during the racing season, and found a horse that had been slightly broken down. He had a physical problem, but he could run short distances. I decided to stage a race, the only race that Man O' War lost in his twenty-one-race career. The horse that beat him was named Upset. Finding an Upset was no problem. We got six jockeys, six horses, a couple of cameras, and camera cars to stage the finish of the race between Man O' War and Upset. But, this horse didn't want to get beat, even though he was a little lame. The jockey couldn't hold the horse back. It was costing us time and money. But finally, after four or five tries, we got him beat right at the wire.

The people who owned the horse were what racetrackers call gypsies. They have a couple of horses and travel around to different half-mile tracks. Now they wanted five thousand dollars because he could no longer run. We gave them the $5,000 after I made a deal with Warner Bros. to make the movie. But the horse had been in the pasture for about a year, nobody looked after him. He gained about 150 to 300 pounds and got so big, he didn't look like a racehorse anymore.

The horse retired—we sold him for a saddle horse. The picture never got made. The name of the horse was Big Ben. All I wound up with was a lot of horseracing footage I'm going to donate to two places, the horse museum in Saratoga and a Churchill Downs museum in Louisville, Kentucky.

MY LION, SUDAN, IS ALIVE AND WELL!

By Hubert Wells
Animal Trainer

My lion Sudan is my favorite animal. He is eleven years old, and he comes from a show business family. I've had him since he was a cub. He did the charges in *Out of Africa*. He's the lion at the end of the movie. By the way, for the scene where the lion and the lioness get shot, there were fanatics who called and said, "You son of a (BLANK), I know you killed that lion!" I told them, "Come out here, you'll see the lion is alive and well!"

SOUNDER HAS A BAD HAIR DAY

———————— ☆ ————————

By Robert B. Radnitz
Producer

In virtually all of my films (*Dog of Flanders, Island of the Blue Dolphins, Misty*) I've used animals in important roles—primarily dogs. Frank Weatherwax has always served as the main trainer. He and his brother, Rudd, are probably best known as the trainers of Lassie. Frank is a wonderful human being. He taught me, early on, about choosing animals for films. Most any trainer can bring in audition animals that can do all sorts of tricks. The thing to look for when you are casting them is this: Can they act normally? The ability to portray normalcy is the most difficult thing for an actor to accomplish. The same is equally true with animals. When Marty Ritt and I did *Sounder* together, he was concerned about one aspect of the film—nervous about it. "The dog is in virtually every scene in the picture. I've never worked with a dog—how do you get them to act?"

"Don't worry about it, Marty," I said. "I'll get Frank Weatherwax on the picture, and we'll have nothing to worry about."

Well, we started shooting the film in Louisiana with Cicely Tyson, Paul Winfield, Kevin Hooks, Taj Mahal, and one of Frank's dogs portraying the pivotal role of Sounder. Then, the roof caved in. One day we were shooting a most important scene. In the script, Sounder had been missing for days, and the boy, heartsick, had searched for him all over the countryside to no avail. One day, working in the fields, he hears a whining. He looks up. Coming at him through the fields is Sounder. Boy and dog approach one another. The boy gets down on his knees, the dog comes to him, and they embrace. That's the scene.

Our planned coverage was simple. A long shot of the boy and the dog in the fields—almost in silhouette—coming toward one another—they meet and embrace. Then, two tight over-the-shoulder close-ups—one on the boy, one on the dog. Well, the long shot went beautifully. We moved in for the close-ups. Suddenly, Sounder just wasn't *there*. I don't quite know what it was, but I believe it was the terrible humidity in the fields. We tried a couple of more times—all to no avail. "I thought you said animals would be no problem on this picture?" Marty asked. "Well, animals, like human beings, sometimes have off days." "I guess so. What are we going to do now?" I thought for a moment and replied, "Listen, why don't we just leave it this way. Believe me, some critic is going to say that as opposed to *milking* the moment, we had taken a much more artistic turn—simply playing the shot in a beautiful long profile fashion." "Maybe you're right—besides, there's nothing else we can do. We're running out of light."

Sure enough, when all the reviews came out they were glorious. *Time* stated something to the effect that an example of the artistry used in the film was the delicate way in which the reunion of the boy and Sounder was shot! Marty and I, along with our cinematographer, John Alonzo, shared many a laugh over this later. When casting animals, the casting couch is never utilized. It's not necessary—besides, animals are too intelligent to fall for that. Sounder went on to get five Academy Award nominations, including Best Picture, Best Actor, Best Actress, and Best Screenplay. Sounder himself was never nominated. As far as I am concerned, the Academy failed in recognizing a truly great performance!

The ability to portray normalcy

is the most difficult thing for an actor to accomplish.

The same is equally true with animals."

—Robert B. Radnitz

Television

They are warm, loving, and adorable. They amuse us, they keep us in suspense, and they would go to the ends of the earth to please us. No, we're not talking about agents. We're talking about animals.

BULLET THE PIG—
BUCK NAKED AND HUNGRY!

——— ☆ ———

By Benay Karp
Animal Trainer, Benay's Bird and Animal Rentals

When I was initially called for the show "Step by Step," they were first doing what is referred to as a cattle call for a little piglet. This meant that they called a large amount of pig owners down for a casting call. When I first arrived with my piglet "Lucy," there were many people with pigs wearing cute sunglasses, bandannas, and outfits. Poor Lucy was buck naked. But, she was much smaller and cuter than all the other pigs. And once she discovered that most people on the show had food, she wanted to be friends with all of them. So she made a pest of herself, went up to everyone, and would tug on their pants, or pull on their shoelaces, or snort at them as only a pig can do. She made a real hog of herself, looking for free handouts. And in the process, she became a hit with everyone (except the other jealous pigs), and she was chosen. In the course of the year on the show, she

was played by eleven pigs (they wanted her character to stay small).
Her name on the show, which stars Patrick Duffy and Suzanne
Somers, was "Bullet."

THE DOG ON "EMPTY NEST"—
A SHOW BIZ LINEAGE

———— ☆ ————

By Gary Gero
Animal Trainer

Dreyfuss, the dog on the long-running series "Empty Nest," came
from a show biz family. His grandfather was rescued from the dog
pound in 1975 and six weeks later he was featured in an After
School Special. Dreyfuss' grandfather also worked with Michael
Landon on "Father Murphy" for forty shows. His brother out of
the same litter was the dog that was used in *Steel Magnolias*. Every
single one of these dogs are just wonderful characters, that whole
genetic line. Dreyfuss showed against a lot of dogs to get that part.
It was an open casting call of all the trainers—it seemed like every
dog in Hollywood was there!

JACK RUSSELL TERRIER
ON "FRASIER"

———— ☆ ————

By Gary Gero
Animal Trainer

Kathy Morrison, our lead person down in Florida, picked up a
little Jack Russell Terrier to train. The breeder wanted to get rid of
this vicious, pesky little dog that was a little wild and nasty. So, when

the producers of "Frasier" asked us to do the show, we were asked to bring in several of our dogs. Among them was this now well-behaved and trained Jack Russell Terrier whom they liked, and who was chosen to star in their hit show "Frasier."

I DON'T DO SHAKESPEARE

By Roy Wood
Fishbusters

I got a call one time from "The Dennis Miller Show" and they wanted a whole group of frogs with full Elizabethan costumes. That was one of my misses. I couldn't get it for them. I called them back and said, "I don't do Shakespeare."

HE'S CUTE . . . BUT CAN HE ACT?
Pokey the Cock-a-Poo and the
Gravy Train Audition

By Sharon M. Ferritto
Associate Producer

Pokey and I were novices when it came to auditions for dogs, but I figured that more than half of the dogs who would be at the Gravy Train audition would have no business being there in the first place. So, I thought we'd have nothing to lose.

Pokey is a Cock-a-Poo, a cross between a Cocker Spaniel and a Poodle. He has a black coat with a white patch on his chest, big brown eyes, and weighs about fifteen pounds. In pictures, he looks like a toy dog you would buy as a gift for a child at F.A.O. Schwarz. Whenever I take him for a walk, people look at him and smile and say, "What a cutie!" His personality manifests all of the traits that make people love dogs—he's loving, attentive, and extremely cuddly.

As I got Pokey ready for the audition, I felt a little guilty about getting him into something he wouldn't understand. When I put his leash and dress bandanna on him, though, he ran eagerly to the door. He had decided that we were headed to Hollywood.

I was surprised at the turnout. There were over one hundred people there even though we arrived about two hours after the auditions had started. Since everyone had to wait outside with their dogs, the line went down the street and around the block. I suddenly realized that everyone secretly thinks that his or her dog has the potential to become a star, if given the chance.

Even though we sat for several hours before it was our turn to audition, Pokey behaved professionally and didn't bark at the other dogs. I was proud of him. By the time it was Pokey's turn to audition, one of the Pit Bulls had attacked the Gravy Train that the dogs were supposed to chase. Now the audition requirements were changed. When he was called, Pokey jumped up the steps to the stage like a pro. He was asked to sit and to stay. Since he wasn't a graduate of dog obedience school he didn't perform on cue, though we both pretended that he could have if he had wanted to. But he sure was cute. In fact, at the end of Pokey's audition the casting director asked him to sit for a close up.

On the way home, I decided to stop at the grocery store to buy Pokey a treat. Once we were back at home, Pokey went to his favorite spot on the sofa and laid there for a long time without moving. I think that the day's events had taken their toll on him. I was so proud of him, though, and I made sure he understood that even if he didn't get the part, I loved him anyway.

CLEO FROM PEOPLE'S CHOICE
The Nervous Basset Hound
Who Liked Doing Charity Work

By Frank Inn
Animal Trainer

When Jackie Cooper and Irving Becker called me in to see them, every trainer in the book was in there with a dog of some kind. I didn't even go in with a dog. They said, "We need a real sad-faced dog. We were thinking about a Bloodhound or a Basset Hound." They asked me to find a Basset Hound.

A couple of weeks later I found a nervous Basset Hound that had three owners, nobody could housetrain it. I made a deal for $85. He puked on me on the way home and chewed up my truck. I trained that dog in two weeks. We did a different thing each week for thirty-nine weeks for three years. Jackie Cooper and I became good friends. We traveled all over on behalf of the March of Dimes.

SIEGFRIED & ROY . . .
AND MORTICIA THE VULTURE

By Hubert Wells
Animal Trainer

One of the animals featured in the spectacular Siegfried & Roy show is my vulture, Morticia. A fisherman had given the vulture to me because it had a knee injury and was not able to make a living in the wild. I took care of Morticia and trained her. She was perfect for the Siegfried & Roy show, and when they wanted to buy Morticia, I suggested trading her for a White Tiger cub. They chose to rent the bird, and have been doing so for a number of years. Morticia appears to be quite happy in her new home.

THE ELEPHANT BOXER SHORTS STORY

By Cheryl Shawver
Elephant Trainer

People are often curious about how much money animals make. The highest paid are: elephants, giraffes, and orangutans—each earning $1,500 per day.

I train many animals, but I am known for training elephants. This is my favorite elephant story.... For an episode of "Full House" there was a birthday party and an elephant was to be a surprise! The actors were dressed in clown outfits and they opened the door and the elephant, Malaika, walked into the room! It was set for her to do a *clown gag* where she would reach into the clown costume with her trunk and pull out some polka-dotted boxer shorts (as if she had reached in and pulled the actor's underwear off). They saved the trick for the live audience. Malaika knew what she was supposed to do. On the first take she performed perfectly! She reached into his pants and pulled out the boxer shorts. However, they didn't *cut* the scene, they kept on filming. . . . So she didn't get rewarded right away. And elephants are used to being rewarded for doing the job right. Because Malaika is very smart, she was wondering what she should do differently, to do the trick *right* so that she would get her reward. She was thinking to herself, *What should I have done differently? We're doing it again, what should I do this time?*

So on the second take, she comes in, reaches in, grabs the shorts from the actor's pants, drops them—then reaches in again! The actors, Bob Saget and David Coulier, thought that was wonderful, because it gave them a chance to ad lib! Malaika still did not get rewarded....

On the third take, Malaika comes in, reaches into the actor's pants, pulls the boxer shorts out correctly, drops them onto the floor—pauses to think—and then takes the boxer shorts and polishes the floor with them!

All three takes were funny! She was being very good! Finally, when the filming was over, I rewarded her amply with her three favorite things: bananas, sugar cubes, and bread!

THE FISH WHO SPIT ON JERRY SEINFELD

By Roy Wood
Fishbusters

I don't know if you've seen the American Express commercials with Jerry Seinfeld and the goldfish in the pet store. There's a series of three or four of them running now. The whole joke throughout the commercial is that the fish spits on him. And I'm supposed to make the fish spit on him—which is impossible. So, when we were shooting the first one we were standing next to Jerry Seinfeld behind this big, black curtain. And just as we were about to roll, the director said, "Okay, Roy, now we want you to make the fish spit." This is where the line between fantasy and reality gets quite blurred.

There were actually three different fish used in the commercials, because there were three different shoots. I gave the first one away to my girlfriend's mother. I told everyone about it and they saw the commercial and now they all wanted the fish. So there was a bidding war on my fish! I sold them to the highest bidder. Normally, the fish end up in someone else's aquarium. The commercial usually buys the fish, but they have no place to put it. So I have a service. I have about fifteen tanks around the city that I service and maintain.

THE PERFECT DOG FOR
"THE GEORGE CARLIN SHOW"

By Benay Karp
Animal Trainer, Benay's Bird and Animal Rentals

When one of the producers for "The George Carlin Show" called, she said they were looking for a cute little dog with attitude. Boy did I have a dog for them. I sent a little dog named Tony down. And from the moment he strutted into their offices like he owned the place, he was a top contender. We showed him against some of the best little dogs in the business. I think his cocky attitude, along with an instant chemistry between Tony and George, is what got him the job. He has become George's sidekick, and is in almost every episode as a sort of doggie co-star. He loves everyone on the show, but takes a real particular liking to George and the creator of the show, Sam Simon. If they don't take the time every day to greet him, he will pout until they do. Tony even has his own dressing room.

"I once asked Mr. McClintock, 'What is your definition of a star?' He replied, 'Any name in lights that will draw a crowd. It could be Lassie, it could be a horse. If crowds go in to see that person, it's a star.' And you know that's brilliant!"

—Jayne Meadows

THE MACAW ON THE
UNITED AIRLINES COMMERCIAL

By Benay Karp
Animal Trainer, Benay's Bird and Animal Rentals

Ranger is a blue and gold macaw that I purchased from an importer about fifteen years ago. When I first brought him back to my home, he was actually quite nasty, with a real flair for biting. I initially purchased him with the thought of taming him down and reselling him as a pet. However, after his superior intelligence began to show (he could pick most locks, and actually dismantled a cage door), I chose to keep him and train him for television and movie work. He immediately became an incredible student, and one of my top performers. He can do over one hundred different trained behaviors, including riding a macaw-sized bike, scooter, and motor car, and is very athletic, enjoying a good game of basketball and bowling. He is a truly brilliant bird. Ranger is that beautiful bird that everyone saw on the award-winning United Airlines commercial, playing the piano. And yes, he did play all the right keys. That really was him playing that song!

ONE SMART CHIMP
WITH A MIND OF HIS OWN

By Hubert Wells
Animal Trainer

Chimpanzees are the closest animals to humans. They are the only animals that can laugh, cry . . . and lie too! By lying I don't mean with words. They can lie to you with their behavior. When working with chimpanzees, you work harder than with any other animal, but at the same time you laugh more than you do with any other animal. We did a show that was a takeoff on James Bond. Chimps did everything, riding motorcycles, skiing, motorboating, karate kicks. In one of the scenes, a chimp was driving a motorcycle with another chimp in the side car. In the first scene, a chimp got into a motorcycle and I started it and led him off. In the second scene, the chimp decided to start his own motorcycle and took off on his own!

ANIMAL LOVER

By Ruth Webb
Talent Agent

I am a great animal lover (I presently have eight cats in my Hollywood Hills office). They all sleep with me in my waterbed, and I have a pet raccoon who swims with me in my pool . . . and a peacock! I used to watch "The Johnny Carson Show." One night he had a singing dog act on—a guy and his pooch. I wrote to Johnny about this, as I not only had a Yorkshire Terrier who sang better, I was taking care of two more Yorkies for my client, Gaylea Byrne. Shirley Wood of "The Tonight Show" answered my letter and arranged a singing dog competition. I arranged for one of Gaylea's little Yorkies to sing with her on this Carson special. I must explain to those who do not know that when the human voice reaches a certain pitch, the dog howls. That's how you get them to sing.

The great day came and Gaylea called in the morning and said, "I'm not going on any darned show with any darned dog, including my own darned dog!" I said, "What shall I do? You and your Yorkie, Higgins, are the stars!" Gaylea said, "I don't care. You go on!" I did. Higgins and I sang a duet of "Can't Help Lovin' That Man" from *Showboat*. We didn't win the fireplug, but it seems this was the start of all Johnny's animal acts. And mine became a Carson classic for which I received residuals for years.

*"Everyone secretly thinks
that his or her dog
has the potential to become a star,
if given the chance."*

—Sharon M. Ferritto

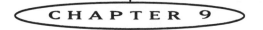

CHAPTER 9

RISKY BUSINESS!

☆

"Thirty feet up. No net.
I was trembling so hard
I looked like a cartoon blur.
But my pride was at stake here.
I was an actress, wasn't I? A method actress.
Ba boom! I became a circus performer.
I swung. I returned.
I pranced prettily like a show horse.
One take. Done."

—JOANNA LEE
Writer/Producer,
from her book, *A Difficult Woman*

Anything to Get the Part

Actors have historically been known to elevate themselves to stratospheric levels of ability, whether they actually possess the qualities demanded for the role or not. From professing to be a world-class pole vaulter to an equestrian, little white lies can be minimally amusing and sometimes even dangerous.

CIRCUS PERFORMER

---- ☆ ----

By Joanna Lee
Writer/Producer

FROM HER BOOK, *A DIFFICULT WOMAN*

I was young and hungry. I was also, I might add, willing to say anything it took to get a job, including bending the truth a little. At a glamorous cocktail party one night, I overheard Collier Young, a distinguished series producer, talking about a show he was having trouble casting. It was a circus episode and he needed a girl who could act and swing on a trapeze. Hey, I was a girl and I could act. True, I was singularly unathletic and had, in fact, flunked gym in high school, but two out of three ain't bad. I presented myself, told the producer who my agent was, and informed him this was his lucky night. I told him I had just returned from Sarasota, Florida, where I was training for the new show with Ringling Bros. Barnum and Bailey. He could see I would look great in a leotard, he believed me, he hired me.

I showed up for hair, makeup, and leotard feeling confident. I knew how they did this stuff. You stand on a little platform a few feet off the ground. Movie magic, right? Wrong. The first thing I saw when I walked out on the set was a real circus rigging, a rope ladder, and a trapeze thirty feet up. No net. There was a stunt coordinator but they were looking for me to set the pace. After all, I was from the circus. My co-star was a great stage actor, Joseph Wiseman. I was going to act with Joseph Wiseman! Or . . . die with Joseph Wiseman. He started gamely up the ladder . . . all he had to do was stand there on the platform and catch me when I swung back. I had to catch the bar and swing out into space, swing back, and raise my hand prettily. I was trembling so hard I looked like a cartoon blur. But my pride was at stake here. I was an actress, wasn't I? A method actress. I was not going to screw this up. Ba boom! I became a circus performer. They threw me the bar. I swung. I returned. I pranced prettily like a show horse. One take. Done. They applauded below.

When I came down, an agent standing there told me I was terrific and he had a great part for me. Someone like me shouldn't have any trouble working six horses at once, right? Show horses. Great part. It was then I ran to the john to throw up.

A ONE-MAN BAND

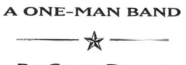

By Gene Perret
Writer/Producer

I was a writer on "Rowan and Martin's Laugh In," and all of us writers, about twelve, were in the office of the producer one day. We had a comedy piece in which we needed a one-man band. So we called this guy in for an audition. He was this old gentleman with all the equipment: a drum on his back, cymbals on his knees, an accordion, flags, etc. He marched around the room playing and we were all laughing at him. He was just what we needed but he began pleading for the job. Finally the producer said, "Look, it's only one day of work. We can't guarantee you'll be on the show when we make the final cut. And we pay scale." The guy said, with a German accent, "That's exactly what I wanted!"

THE EIGHTEEN WHEELER BLUFF

———— ☆ ————

By Marty Ratigan
Actor

My agent called and asked if I could handle a semi. I was so desperate for work that I said, "Yes!" I hung up the phone and ran to the nearest truck stop and bribed a truck driver to give me a crash course in trucker terminology and technique. I bluffed my way through the auditions, and got the job.

I was extremely nervous the day of the shoot, since I really had no clue how to drive the thing. Fortunately, the real acting came when they explained that it was a new truck and the dealership wanted their own man to do the moving shots. "Aw gee, that's too bad. You only want me for the close-ups?" Whew!

"I once lost a part in 'L.A. LAW' because I couldn't take my hair off. Mine is unremovable!"

—Jack Carter

SHOES TOO SMALL

By Marty Ratigan
Actor

I got to a callback on a tennis shoe commercial and they said, "You have the job, but you must be able to fit into this size eight pair of shoes. They are specially made by the ad agency." Well, I wear a size eleven, so naturally I said, "I can do it." I crammed those things on my feet and worked four hours doing sit-ups and calisthenics as they photographed my feet. To truly add insult to injury, they called me at home that night. They had lost the shoes and wanted to know if I had taken them!

MOVE OVER JAMES BOND, THESE ACTORS DO IT ALL!

By Dee Miller and Kim Nammoto
Casting Directors, The Casting Directors

During a casting session, the talent will answer without even thinking about what is being asked of them. The standard answer is, "Sure, no problem." This is mainly because the talent is too busy watching themselves on the monitor. Also they really, really want the part.

To prove this theory, we were casting for a beer company that was to be shooting two different commercials. Talent was required to be able to play softball while roller blading . . . and play volleyball while on a trampoline. When questioning the talent we decided to combine all questions to prove our theory—and see if they would respond differently. They were asked, "So, you are saying that you can on-line roller blade while playing softball on a trampoline while playing volleyball?" Talent response, "Sure, no problem," said with a big smile. . .Theory proven.

Another example. We were casting a commercial that required Black people. When told why they were not being considered for the role, their response: "I could be Black!"

LADY IN COAT WITH PASTIES

— ☆ —

By Eddie Foy III
Casting Director

I started working at Twentieth Century-Fox. They had a new talent program there and I was meeting the people they had under contract. This woman comes through my door and she's late by one and a half hours. She is wearing a coat—and it's the middle of the summer. She sits down. I asked, "Don't you think it's a little strange that you're wearing a full-length jacket today?" So she stood up, opened her coat, and all she was wearing were two pasties and a postage stamp. I'm sitting there staring at this and I said, "You have to understand something. I am a very happily married man. You have a gorgeous figure, but my wife's figure beats the bejesus out of yours. So why don't you cover up."

"We had clean sex on the screen in my day.

My sarong was thought very daring.

But it seems like long underwear now."

—Dorothy Lamour

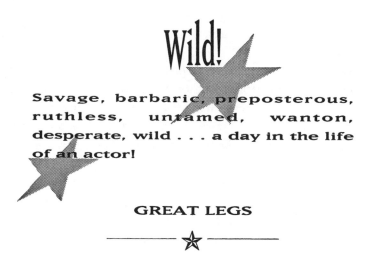

Wild!

Savage, barbaric, preposterous, ruthless, untamed, wanton, desperate, wild . . . a day in the life of an actor!

GREAT LEGS

By Cynthia Garris
Actress

This audition called for great legs. I walked in and right away they said, "Okay, you got it!" I didn't even know what I'd be doing. They sent me over to wardrobe. The wardrobe lady said, "Okay, let's get the hanging harness out." Hanging harness! Nobody told me I'd be hanging!

The show was "Tequila and Bonetti." I was paid $1,200 to dangle dead and do a background voice-over in the next scene, and it wasn't even acting. It was very, very strange.

CLEAN AND SOBER . . . AND NAKED

By Linnea Quigley
Actress

I had an interview at Warner Bros., so I got all dressed up. I'm auditioning for a scene with Michael Keaton. I thought, *Wow, here's a great big movie with Michael Keaton, a star!* Plus, I was getting to see the producer and director right away instead of just the casting director.

When I arrived at the studio they asked me some questions, and looked at my photos. Then they left the room and had me disrobe into my underwear. I had to lay down on my stomach on the couch and yell "okay" for them to come in. The producer, the director, and the casting lady filed in, looked me over, said "thank you," and left.

My husband and I went to see the movie which was *Clean and Sober*. I said, "That's the part I auditioned for!" My husband was mortified. It was for a dead, naked girl lying in bed with Michael Keaton . . . I guess I don't do dead naked well.

DANIEL TRAVANTI, CONSUMMATE ACTOR

───── ✭ ─────

By Eddie Foy III
Casting Director

There are only a couple of producers who are as good as Danny Arnold. Danny is a screamer, he's a fighter, he's a unique wonderful human being and he's a genius. We were casting *The Wackiest Ship in the Army* at Screen Gems and I brought in Daniel Travanti. I didn't know if he had a sense of humor or not. He had just come from New York and was hot as a firecracker—a new face in town.

Meanwhile, they had warned us that they were going to be doing some remodeling in the office. Danny had a couch set up against a wall. Dan Travanti and I start reading together. As Dan reads, a pick came through the wall, right past his right ear, and lodged in front of the script. And he didn't miss a beat. He kept reading. And Danny stared at him. Now the guy is trying to take the pick back, and Dan kept right on going, didn't break a sweat. The pick is moving back and the wall is starting to give way. Finally Arnold can't go on any further, he's starting to break up. He said, "Stop!" And Travanti said, "What did I do wrong?" And he looked and said, "What is that?!!" One more inch and that pick would have killed Dan Travanti. Wild. . . .

SHOW AND TELL

───────── ☆ ─────────

By Robert Easton
Actor/Dialect Coach

In 1971 my agent sent me on an interview to read for the role of a charismatic cult leader in a TV movie starring Eve Arden, Julie Newmar, and Pat Morita. At the time I had very long hair and a long beard left over from another job so I knew I looked right for the role and I went in with confidence. The interview went very harmoniously. The vibes couldn't have been friendlier. But all of a sudden the director, producer, and writer were standing up, thanking me for having come in. I suddenly realized they were not going to even let me read for the role. Intuitively I knew they had already decided I was too normal for the part. I had made the big mistake of talking to them as a polite professional, who, if given the chance, could create a bizarre character. But clearly they weren't going to give me the chance.

Instant anger kicked in and with the guts generated by massive adrenalin flow I grabbed the script off the director's desk and bellowed, "What page does this scene start on?" Startled, he told me and I sight read a blood-curdling monologue in which I bombastically assured him and his cohorts that they were going to burn in hellfire forever because of their stupidity, viciousness, and depravity. I snarled in their faces and glowered at them as though they were human garbage. Then I threw the script down and thundered out of the room.

My agent called me that night. He said, "I don't know what you said to those people, but they think you're a maniac." I told him I was sorry but I had gotten angry that they didn't think I was right for the part. "But they do," he said. "They just made a great offer." I took it, and ever since then I have realized that at a casting session the performer can never underestimate the lack of imagination in those who do the casting. It's show and tell time!

CASTING MY HUSBAND IN A TELEVISION PILOT

By Liz Herszage
Writer/Actress

I knew it was risky, I had been told by too many people, "Liz, you're asking for trouble . . . casting your husband in the television pilot." It seemed like such a good idea. After all, it was a small part. He was from South America, suave, debonair, adorable . . . the only problem was, he couldn't act. He was just fine during rehearsal, but once the red light on the camera came on, he stuttered and stammered and couldn't remember a thing. He somehow thought he was doing great; he never was one to admit to failure of any kind. His English wasn't very good either. His line might be, "That was fantastico, magnifico, perfecto . . . darling." When it came time to tape, he'd say, "Perfecto, ah, ah, that is fantastico, I mean, darling." It was a mess. The producer hated me for the unabashed nepotism I was indulging in, and I didn't know how to handle the situation. When the ax finally came, I was the one who had to tell him. To this day he blames me. He thinks I wrote a too-complicated part for him. He's probably right, those three lines were difficult, each one of them was over four words long. By the way, we're divorced.

VERONICA LAKE WOULDN'T BE FLIPPED BY CHRISTOPHER WALKEN

By Edmund Gaynes
Producer/Actor

I was doing a show with Liza Minnelli, Christopher Walken, and Veronica Lake, who played the part of a has-been movie star—which she was at the time. I was sixteen years old, Chris was twenty, and Veronica was forty-two, but she looked sixty. She was a nice lady but she had a drinking problem and had led a hard life. She would often walk off stage because she wasn't feeling well, leaving us on stage having to ad lib. That is a real actor's nightmare.

There was one number where Christopher Walken was to start dancing with Veronica Lake and they would go back to back and he was to flip her over his back and she would land on her feet. This poor woman was so petrified, she wouldn't even attempt to do it. So, the choreographer—in order not to lose that bit—created a scenario where, in the confusion of the tango, I got caught in the middle of it and Chris mistakenly would flip me over while I was protesting.

We rehearsed it once and my feet came down a little too early. The choreographer said, "Don't land quite so soon." The next time I did it I woke up in the hospital because I fell right on my head! I'm amazed I didn't get killed because it was a very hard floor. Theater is not necessarily the safest thing in the world.

"I don't like to tell people I'm an actress, it's too much like, 'What can you do for me?'"

—Katherine Soler

IS THAT YOUR REAL HAIR?

By Jane Brody
Casting Director

My associate, Mickie Paskal, has very long hair and she always wears it in a long braid down her back. Mickie was prereading people for a film. And she was giving this one lady some very intense direction, all about the tragedy of the role and how this woman is desperate for her father's love, and how she's got to really find that spine of pain—and she's going on and on. And in the middle of all of this, the actress looks at Mickie and says, "Is that your real hair?"

TINA TURNER
AND SMOKEY ROBINSON

By Steve Binder
Director/Producer

Basically the 666 story was pretty amusing. I had offices on Robertson Boulevard in West Hollywood, where I operated a production and management company. That building is actually a historical site in Hollywood because it was the original home of Panavision. My partner at the time was very good friends with Tina Turner. I had spent some time talking to Tina, and we had convinced her to come over and talk to us about management. This was just at the time when she was switching managers. She set up a meeting at my office, then she never showed up. I wondered what happened.

My partner called Tina and she said, "Well, I actually did show up but when I got to the front door I realized your address was 666, and I wouldn't cross it and come up to the office." So we were kind of amused by the whole thing . . . we are still good friends. It never occurred to me in a million years that anybody would find our address *disturbing*. Yet, within a year I was hired to produce and direct the weekly variety "Smokey Robinson Motown" series on NBC. We had made a deal basically to produce the show. Also, our company would become the headquarters for the offices for the show.

We set our first production meeting and Smokey was supposed to come over to the office at a certain time. Next thing I know I receive a telephone call from his manager saying, "We have a problem." And I said, "What's the problem?" He said, "We can't have our offices at your offices." I said, "Why?" He said, "Because Smokey saw your address when he came over and it was 666." We ended up moving to NBC. Because at that point I decided, I've got to get out of this building!

CLONED

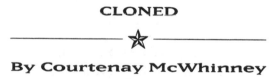

By Courtenay McWhinney
Actress

I've never known anyone with my first name, and I've never known anyone who looked like me. I was going to read for a pilot at the black tower at Universal. When I got off of the elevator I saw five clones of myself at different stages of my life! Three of them were younger, two of them were older. It was the darndest thing! I looked in the mirror and couldn't tell who I was, me or them? It was spooky! These people looked identical! And for somebody who has been an individual all of her life, it was quite a shock. As it turned out I was second up for the part. The person who got the part looked more like me than I did!

PLATOON GOES AWOL

———— ☆ ————

By Pat Golden
Director

Platoon, Oliver Stone's second directing venture, which went over so successfully, was shot in the Philippines. We'd cast just about everybody, and Oliver had gone on location. From there, he called every cast member at home to give them his drill sergeant, boot camp, gung ho speech. I guess he must have really gotten into it, because the next day I received calls from four or five of the actor's agents saying that they'd have to bow out. After a flurry of transcontinental calls and telexes, we recast the roles. And so it goes, you never know.

NERVOUS BREAKDOWN

———— ☆ ————

By Scott Kaske
Performer at the Queen Mary

Basically, I portray a female in a show at the Queen Mary. One night I was performing and some people in the audience were studying me just a little too hard. After the show my boss came up to me and said, "There are some people in the audience who are thinking of casting you in a movie." And I said, "Yeah, right." Actually, I had just finished playing a transvestite in a horror film. It was a lot of fun. But it went straight to video. Boo hoo.

Next, they talked about me coming down and auditioning. I went to the producer's house dressed as a boy and they didn't know who I was! I told them, "I'm applying for the part of Angel." . . . It was a very emotional part. I was very nervous and very scared because I wanted this part so badly. They gave me the script. I was having a hard time reading it because I'm dyslexic. I said, "Can I go home and study it?" They let me. I went home and read the whole thing.

When I returned they put me in a room by myself and said, "Think of all the depressing things that have happened in your life— whatever it is you've gone through." And I come from a dysfunctional family, so that wasn't really difficult to do. I made the part like it was really me, like it really happened. I had no control over what was going on. Basically I had a nervous breakdown . . . and I got the part!

After the movie was shot—during a screening—the producer told my parents that the original person who was supposed to have played this part was Bud Cort.

YOU'RE JUST NOT OFFICER MATERIAL

By Robert Easton
Actor/Dialect Coach

In war film after war film I was always cast as an enlisted man. In John Huston's *The Red Badge of Courage* I played a Union private. In a number of other Civil War films I played Confederate privates. I also was cast as a private in many World War II films including *The Bold and the Brave* and *Combat Squad* and many Korean War films. . . . I fared no better in the earlier wars, playing American Revolutionary War privates, even a World War I private.

With the passage of time I thought I would mature and get officer roles. It didn't happen. As I got older I finally was cast as a corporal in Robert Wise's *Somebody Up There Likes Me*, and then I got to play a sergeant as Charlie Bronson's comic relief buddy in *When Hell Broke Loose*. But the promotions stopped there. Again and again I auditioned for officer roles. I never got them. Finally one director leveled with me: "I'm sorry, Bob, but you're just not officer material!" It frustrated the heck out of me. Why couldn't I ever get a part as an officer and a gentleman? I resigned myself to a military career of playing noncoms.

In the early 1960s I went to England and much to my amazement one of the first parts offered to me was that of an American colonel. I had never portrayed a lieutenant nor a captain nor a major and here I was playing a colonel! I said to the British director, "Which is it? Do you have a very high opinion of me or a very low opinion of American colonels?"

MY INTRODUCTION TO NORMAN LEAR

———— ☆ ————

By Gina Francis
Actress

My wonderful, fantastic, terrific Dad saved Norman Lear's life in World War II, the Big One. He pulled him from a burning bunker, and as he did, Norman raspily whispered in my Dad's ear, "If you ever marry, and have a really talented daughter who wants to become an actress, tell her to move to Hollywood and call me because I'll be an incredibly successful producer who can help her . . . all because you saved my life." Or something like that.

So, after moving to Hollywood, I gave Mr. Lear a call, and he was nice enough to invite me over to his humble 106-room abode. His butler let me in, led me to the living room, and said, "Mr. Lear will be right with you." I said, "Thank you, Mr. French." I guess they're paid not to respond to humor.

So, I'm waiting, looking around, hugely impressed with myself sitting in his grandiose room. Still waiting. I get up, do a couple of twirls, and start inspecting things. Spying a large candy dish, I dance over, help myself to most of the bowl, depositing the contents in my purse. I continue my investigation. Another candy dish is spotted. In a move worthy of Twyla Tharp, I spin and dump the goodies in my bag. This was fun. There were candy dishes all over. My bag is stretching completely out of proportion.

Without warning I hear from behind me, "There's some on the piano." Not missing a beat (timing is everything), I respond, "Got 'em." Then I turned to meet the great man himself. He was wonderfully gracious, complimentary, and made me feel completely at ease. I wasn't intimidated in the least. Due, perhaps, to the little chunk of cottage cheese stuck to his cheek. A nice guy, to be sure. But so far, besides the tonnage gained from all that candy, I'm still waiting for my series.

A BLOODY SHAME

———— ✭ ————

By Sandra Caruso
Actress / Director / Acting Teacher

Whenever I'm called to audition for commercials, they are usually very proper female roles—like moms in cereal commercials—or for products like Ford or IBM. So, I'm always dressed very conservatively when I go for readings. I am, you might say, excessively neat.

On my way to this one audition, I stopped to help a guy who had just been in a motorcycle accident. He was okay, although he had to be taken to the hospital. He was covered with blood and, helping him, I too got covered with blood. As an actress, one never passes up an audition, no matter what! I didn't have time to change, so when I arrived at the audition and went to shake the hand of another actor, he was horrified. I explained what had happened, but his reaction—one of pure terror and shock—made me decide not to explain what had happened to me when I went into the room. I walked in with a big smile and never said a word about why I was covered with blood. I handed the producers and director and casting director my picture and resume covered with blood. I gave the reading. Nobody said anything. I thanked them and left. Needless to say, I didn't get a callback.

THE TRUE "CRAZY ACTOR WITH GUN" STORY

─────── ☆ ───────

by Eddie Foy III
Casting Director

I get an offer from the brilliant producer Danny Arnold to leave Screen Gems and join him as his associate producer on the series "That Girl." Marlo Thomas is the lead and I think the world of her. I wanted the job. Two weeks later I'm in my office packing to leave Screen Gems. My secretary, Trudy Soss, comes into my office and says there's a guy in the outer office and he wants me to sign for a package. She tells me he won't take no for an answer. Then this guy walks into my office, he's wearing sunglasses, a T-shirt with something scribbled on the front, a ball cap, and pulls out a .22 pistol. He hands me this envelope and asks me to sign it because he wants an autograph for his grandmother. While this is going on, Trudy sees what's happening, and calls the guards at the front gate telling them about the guy with the gun. The guy now throws the envelope on the ground and starts to cry. Trudy says to the guard on the phone, "What do you mean you have four cars backed up at the gate?! . . . The man has a gun . . . You're too busy?! . . . In a few minutes?!" She hangs up the phone. By this time, I've backed into the desk and reach down for a cigarette. He asks why I'm doing that and I said, "It's better than what's going on in my underwear . . . Sears is going to get my business today."

He then drops to the floor, lets go of the gun, pulls a knife, and starts to stab the floor. He stands up, pulls off the mustache, takes off the hat, glasses, and with a big smile says his name and, "I'm an actor and I want to audition for you."

Trudy said, "I think you'd better get out of here." The actor turns and leaves. I heard later that he attacked a female casting director in a reading. He was a crazy person. I have had this same exact story told to me by other casting directors. . . . Now you have the truth!

RONALD REAGAN TWIRLS "CASABLANCA" BATON TO BOGEY

———— ☆ ————

By Armand Deutsch
Writer

Ronald Reagan was president of the United States for eight years, governor of the state of California for eight years, and a motion picture star at Warner Bros. Studios for twenty-seven years. He made over forty films. His favorites were *Kings Row* and *Knute Rockne, All American*. He has always had, however, one major regret. He turned down the role played by Humphrey Bogart in *Casablanca*. At the time it did not seem worthy of a second thought. He was given two choices and opted for a movie called *International Squadron*. *International Squadron* had its tiny moment in the sun and disappeared forever; *Casablanca* is eternal.

Humphrey Bogart was far from overjoyed at being chosen by the studio to play the role of Rick. He fought it like a tiger, but in those days the studio was the boss and he finally gave in. His objections did not lack merit. Shooting started with a half-finished script. Each day the cast would receive the pages for the day's work. No one knew where the picture was going or how it would end. Bogart complained to anyone who would listen, "This picture will end my career. What does Jack Warner care about me? I'll be out on the street and he'll be sitting at his big desk in his huge office." History records it differently. *Casablanca* is forever and so is Bogart's portrayal of Rick. Reagan, however, was not left out. He became immortal.

"Play it again, Sam."

"To have talent is not enough.
One must also have
a talent for luck."

—Berloiz

CHAPTER 10

SEX, SEX, SEX!

☆

THE LADY'S A STAR!

She can greet with grace and good humor
All the cruel things that are said
She can smile and shrug at the rumor
That she won her Oscar in bed

'Cause the truth is she did it the hard way
In a small Italian car!

The lady's a star!
The lady's a star!

—MARSHALL BARER
Lyricist/Author,
Written for Wayland Flowers & Madam

Nudity Required

Auditioning nude women is a tough job, but someone's got to do it . . . and they're usually men!

AUDITIONING TOPLESS FOR THE FOLIES BERGÉRE
The Bare Essentials

☆

By Robyn Whitney
Former Dancer/Choreographer

I auditioned for The Folies Bergére at the Tropicana Hotel in Las Vegas as a dare from one of my friends who was dancing in a local ballet company with me. In a dance studio in Hollywood, one hundred female jazz dancers auditioned for Jerry Jackson, one of the most wonderful choreographers ever.

Jerry put us through our paces and kept eliminating candidates until he had the twenty girls he thought worked for the roles in the Folies. My friend and I were left nervously standing in line wondering what we'd say if they did indeed offer us the jobs. Jerry, wringing his hands with a look of total embarrassment on his face stood up and said, "You are all lovely and very good dancers, but before we can offer you the gig, the show wants me to make sure you have all the essentials that are required for the job. Could you please just take off your tops. As you know you will be dancing wearing very little, so I have to audition your Ho Ho's." We were all laughing so hard it was easy to comply with such a sweet request.

Later on I asked the Folies stage manager why Jerry called female breasts "Ho Ho's." He said it was because that's the sound that male tourists make when the curtain goes up on a stage full of topless showgirls.

On opening night we discovered Jerry was right!

THE LOVE MACHINE

———— ☆ ————

By Jack Haley, Jr.
Producer/Director

I was hired to direct my second picture, *The Love Machine*, at Columbia Studios. From the onset, producer Mike Frankovich insisted this was to be an "R" rated film. Based on the best-selling sexually-charged novel by Jacqueline Susann (*Valley of the Dolls*), this movie would be, by design, a highly controversial project.

By today's standards, *The Love Machine* is pretty tame. There are flashes of nudity (female of course) and depictions of infidelity abound. But, let's go back to the late 1960s—The Age of Permissiveness—and what was happening in Hollywood. I was in my mid-thirties—a bachelor—a novice director—and about to take on a high-budget film that was centered on a womanizing television executive. I opted for the side of the angels. I was really nervous about auditions. In a movie that required many gorgeous creatures, there would be no accusations about casting couch sessions on my part. I decided to keep the door between my office and the adjacent secretarial area open at all times.

Just before shooting was to start, the leading lady, Dyan Cannon, stopped by my office to chat. We had been good friends for some time and were looking forward to working together. Dyan asked me why I left the door open and I told her "I'm scared to death about getting a casting couch rap." She laughed that remarkable laugh of hers and said, "Knowing your reputation, I don't blame you."

So at any rate, I'm in the last weeks of pre-production for *The Love Machine*, and most of the stars have been set for the picture. There was a fashion show sequence that required about two dozen models, but it was scheduled toward the end of shooting and therefore not an immediate priority.

On an early Saturday morning my girlfriend wakes me up and says, "There are a lot of people in the living room." I said, "No, that's impossible." Sure enough, I looked through some louvers and saw about thirty beautiful models sitting around on the couches. It turned out, that a temporary houseguest of mine, whose intent was to get their phone numbers, had invited them to *audition*.

My heart started to palpitate, because, if you're caught doing something like this, having a cattle call on a weekend at your private home, you could be drummed out of every guild known to man. I looked out into the living room and saw my whole career going down the toilet.

I buzzed him on the intercom and said, "Get every girl out of the house right now. The studio will fire me, the Directors Guild will throw me out, the Screen Actors Guild will take me to court."

Finally, he got all the girls out the door and I said, "Don't ever do that to me again. You could have cost me my career." But he didn't care. He had all of these eight-by-ten-inch pictures of these beautiful models with their phone numbers on each and every one of them!

When you have sex with a producer,

he or she doesn't want to see you the next day,

much less give you a job."

—Hollywood Producer

WORKING WITH BARBRA STREISAND
Up the Sandbox

By Carole Ita White
Actress / Writer

The first movie I ever auditioned for was *Up the Sandbox*, starring Barbra Streisand. It was for the part of Bernice Spittlemeister, her baby-sitter. I was so excited, because Barbra was one of my heroes. I went over to Twentieth Century-Fox to meet Cis Corman, who was casting the film. She liked me, and showed me a photo of a girl they met in New York for the role. "I'm going to have you back to meet Irvin Kershner the director," she said. "Try to look a little more like the girl in the picture. And, by the way, if you get the role, one of your scenes is a nude scene. Is that okay?"

She could have said, "You'll have to jump out of an airplane without a parachute," and I'd have still said, "GREAT!" Anything to work with Barbra Streisand. Well, I got the role.

Now I'm thinking, *How the heck am I going to tell my parents? I'm not exactly the nude scene type.* "Hey mom, I finally got my big break, but I have to take my clothes off!" I tried to explain to them that since it was Barbra Streisand, there wouldn't be any crotch shots. It would be tasteful. (I hoped!)

The nude scene shot on a Monday, so I figured I'd go down to Palm Springs and get a tan. Well, I'm a redhead—I've never had a tan in my life. I BURNED! I got these huge blisters all over my body. *They'll cover these with makeup,* I told myself. Nothing was going to break my spirit.

Monday finally came. Time to shoot the nude scene. Barbra called me into her trailer to ask if I was nervous. She told me I had a lot of guts, and tried to calm my fears by telling me the set would be completely closed. It wasn't. Everyone took a peek.

The scene involved Barbra's character and her husband, played by David Selby, coming home from a party in the midst of a fight. Barbra slams into her bedroom, and there I am on her bed, having sex with my boyfriend/biology partner. The poor guy who played my boyfriend was so nervous he had flop sweat, and I kept sliding off him. All you end up seeing is my right breast for one second.

It's the only nude scene I ever did, and I don't know if my folks ever saw the movie, though it does play a lot on cable. When I least expect it someone will say to me, "Hey, I saw you in that Barbra Streisand movie. I saw your right breast."

SWEATING IT OUT AT THE *STEAMBATH* AUDITION!

By Gina Francis
Actress

I'd been after my agent forever to get me an audition for a play. Finally he did and I went in and met with the director. The interview went really well. We got along great. Fast friends. I kept waiting for the other shoe to drop. Eventually it did. "You know, of course, this play involves nudity."

"Well, actually, no, I didn't," I said.

He told me the play was *Steambath* and everyone on stage will be nude. Did I have a problem with that? "Oh, no," I assured him, "not at all." Only a HUGE problem with it. I mean, didn't he want to sell tickets and fill the theater? However, I agreed to audition because I wanted him to hear me read and then perhaps he'd think of me for some future project, requiring attire.

The audition was one of my best. I probably did so well knowing I didn't want the part anyway. There were several more days of intense auditioning. The competition was fierce. I was asked to attend the final callback, and told on this day we all must do the reading sans clothing. Completely nude. Not even socks. Naked, naked. I hadn't yet told them I couldn't do it. In fact, the play and part were so good I was desperately trying to convince myself I could handle it. However, when I got to that last day of auditions, I knew I couldn't. I was a wreck. My palms are sweaty just thinking about it. It was horrible. I could hardly tell them now, after going through all those auditions, that I was too chicken to take my clothes off. What was I to do?

I called my best friend Patrick. "Patrick, Patrick, you have got to help me get out of this. Please call these guys and ask for me. Make up some dire emergency, like a water pipe in my apartment burst, or something, anything to get me outta here. Then you can tell me, 'I told you so' later." He promised he would think of something and call me during the reading.

I'm sitting in the waiting area when the producer calls me into a private room. He's avoiding my eyes, and I notice now he's the one perspiring. He takes my hand. "I don't know how to tell you this, Gina. Your parents have been killed in a car crash." Tears appropriately welled in my eyes as I bit my tongue to avoid bursting out laughing. I was hysterical. This was the story Patrick had come up with? I cried and cried, from relief, actually, but nonetheless, quite a performance. But at least for this I could keep my clothes on.

Oh, and just as an aside, the woman who eventually was cast in my part went on to win all sorts of awards. That's show biz!

OH, CALCUTTA!
Total Nudity

---- ☆ ----

By Hillard Elkins
Producer / Personal Manager

We produced a play called *Oh, Calcutta!*, which was the first time there was total nudity—male and female—on the stage. And we were in a real conundrum because Equity had no rules, and we really had no rules or regulations. Fortunately Jacques Levy, our director, had been a psychologist at Menniger Clinic.

After we had auditioned the talent as singers and actors and dancers—we had limited it to the people we wanted—we had to have them take their clothes off and see them perform in total nudity. So, what Jacques did was to give the actors an improvisation!

When you take your clothes off it's hard to tell the stars from the supporting actors . . . but Bill Macy of course was the oldest and most mature and I must say the least concerned about his dress. What was fascinating to me was that the better the actor—the more deeply he got into the improvisation, the easier it was for him to work without clothes!

AROUND THE WORLD
IN 80 MINUTES

By Jennie Louise Frankel
Writer

The ad in the *Chicago Sun Times* read:

WANTED—
SHOWGIRLS FOR THEATRICAL REVIEW

My twin sister and I were very young (eighteen years old) and had no idea whatsoever what a *showgirl* was, or what she does. For those of you who also don't know, a showgirl is usually someone who walks around a stage, half-naked, wearing a forty-pound headdress and high heels. Her primary job is to point at the other girls in the review, who are dancing and singing.

We showed up at the audition with our forty-pound accordions in hand, hoping to get a chance to *show them our stuff.* Thinking back, perhaps these people figured since we carried forty-pound accordions, the headdresses would be a piece of cake. What we didn't realize at the time was that the woman who interviewed us couldn't care less about our accordion playing and was only interested in our firm young breasts.

We hoisted on the headdresses and, following direction, paraded around the small hotel room, smiling and pointing. The woman was taken with our performance and the fact that we were twins. When we told her we had no intention of taking our tops off she looked worried, and called in two male partners who had been waiting in the adjoining hotel room peering through the half-open door. The men decided we were at least young enough and seemed to walk and point with a profound proficiency—talents that led them to make an offer too good for us to refuse. Since we couldn't have cared less about parading around on the stage, imagine our unbridled joy when they told us we could play two songs on our accordions. We were delighted. Ten years of lessons no longer for naught. For the exorbitant sum of fifty dollars each per night, we were to become the two new showgirls of the revue, "Around the World in Eighty Minutes."

We opened in Rockford, Illinois, to rave reviews. Each night we'd don the headdresses, high heels, and sequined tops, and once the walking and pointing was out of the way, we'd launch into perfect executions of "Lady of Spain" and "Rhapsody in Blue." We were marvelous!

Our showgirl careers came to an abrupt end when, after a two-weekend run, we were told that if we wanted to continue with this career and be allowed to play our accordions, we HAD TO strip off the sequined tops and expose our, how shall I say it delicately . . . our Bombay mangoes. The stakes increased as they told us we could actually add one more accordion tune to our repertoire. The tension mounted. We excused ourselves to talk privately in a four-by-six-foot bathroom. As we frantically whispered, discussing the pros and cons—the con being ... well ... Can you imagine the consequences of playing "Flight of the Bumblebee" topless? Bruised mangoes! They left us no choice.

The image of two men and a woman, holding four sequined pasties in a confrontational fashion, will be forever ingrained in our minds. And so, we turned in our costumes, packed up our accordions and, modesty intact, went on to perform in Vietnam with the USO. Much to our amazement, the transfixed servicemen could not get enough of our accordion playing. They loved our "Flight of the Bumble Bee," and seemed to enjoy thinking about our Bombay mangoes, without ever needing to see them.

WILL SUCCESS SPOIL JAYNE MEADOWS?

— ☆ —

By Jayne Meadows
Actress

Jule Styne, the brilliant Broadway composer/producer (*Gypsy, High Button Shoes*) offered me the female lead opposite newcomer Walter Matthau in the Broadway play *Will Success Spoil Rock Hunter?* My husband, Steve Allen, was very upset when he read the first scene, which involved my character being massaged naked by a masseur.

"I can't believe that you, a minister's daughter," he said, "would actually play a part like this."

I explained to him that I had played a psychopathic murderess in *Lady in the Lake* and a nymphomaniac opposite Tyrone Power in *The Luck of the Irish*, and neither role seemed to have hurt my reputation. In any event, I would actually be wearing a bathing suit under the sheet that covered my body during the scene.

Steve was as unmovable as Gibraltar. However, Jule rushed me up to meet the author, George Axelrod, who clapped his hands and said, "I can't believe it. You're exactly what I wrote." The play was a satire on Hollywood sex queens. My role was fabulous; a composite of Marilyn Monroe, Ava Gardner, Rita Hayworth, etc. The play was hilarious. Of course I agreed to do it.

Rehearsals were not scheduled to start for six months. But, as we got nearer to production, Steve became more upset and I more and more ambivalent. I didn't want to risk a divorce, so, a week before rehearsals were to begin, I decided against the role. Steve was pleased, my agent was upset, and Axelrod was furious. Jule warned me, "Don't ever try to speak to Axelrod again. Your name is mud with him."

They tried another actress in the part for a few days, but unfortunately she lacked a sense of comedy. A casting call went out. They read almost every actress in New York and Hollywood. Finally an agent arrived with a folder full of sexy stills of an unknown and practically nude young woman named Jayne Mansfield. Jule told me that Axelrod studied the pictures, noted her name Jayne was even spelled like mine, and laughed out loud.

"Hire her," he said. "I don't care if she can act or not. I'll coach her twenty-four hours a day if necessary. This part will make a star out of her. I'll fix Meadows. With the similarity of their names, I'll run Meadows out of the business."

There was one thing George forgot. He was talking about a local play, but I was seen weekly on the nationally televised program "I've Got a Secret," which was always one of the top five shows in the ratings for the seven years I was on it.

The play was an enormous hit. Fox made the movie with Mansfield. Jayne, George, Steve, and I all moved to Los Angeles and soon became good friends again, going to each other's parties, which is, after all, the Hollywood way.

Ready, Willing, and Wacky!

Who says sex isn't funny? The following titillating tales will arouse your libido, kick start your kundelini energy, *and* make you laugh.

"IF YOU KNOW WHAT I MEAN!"

———————— ☆ ————————

By Meredith MacRae
Actress/Producer

I think that because my parents were famous, I didn't have as many casting couch experiences as most other young actresses did. I think people thought it might get back to my parents. . . . However, I remember going up for a movie and I walked into this sleazy office, and the producer was sitting with his feet on the desk and he had a big cigar in his mouth—the epitome of the horrible producer that you want to avoid. He didn't even get up when I entered the room. He said, "Sit down, tell me about yourself." After every sentence he would always say, "IF you know what I mean." So, the first thing he said was, "There may be some nudity involved, if you know what I mean! Is that a problem for you?" And I said in a halting voice, "Well . . . it depends. I've never done nudity."

"Now, it's going to be hot," he said. "It will be shot in Arizona. We found some swampy place there. I hope you don't mind getting muddy. It won't be the greatest location . . . if you know what I mean!" Then he said, "Let me tell you the story. You're the young love interest, if you know what I mean!" And I said,

"Yeah, uh huh." And he said, "There's you and this young kid and you're off on a romantic picnic and there's this Bog Man who's been causing havoc in the swamps. But you guys are not aware of this. You go off on this picnic and after you've finished eating it's time for a little romance, if you know what I mean! You're lying back and your boyfriend's kissing you and you'll go a little further, if you know what I mean! Just at that moment, the Bog Man comes out of the swamp and grabs you and takes you off into the swamp and he gives you the best (blank) you've ever had in your life! If you know what I mean!"

I just couldn't believe it! I sat there not knowing what to say—trying to be nice. Obviously I wasn't interested in the picture but I thought I would let him finish. He continued, "So after the Bog Man is finished with you, he leaves you at this church. There's this minister, and he finds you there and he's attracted to you also. You're semi-conscious and he starts to undress you. Then he starts to make love to you, if you know what I mean. And just at the peak of his passion, as he's reaching his climax, he has a heart attack and dies inside you! If you know what I mean!"

This was truly the most terrible and definitely the most unforgettable casting experience I ever had. I just smiled and said, "Thank you very much," and got out of there as fast as I could. (If you know what I mean!)

WET T-SHIRTS

———— ☆ ————

By Linda Day
Director

It's amazing how actresses will dress if they think they're reading for a male director. I was casting for a female chauffeur on a sitcom. All the actresses thought they were reading for a male director, so they all came in wearing either low-cut or see-through blouses. They dressed like they thought a male would want them to dress. One girl came in with a wet T-shirt and no bra. She totally soaked herself down before she came in! And when these women discovered they were casting for a female director, half of them went out and changed their wardrobe and came back in! The girl who got the part was wearing Levi's and a plaid shirt! She actually gave the best reading.

PAID TO KEEP MY CLOTHES ON!

By Gina Francis
Actress/Comedienne

A friend I'd worked with on several occasions wrote a funny two-character piece that he would also direct for the Playboy Channel. It was called *Love and Humor.* The female role was written with me in mind, the character even being called Gina. I was very flattered, but told him in no uncertain terms that I would never ever consider taking my clothes off. (However, if Martin Scorsese were to ask. . . .)

He assured me that although the women in all the other pieces he was also shooting would be at least partially nude, I could get away with wearing a sexy little teddy. That would be OK. My segment required someone who could act.

So I was called in to read with actors auditioning for the part opposite me. I show up and am forced to wait in a room filled with voluptuous eighteen-year-old Meryl Streeps. I strongly recommend it for building self-esteem.

My friend came out of the casting room and went to get himself something to eat. I guess seeing all those naked women worked up his appetite. As the door closed behind him, I was called in. Facing me was a row of guys sitting behind a long table. We all say "Hi . . . marr marr marr, etc." and I'm noticing little glances passing between them. I keep waiting for actors to be called in to read with me, but instead some sleaze says, "I guess we all know what comes next." They laugh, I laugh, but what was funny? "You can put your clothes over there," one offers. Uh, I don't think so. "There's no nudity in this," I say. "Except for the part where she walks in naked," another guy returns. More laughter. "No, no," I explain, "this part was written for me, didn't my friend tell you that? The character even has my name, and she's not naked." They inform me there is a room full of women out there more than willing to drop their duds at a moment's notice. Even faster. We start arguing. It was totally embarrassing with all these guys just leering and yelling at me.

In the nick of time my friend walks in and says, "No, no, no, we don't want to see her naked." And some guy coming in with him shoots me a glance and says, "That's for sure."

Well, I did the show, didn't take my clothes off, and the world will just have to wonder what its missing.

RELAX, YOU'RE GOING TO BE A STAR!

By James Komack
Producer

I used to have a sign on my ceiling that read, "RELAX, YOU'RE GOING TO BE A STAR." I would have people lie down on my couch and look up and they would laugh. In order to do this, I'd have to say, "Do me a favor and lie down on the couch," and they'd get real nervous and say, "NO!" And I'd say, "Please." And they'd lie down and see the sign and they'd laugh.

One day I had Yvonne Craig (who played Batgirl on "Batman") in the office. I said, "Yvonne, lie down on the couch." She said, "I'm not doing it!" I said, "Just lie down." So she did. And she didn't laugh. And now I'm thinking I'm in trouble. I said, "Don't you see the sign?" She said, "I don't have my glasses on."

PUT THEM AWAY
FOR A RAINY DAY

——————— ☆ ———————

By Eddie Foy III
Casting Director

This lady comes through the door wearing a low-cut dress. It was in the days when people went braless. It was also in the days when people handed you their picture book. And I tell people when I conduct a workshop, "Don't hand them your picture book, because you might knock over something on the desk."

Well, she bends over and two of the biggest breasts you've ever seen fall out of her dress. She doesn't move. And I don't move. I'm staring at them. And she says, "Do you like what you see?" And I say, "They are really something." Now I'm starting to sweat. I said, "But I wish you would put them away for a rainy day." And this lady stared at me. Now, this lady inserts her breasts back into her dress while I'm sitting there watching. I was so nervous. I have yet to look at her face. To this day I don't know what this lady looks like!

UNDRESS,
AND I'LL BE RIGHT BACK!

——————— ☆ ———————

By Angelyne
Hollywood Icon / Billboard Queen

I like to use my mind and do clever things to get even with people who are mean to me. One time I went to a major studio to read a screenplay. The guy wanted me to reenact the *newlywed* part with him—including the sex! As he put it, "Starting out easy and going all the way!"

I told him, "Why don't you take off all your clothes, I'll go to the ladies room, freshen up, and be right back. Then you'll be ready for me!" I left him eagerly undoing his tie. I then told his secretary, "Your boss wants you to go in and see him in five minutes!" ... Then I left!

THE VERY SUAVE
AND OH, SO ELEGANT "MR. BIG"

───── ☆ ─────

By Anonymous
Actress

In the "good old days" it wasn't unusual to be under contract for years without meeting the head of the studio. So it wasn't until I had made several films that I finally met "Mr. Big." I can't remember how I happened to be invited to a small, exclusive Christmas party on the lot, but there I was, drinking champagne with lots of stars and executives. Although the studio was promoting me as a *sexpot*, I was actually young and innocent; on the other hand, "Mr. Big" was suave and elegant looking—had a very fancy car and a socially prominent wife. When I left the party, he surprised me with a very nice kiss on the lips!

Weeks later, we passed each other on the lot and he invited me into the projection room to watch dailies with him. I was thrilled! When the lights went out he put his hand on my knee and kept it there till the lights came back on. He asked me to walk him back to his office. As we got to the door he said, "Do you know what I'm going to do now?" "No," I replied, looking with admiration at this very suave, extremely elegant man. "I'm going to go into my office and jerk off!"

I had no further contact with him, but my career continued to flourish until "Mr. Big" left the studio, to be replaced by a new "Mr. Big," who dropped my contract!

MERCY READ

By Jane Brody
Casting Director

We were auditioning for a role in a video for two weeks. The director didn't like anybody and we were looking and searching. By this time everybody on the production is saying, "Well, why don't you see my cousin?" So we're doing all these courtesy reads. And one tech guy sent us a whole bunch of women to read and guaranteed all of them would be beautiful—because we needed a beautiful girl in the role. When the girls arrived, we had a room full of very hard-looking women—I wouldn't say *hooker-like*, let's just say *club-like*. So, my associate, Rachel Tenner, looked up to see a woman who was wearing a bra for the reading. The role had nothing to do with her being in a bra. For us, that was as funny as it gets!

THE PRODUCER

By A. N. Onymous

A prolific filmmaker once convinced me to finance one of his now over fifty films—each of which has achieved instant oblivion—regrettably mine didn't break the chain. Normally I am a dispassionate and rational businessman, but in this case I was seduced by the glamour of the screen. It was a comedy of errors, a movie shot in Korea. The Korean government was extremely helpful (lent us planes, boats, and soldiers); the cast enthusiastic; the overall undertaking poorly thought out; and the marketing of the film appalling.

The starlet's chief claim to fame was having been boldly revealed in two of the better-known glossy publications repugnant to the Christian right. Sitting on the casting couch, it was not readily apparent that her physical attributes—uncovered as they were—camouflaged a complete lack of intellectual, spiritual, and mental gifts, proclivities, or attributes. Dorothy Parker beat me in her acerbic comment about covering the gamut of emotions "from A to B." My central and ultimately fatal miscalculation was the foolish belief that "sex sells." God knows she tried. When it was all said and done I was the only one in the production who didn't enjoy her wily gifts. For an outsider to the business it was extremely humorous. She was planning on being a great star. Once again, another fond ambition dashed.

I stand before you slightly poorer—infinitely wiser.

NUDE WITH VIOLIN

———— ☆ ————

By Marshall Barer
Lyricist/Author

Checking out the Dramatis Personae of Noel Coward's later plays, one cannot fail to note that the same character (with slight variations) turns up in all of them: young and (need I say?) male. His role is always a small one, unimportant, and clearly undemanding: one or two brief appearances as a bellhop, chauffeur, messenger, or the like, is all that will be required. . . . But in casting these plays, it had become a sort of tradition that one full eight-hour day be devoted exclusively to the auditions for this particular part! In the instance of the Bocaccian tale I'm about to tell, upwards of ninety chaps had shown up; all handsome, some beautiful, two or three very beautiful! . . .

THE TIME: LATER AFTERNOON, SOME YEARS AGO
THE SEASON: AUTUMN (OF COURSE . . .)
THE PLACE: A SMALL THEATER ON SHAFTESBURY AVENUE,
            IN LONDON'S WEST END

Out front, in the stalls (Brit word for orchestra) somewhere between rows E and G (as is customary) sits the Power Panel, the Jury, Keepers of the Fate. In this case they number three, but their identities are of no importance, because the ultimate Power, the Deciding Vote, the Captain of the Jury is not among them. Conspicuously absent is the author/director, Sir Noel himself. But he is out there . . . He just doesn't like to be seen from the stage in such circumstances, and it is his custom to view the Parade from the back row, totally obscured in the shadows.

The play is called *Nude with Violin,* and the mood at the moment is desultory, if not stultifying. It's been a long, unspeakably monotonous day; out front a numbness resembling rigor mortis has begun to set in . . . but mercifully the ordeal will soon be over . . . only a handful of hopefuls left . . .

Backstage, the remaining Twinkies, equally bored, await their turns, "sides" in hand, wishing, by now, they hadn't come. But one of them, determined to make the most of what seems to him Main Chance, is about to prove himself a tad more resourceful than his peers! Now it's his turn. But before he goes on, he informs the stage manager that he will perform a brief pantomime prior to his reading. "No, no! No panto! Just read the side and get off!" But the boy persists: dropping to his knees, Dickensian to the max, he sobs: "Please sir! It's only ten seconds!"

Feeling, perhaps, that at this point a little break in the monotony might not be such a bad thing, the weary stage manager gives in . . . "But only ten seconds, mind!" Now the lad is up and smiling: This is it!! A brisk stride takes him to center stage where, in less than ten seconds he manages to remove every stitch of clothing! Including shoes and socks!

A stunned silence descends upon the theater, lasting perhaps more than ten seconds, during which the Barefoot Boy with Cheek stands frozen in panic, wildly wondering, *What must I do now?* (He hadn't planned this far ahead.) Why doesn't someone say something? . . . Eventually someone does. Out of the shadows, slicing the silence like a Lavender Laser, a familiar, clipped voice makes a polite request. Brief, and to the point, it tells the boy exactly what he must do next. And at the same time grants the rest of us an unforgettable moment of pure theater: viz. and to wit:

"Would you turn a little to the left, please?"

TASTEFUL NUDITY REQUIRED
The Hollywood Cabaret
Story Conference

By Jennie Louise Frankel
Writer

My sister Terrie and I wrote a feature film that ended up starring Morton Downey, Jr., Jessica Hahn, and a bevy of beautiful *Playboy* and *Penthouse* centerfolds. The final title of the movie was *Hollywood Cabaret*. The following took place at our first story conference with the two producers who commissioned us to write this *monumental epic*. The meeting went something like this. . . .

PRODUCER DAN: Yeah, we want lots of sexy girls, hardly wearing anything and we want to call it *The Great Silver Cream Machine*.

PRODUCER BOB: Yes, and we want the girls to dance a lot and sing and we want them to take their clothes off . . . got it? Maybe have them land in a spaceship wearing tight clothes, sexy . . .

JENNIE & TERRIE: Got it!

> *At this point Sandy, the assistant to the producers, gingerly peeks in the door.*

SANDY: Bob, the girls are starting to arrive, shall I send them in?

PRODUCER DAN (*smiling*): Yes, send them in one at a time, every five minutes. Hey, Jennie and Terrie, do you girls want to sit in on the casting?

JENNIE & TERRIE: Casting??!! We just had our first story meeting. The script isn't even written yet!

PRODUCER DAN (*smiling*): We work fast. Besides, we like casting.

JENNIE & TERRIE: Sure.

> *A beautiful, young, blonde, blue-eyed actress enters. She hands over her eight-by-ten glossy photograph. Producer Bob stares at it and with authority, speaks . . .*

PRODUCER BOB: Do you have any acting experience Bambi?

BLONDE ACTRESS: No.

PRODUCER BOB: Are you in any unions? Like SAG or AFTRA?

> *Beautiful blonde has a blank expression. She pouts and gives a seductive look.*

BLONDE ACTRESS: No. Do I have to???

PRODUCER BOB: Have you been told there would be some tasteful nudity?

BLONDE ACTRESS: Yes.

PRODUCER DAN: Does that bother you?

BLONDE ACTRESS: No. Would you like to see my body?

Before the men can give a resounding yes, the actress takes off her white-lace-and-blue-satin-ribbon bustier.

PRODUCER BOB: They're very nice.

The men seem to be enjoying the view. After a couple of minutes of silence, the girl is thanked, she gets dressed, and is excused from the room.

JENNIE & TERRIE: Do you need some dialogue, so you can read these girls?

PRODUCER DAN: Oh, no, no, no, we don't need to get into their acting abilities, that comes much later . . . at another casting session . . . after we get the financing!

SLEEPING WITH EVERYONE IN TOWN, NOT!

———— ☆ ————

By Angelyne
Hollywood Icon/Billboard Queen

People wonder about my billboards . . . I made a business deal in 1983 with an investor to get my billboards around town. It was strictly a business deal, I had to give 50 percent of my earnings for five years, NO SLEEPING!

My time is precious and I've been very particular with whom I spend it. . . . So, every time people approach me and don't want to pay me I say, "If you don't pay me I'll have to sleep with everybody in town, and you wouldn't want me to do that, would you?"

I've earned fame in a rebellious form—anti-Hollywood. I've gotta have what I want when I want it, right now! I will go to the ends of the earth and the top of the world to get it!

Seductions

When Lauren Bacall told Humphrey Bogart, "You know how to whistle, don't you? Just put your lips together . . . and blow," that look and lip placement launched a hit movie, an acting career, and an unforgettable, historic marriage.

THE OCTOPUS DIRECTOR

———— ☆ ————

By Angelyne
Hollywood Icon Billboard Queen

I did not go out with this director with the intention of getting a part, but he kept insisting, "Oh, you'd be so perfect for this part! I want to give you this part!" We ended up at his house where he waited on me hand and foot. Suddenly he was taking my shoes off and kissing my feet! He got me to a point where I was very drunk and had all of my clothes off! He was really getting very intimate with me, trying to kiss me everywhere. Usually I'm not in control when I'm drunk, but I managed to be in control somehow. I told him, "I've got to go to the bathroom! Let me go, please!" He was like an octopus, all over me and he would not let up!

Finally, after about fifteen minutes—which seemed like an hour—he let me go to the bathroom. So I ran outside totally naked! He was upset because he thought the neighbors would see. He kept begging me to come back in. I wouldn't. I said, "Give me my clothes!" He said, "Come in and get them!" I said, "No, no!" I finally came back in to get my clothes and he started in again! I couldn't believe it! This time I got my clothes, took them with me, and managed to get away to a neighbor's house—a high-powered attorney for the White House. Thankfully, he helped me out of there.

The next day the director called and said, "I really love you and I want you to have the part—you've got the part!" I said, "That's nice, I'll call you later." Of course I didn't call. The nerve! How can you trust an *octopus* like that?!

LET'S MAKE A DEAL

———————— ★ · ————————

By Robyn Whitney
Former Dancer/Choreographer

I was auditioning for a part at a Hollywood casting office. The older male director told me I was physically right for the part, my reading of the script was "superior," and my agent had worked out the right price for my services.

However, if I wanted the role, he said I would need—to paraphrase him—to supply oral suction to his genitalia . . . He waited with a Cheshire cat grin for my Squirm Response. I would not give him the pleasure. Instead, I answered in the same businesslike tone we had been talking in. "In that case, my fee will have to be considerably renegotiated."

"You can't sleep your way into being a star,

it takes much, much more.

But it helps!"

—Marilyn Monroe

WHAM, BAM, I GOT THE LEAD!

By Anonymous
Actress

There was a free-lance producer in the early fifties—he was pretty well known. I don't know how I ended up in his office, but I ended up there. I guess my agent sent me. After a few minutes, he chased me around the office, pinned me against the wall, and thrust himself against me. I was absolutely paralyzed. Wham bam, thank you ma'am, without even unzipping his pants. We were fully dressed and he had an orgasm! . . . I fled his office.

I was like Alice in Wonderland at the time. I was a virgin, and looked it. Nothing like that had ever happened to me. . . . The next thing I knew—from this weird little incident—I got the lead in a major motion picture from a director friend of his who cast me and never laid a hand on me.

AN HONEST ANSWER

By Vanessa Brown
Actress/Journalist/Documentarian

I once asked famed director Elia Kazan, "Does a person have to sleep with a producer to get a part?" And Kazan looked at me intently and said, "It depends on the part."

You know, I did twenty-six motion pictures and about four hundred radio and television shows and it never happened that I had to sleep with someone or take someone's advances to get a part. There are small people and there are cheap people and there are people who take advantage of their position of power. If the actress is weak-minded and if the part is small enough, she will get approached. But it's up to the person approached to take the initiative as to how she wants to deal with her career. With me, it was a living; it was not a business of making it to the top. I didn't care whether I got to the top or not.

It is my firm belief that you do not have to sleep with anybody to get a part. Nor do you have to cater to any advances or make any concessions upon your virginity or anything. You are you and the heck with everybody else.

SUSPICIOUS SCENE

By Donna Mills
Actress

When I was first starting out in New York, it was common for actresses to go around to various agents with their pictures and resumés—hoping to get agency representation. I went to one agent and he said, "I like your picture, but I'd like to see you do a scene. Take this scene home with you tonight, learn it, and we'll do it together tomorrow." I said, "Who shall I do the scene with? Shall I bring a partner?" He said, "No, no, we'll read it together. *I'll* do it with you."

I went home and soon realized the scene was like soft porn! I went back the next day—though I was very skeptical. The agent said, "Okay, we'll read this scene together." I reluctantly agreed. Then he started sitting on the couch next to me and putting his arms around me—while we were reading the scene! I said, "Wait a minute! . . . No! . . ." Apparently that was what he did to all of the young actresses who came in there. Some of the actresses must have thought, *Well, it's in the scene, maybe I should do this.* Things like this may still be going on. I found it really tacky.

THE MURPHY BED STORY

——— ☆ ———

By Edward Asner
Actor/Producer

A friend of mine told me about how she went to see an agent on Sunset Boulevard. Once inside his office, the door closed behind her and locked and a Murphy bed came out of the wall. The experience encouraged our would-be starlet to get into production rather than being in front of a camera.

PROMISE HIM ANYTHING

——— ☆ ———

By Alpha Blair
Actress

As a teenage aspiring actress, I was very dedicated about answering all of the casting notices in the show business trade papers. Unfortunately, a number turned out to be from unscrupulous individuals who were dedicated to trying to combine their work life with their sex life. Sometimes, to get out of unpleasant situations, I'd have to plead and cry. Finally, I got inventive and I'd demurely mention my dad was with the police department. I graduated my dad to the FBI and the mayor's office. Strangely, none of these positions of power my dad supposedly held were as much of a deterrent as I'd hoped for. Then I found a job for my dad that really made those casting couch guys hurry to unlock their doors and usher me out. I said my dad was in the Mafia.

At one interview in California, a producer of convention shows utilizing models said he would like to hire me. Then he threw his arm around me and tried to pull me into a sweaty embrace, saying I should be grateful he was giving me the job even though I wasn't a blonde. Thinking quickly, I told him that I had several gorgeous, very blonde girlfriends who liked to work a lot and didn't mind partying for jobs. If he let me go, I'd call back with their names and telephone numbers. I didn't think he'd believe such a lame story, but he did. Requesting assurances from me that I'd be calling him with the names and numbers of my friends, he opened the door and let me out. . . . He's still waiting.

YOU CAN'T WIN

By Allan Byrns
Writer/Producer

I was a commercial director. We were doing a spot for a major advertising agency. We auditioned the top fashion models in New York. I was waiting at the elevators after the audition. One top model walked up to me, took my hand, and said, "Mr. Byrns, I will do *anything* to get this job." I bravely and honorably told her, "You've done everything necessary to get the job. The tape will go to the client who will make the final decision." I put her on the elevator and wished her good luck. The producer came up to me and said, "Are you crazy? You've ruined it for all of us. If it were up to me, you'd never work again!" Which goes to prove that no good deed goes unpunished!

"Did you hear about the actress who landed the part by signing on the dotted couch?"

—**Milton Berle**

FALSE PRETENSES

——————— ☆ ———————

By Carmen D'Amico
Professional Speaker

I once met a producer who told me he was taking time off from business. He asked me if I could see him at his home office. He said he was interested in discussing the possibility of casting me in a new movie that was in the works reminiscent of the old Gloria Swanson flick *Sunset Boulevard*. In the new movie the character of the aging star was fashioned after Liz Taylor and my resemblance to her might be a great opportunity for me. Having had some training in drama and some stage experience, followed by my career as a professional speaker, I felt that here might be the chance of a lifetime to do something very special, as Liz Taylor is my role model.

Arriving at his home, the producer showed me into his office and we sat and talked for awhile. Presently he showed me a contractual agreement and told me how lucky I would be if I "really wanted it." I glanced hungrily at the impressive paper and when I reached out to read it more closely, he swept it from my hands and glided toward the door saying he'd be right back for more "serious discussion." When he reentered, he had removed his pants and was standing in the doorway in his shirt, socks, and boxer shorts, explaining that he felt more comfortable in loose attire.

As he talked about my "beautiful features" his eyes went to my breasts. And didn't I catch a hint of sweat beading up on his upper lip? In an instant he was standing before me, the contract in one hand and his other hand on his bulging crotch. I almost wanted to laugh, seeing his little spindly bowed legs peering out from under his baggy boxer shorts. Instantly, I thought that I should take a good look at this scenario, for this is what I should expect if I ever fell in love somewhere in my seventies or eighties.

In a desperate effort to unscramble the turmoil in my brain, I managed to hear parts of his offer which included benefits and compensations which somehow seemed to belong to him and not me. Some of the phrases I managed to catch sounded like you need to audition and how important his decision would be based upon my desire to perform. Why did I have this foreboding premonition that somehow my so-called performance would be like the thousands of feet of film that would end up on the cutting room floor along with my bra and panties?

Driving back home to Fort Lauderdale, I wanted to laugh and cry at what I had just experienced, and the old cliché I once heard kept haunting me. You know the one that goes, "Fool me once, shame on you. Fool me twice, shame on me!"

A NECK MASSAGE

By Stephen Heilpern
Producer

A famous model from New York was trying to break into the acting business. One evening I took her to dinner and she was enraged at what had just happened to her. She had been in a meeting with a fairly big producer. It was during the summer and she was wearing a backless dress. He had a large office and as they spoke, he got up from his desk and started circling in back of her. She assumed it was just to see what she looked like from different angles. She proceeded to look straight ahead through the window and before long, she felt something on her back, an *unmistakable touch*. This producer was massaging her with his sex organ! She was nonplussed, to say the least. She looked back, gasped and . . . didn't get the part.

THE GIRDLE SNAPPER!

By Ruth Webb
Talent Agent

FROM HER BOOK, *WON'T YOU STEP INTO MY PARLOUR?*

Prior to becoming a star talent agent for legends like Mickey Rooney, Claudette Colbert, and many others, I was a Broadway actress. In fact, I was a star represented by the late, great, NYC agent Lester Shurr. I did five Broadway shows. Lester Shurr never got me a job, but he tried his best to get into my pants. Only in those days I wore a girdle. Lester would chase me around his office and grab at me every time I was called in for an *audition*. But the only thing Lester got hold of was the back of my girdle, which repeatedly snapped back in his face. He was about the size of Mickey Rooney! He finally got so mad that he tore up my contract and threw me out of his office. Nonetheless, I succeeded as my own agent, using a different name of course.

ANGELYNE, TRIUMPHANT!

By Angelyne
Hollywood Icon/Billboard Queen

When I was fifteen years old I was invited to this big studio party where a director started talking to me and said he could make me a *big star*. Of course I fell for it. I was young and naive and had wanted to become a star since the age of three! He offered to drive me home and I accepted. On the way home he started to tell me what he could do for me—but he needed to know how I kissed, and all that. So he parked the car and asked me to kiss him. I wouldn't kiss him. He then said, "Well, I need to see what you look like without your clothes on."

He had me there for an hour trying to convince me that he was going to make me a star if I took my clothes off. This guy was the best con artist I'd ever met. I really believed him. I took off all my clothes except for my bra and panties—which is more than I had done for anyone who had ever tried to con me before. He wanted me to take everything off. I refused. He said I would "never make it" if I didn't take off my bra and panties and show him my body. He just wanted to have sex with me in the car. I didn't do anything with him, but by the time I got home I was very upset.

Five years later I became famous on the billboards. I got cast in a film he was working on. He was always afraid I was going to say something to him—because he had upset me and conned me. Of course I was too cool to say anything to him, but just the thought that I might confront him scared him.

Anyway, I think I was triumphant in winning and succeeding without taking my bra and panties off. It was wonderful to succeed in the glory of being avenged in success! I love winning. The "Win Win Fairies" are always with me!

"I can't for the life of me
see what nudity has to do with good acting.
But perhaps if I were younger
I would feel differently."

—Julie Harris

Hot!

Sex can run the gamut from titillating to tasteless. The following Hollywood casting stories go off the scale!

TRANSVESTITE FOR A DAY

☆

By Marty Ratigan
Actor

After two years in Los Angeles, I'd had many commercial auditions, but no readings for feature films. Then, one day, there it was in the trade paper, "PRINCIPAL ROLE, MUST PLAY A TV, PARTIAL NUDITY." Well, I'm from a small town in the Midwest and only recently learned that TV means transvestite, not television! So, I looked in the mirror and asked, "Are you willing to do ANYTHING for scale?" Brief pause ... "YES!" ... "Do you want it THIS bad? ...YES!"

Well, I bit off more than I could chew. I approached my wife, curious about her reaction to the idea. Her enthusiasm for dressing and making me up was a bit of a surprise (after she stopped laughing). All of a sudden, I'm in her black, sheer evening gown, black pumps, socks in a bra, and all the trimmings.

When I got to the audition I needed to use the bathroom. But which one? I didn't want any guys to see me like that, but I didn't have enough nerve to use the ladies room. So I decided to wait it out!

During the audition I died like the *straight* dog that I am. I just couldn't relax in that get-up. My reading was poor, and when asked, I didn't know the difference between transsexual and transvestite. To add insult to injury, my smart-aleck wife snapped a few photos of me and to this day uses them (very effectively) to get her own way.

10 PERCENT FOR MY AGENT

By Anonymous
Actress

While I was under contract to Universal in the fifties, a well-known writer/director (M. G.) on the lot sent for me to discuss my appearing in his next film. After chatting with me for awhile, he unzipped his fly and started "pleasuring himself." When he saw the shocked look on my face he said, "Mental hospitals are filled with people who'd like to do this, but don't have the nerve!"

Some years later, M. G. was at Paramount and I was now free-lancing. My agent called me one day and said, "M. G. would like you to come in to read for his new project." I told my agent that I didn't want to be alone with this man and that I would only go to the audition if my agent would promise to stay with me, no matter what. He promised.

My agent and I arrived in the outer office and a secretary announced us. I grabbed my agent's arm as we walked through the door into the inner office. When M. G. saw my agent he said, "You can wait for her out there." So, in spite of his promise, my agent deserted me. I read a couple of scenes and then the dreaded event started! He unzipped and was on the brink of orgasm in no time. He grabbed my hand and ejaculated on my open palm before I even knew what was happening. I whirled around and headed for the door. "Where are you going?" he asked. "I'm going to give 10 percent to my agent!" I answered.

WEEKEND TRIPS

———— ☆ ————

By Alpha Blair
Actress

Shortly after I came to California I had an interview with a film company in the Valley. It took me two hours and several buses to get there. The man interviewing me informed me that I was "just right" for the part. But he wanted to "get to know me better." He suggested a weekend in San Francisco. I said "No!"—and sat on the bus on the way home with tears of disillusionment clouding my eyes.

At about the same time, I went on an interview for a popular TV series. The producer's assistant told me I could have a small speaking part in an upcoming episode, but, in exchange, I would have to go out on the producer's boat over the weekend with some other actors and make a porno movie for the producer's private collection. Needless to say, I declined.

THE VIBRATOR-WIELDING DIRECTOR

By Anonymous
Actress

I was under contract to a major studio. There was a very macho director, B. B., who invited me to his office very late one afternoon. After a few minutes of chit chat he asked me to close my eyes. Before I knew it he had locked the door and was chasing me around the room—with a vibrator! I think it was an electric one on a long cord. First of all, I did not like him. Second, I was absolutely appalled. Finally I was able to unlock the door and I ran out into the hall. I was in tears. I was outraged and offended and frightened, because I thought he was going to rape me. I don't know where he got off chasing me around with that vibrator. In those days, I was naive and innocent, but I wasn't stupid.

As I burst out of his office, I bumped into the janitor, who was coming to clean the office. The janitor walked in to find B. B., vibrator in hand, zipping up his fly! When I think about it now, it makes me laugh. But it wasn't funny then.

TOPS OFF, BOTTOMS UP

By Donna Lee
Writer/Producer, Founder/Director, Hollywood Scriptwriting Institute

This incident happened many years ago. I was looking into ways to finance my new venture, the Hollywood Scriptwriting Institute, and I had been told that low-budget movies, if done right, can be virtual gold mines. An attorney friend, a filmmaker, and I decided to go into business together. I would write the script, they would take care of the rest. After writing what I considered to be one of the more extravagant, yet tastefully sexy, low-budget features about, what else—the world's highest-paid prostitute—we began casting. That's how it's done, isn't it? At least we thought so at the time. You write the script, get the cast, then go for the financing.

After putting an ad in the trades, twenty gorgeous young ladies arrived to read at the home of my attorney friend. I watched as the men involved with the film asked the women questions. They offered them beverages and talked small talk. When my partner casually asked the bevy of beauties to take their tops off, to my surprise, one by one, they all complied . . . responding as if we had asked them the time of day. It really was startling to all of us that the girls just whipped off their clothes. And so, here were twenty gorgeous, topless women, talking, schmoozing, drinking their beverage of choice, acting like they were at a Girl Scouts troop meeting—while the men were groping for something sensible to say.

I had an education that day, a look at the other side of the casting process, and was truly amazed at the girls' ability to readily comply with any and all requests made of them.

P.S.: The movie was never financed, but for the men involved in this project, the memory remains. That's probably the only time in their lives they ever told twenty women to disrobe and they all eagerly cooperated!

FOOT FETISH

——— ☆ ———

By Delia Salvi
Actress/UCLA Drama Instructor

I was working at a typing service. A writer came in one day. According to my boss, Ruth, he was "one of the biggest, hottest, most important screenwriters in town!" Well, he took a big fancy to me and offered to take me to lunch. And Ruth was saying, "Go, go!" I thought, *Oh, gee. I don't know how to play the game.*

I went to lunch with him to a famous place in Hollywood and he starts talking to me about Napoleon and Josephine. The guy had a foot fetish! He was trying to teach me about foot fetishes.

He took me to lunch again and this time he's telling me more and more how beautiful my feet were. And then he started calling me up at home and telling me he would be willing to sacrifice himself at the altar of my feet!

In the meantime, my boss is going, "Go for it! Go for it! He can write parts for you." He can do this, he can do that . . . That's the kind of insanity that young actresses are subjected to.

LIST OF CONTRIBUTORS

*Our heartfelt thanks to the following industry people
who generously shared their experiences:*

MARTY ALLEN, ACTOR/COMEDIAN
STEVE ALLEN, ACTOR/AUTHOR/COMPOSER/PERSONALITY
ANGELYNE, HOLLYWOOD ICON BILLBOARD QUEEN
RALPH ARCHBOLD, ACTOR
EDWARD ASNER, ACTOR/PRODUCER
ARTHUR AXELMAN, PRODUCER
MARSHALL BARER, WRITER/LYRICIST
FRAN F. BASCOM, CASTING DIRECTOR
MILTON BERLE, COMEDIAN
STEVE BINDER, DIRECTOR/PRODUCER
ALPHA BLAIR, ACTRESS
STEVE BLUESTONE, ACTOR/COMEDIAN
JEFF BLYTH, DIRECTOR
JANE BRODY, CASTING DIRECTOR
VANESSA BROWN, ACTRESS/JOURNALIST/DOCUMENTARIAN
ALLAN BYRNS, WRITER/PRODUCER
JACK CARTER, ACTOR/COMEDIAN
SANDRA CARUSO, ACTRESS/DIRECTOR/ACTING TEACHER
GIL CATES, PRODUCER/DIRECTOR
FERN CHAMPION, CASTING DIRECTOR
BARBARA CLAMAN, CASTING DIRECTOR
JOHN FORD COLEY, ACTOR/MUSICIAN
PAT CRONIN, ACTOR
FRED CURT, DANCER
BILLY DaMOTA, CASTING DIRECTOR
CARMEN D'AMICO, PROFESSIONAL SPEAKER
ARI DANE, SINGER/ACTOR/PERFORMER
EILEEN DAVIDSON, ACTRESS
LINDA DAY, DIRECTOR
PATTE DEE, ACTRESS/UCLA DRAMA INSTRUCTOR
RICHARD DEVIN, ACTOR
TONY DIAMOND, COMEDIAN/PRODUCER/HEAD OF BRAVO NETWORK
PHYLLIS DILLER, COMEDIENNE
JOSEPH DiSANTE, ACTOR/ABC EXECUTIVE
DENNIS DOTY, PRODUCER
JOHN DOWNEY III, ACTOR/PRODUCER
CAROLYN DYER, DANCE CHOREOGRAPHER
ROBERT EASTON, ACTOR/DIALECT COACH
MICHAEL ECONOMOU, PRODUCER
BARBARA EDEN, ACTRESS
HILLARD ELKINS, PERSONAL MANAGER
MARK EDWARDS, NEWSCASTER
SHARON M. FERRITTO, ASSOCIATE PRODUCER
BOB FINKEL, DIRECTOR/PRODUCER
ROBERT FORSTER, ACTOR
EDDIE FOY III, CASTING DIRECTOR
GINA FRANCIS, ACTRESS/COMEDIENNE
JENNIE LOUISE FRANKEL, WRITER
TERRIE MAXINE FRANKEL, WRITER/PRODUCER
JOEL FREEMAN, PRODUCER

DENNIS GALLEGOS, CASTING DIRECTOR
GARY GARDNER, ACTOR/DRAMA TEACHER
CYNTHIA GARRIS, ACTRESS
EDMUND GAYNES, PRODUCER/ACTOR/CASTING DIRECTOR
GARY GERO, ANIMAL TRAINER
PAUL GILBERT, PRODUCER
PHIL GILBRETH, MUSICIAN
PAT GOLDEN, DIRECTOR
GENE GRIESSMAN, ACTOR
CHARLIE HAUCK, WRITER/PRODUCER/AUTHOR
JACK HALEY, JR., PRODUCER/DIRECTOR
CAMILLE HARRIS, PRODUCER
EDNA HARRIS, ACTRESS/COMEDIENNE
JOE HART, ACTOR/PRODUCER/MULTI-AUDITIONER
BEVERLY HECHT, COMMERCIAL TALENT AGENT
STEPHEN HEILPERN, PRODUCER
LIZ HERSZAGE, WRITER/ACTRESS
LAURA HILL, ACTRESS
JANET HIRSHENSON, CASTING DIRECTOR
MICHAEL HIRSHENSON, CASTING DIRECTOR
RANCE HOWARD, ACTOR
KATHLEEN HUGHES, ACTRESS
FRANK INN, ANIMAL TRAINER
DOROTHY JAMES, ACTRESS
ANNE JEFFREYS, ACTRESS
JANE JENKINS, CASTING DIRECTOR
CHAROLE FLOYD JOHNSON, PRODUCER
JEREMY KAGAN, DIRECTOR/PRODUCER/WRITER
BENAY KARP, ANIMAL TRAINER
SCOTT KASKE, PERFORMER
JAMES KOMACK, WRITER/PRODUCER
KAREN KONDAZIAN, ACTRESS
HENRY KAPONO, ACTOR/SINGER/SONGWRITER
SYDNEY LASSICK, ACTOR
DONNA LEE, WRITER/PRODUCER
JOANNA LEE, WRITER/PRODUCER
SAMANTHA LEFFEL, STUDENT/ACTRESS
SHELDON LEONARD, PRODUCER
JOHN THOMAS LENOX, PRODUCER/DIRECTOR
MICHAEL LEVINE, PUBLICIST/AUTHOR
HARRY LEWIS, ACTOR/RESTAURATEUR
SID LUFT, PRODUCER
WARREN LYONS, ENTERTAINER/PRODUCER/TEACHER
SAM MANNERS, PRODUCER
COURTENAY McWHINNEY, ACTRESS
PATRICK MACNEE, ACTOR/AUTHOR
MEREDITH MacRAE, ACTRESS/PRODUCER
DON MANKIEWICZ, PRODUCER
SAM MANNERS, PRODUCER
KENNETH MARS, ACTOR
TRUDY MARSHALL, ACTRESS
MITCH MATOVICH, PRODUCER
JAYNE MEADOWS, ACTRESS
DEE MILLER, CASTING DIRECTOR

DONNA MILLS, ACTRESS
GARY MORRIS, ACTOR/SINGER
JEREMIAH MORRIS, DIRECTOR/ACTOR/WRITER
KIMBERLY NAMMOTO, CASTING DIRECTOR
FAYARD NICHOLAS, DANCER/ACTOR
GARY OWENS, BROADCASTER/ACTOR
MARVIN PAIGE, CASTING DIRECTOR
GENE PERRET, WRITER/PRODUCER
BUDDY POWELL, ACTOR
LINNEA QUIGLEY, ACTRESS
ALAN RACHINS, ACTOR
ROBERT B. RADNITZ, PRODUCER
MARTY RATIGAN, ACTOR
JOHN RATZENBERGER, ACTOR/DIRECTOR/PRODUCER
BARBARA REMSEN, CASTING DIRECTOR
DEBBIE REYNOLDS, ACTRESS
JOHN RITTER, ACTOR
DIANE ROBISON, PRODUCER
BARNEY ROSENZWEIG, EXECUTIVE PRODUCER
STANLEY RUBIN, PRODUCER
SIG SAKOWICZ, RADIO/TV PERSONALITY
DELIA SALVI, ACTRESS/UCLA DRAMA INSTRUCTOR
PHIL SAVENICK, PRODUCER
KURT SCHWOEBEL, ACTOR
GLENN SHADIX, ACTOR
CHERYL SHAWVER, ELEPHANT TRAINER
MELISSA SKOFF, CASTING DIRECTOR
BOB SOLER, PRODUCER/COMPOSER
KATHERINE SOLER, ACTRESS
TOM SPALDING, PRODUCER/DIRECTOR
LEONARD STERN, WRITER/PRODUCER
DAVID STONE, ACTOR
GEORGE SUNGA, PRODUCER
R. THAD TAYLOR, FOUNDER & PRESIDENT, SHAKESPEARE SOCIETY OF AMERICA
JEAN THORPE, ACTRESS
CONSTANCE TOWERS, MUSICAL ACTRESS
RENÉE VALENTE PRODUCER
BRAD WAISBREN, PRODUCER
MALVIN WALD, WRITER/PRODUCER
LILLY WALTERS, ACTRESS
JAMES A. WATSON, JR., ACTOR
RUTH WEBB, TALENT AGENT
BERNARD WEITZMAN, NETWORK EXECUTIVE
HUBERT WELLS, ANIMAL TRAINER
LOUISE WESTERGAARD, PRODUCER
CAROLE ITA WHITE, ACTRESS/PRODUCER
JESSE WHITE, ACTOR
ROBYN WHITNEY, FORMER DANCER/CHOREOGRAPHER
ROY WOOD, FISHBUSTERS
RICHARD YNIGUEZ, ACTOR
MICHAEL YORK, ACTOR
GRACE ZABRISKIE, ACTRESS
BOBBY ZEE, PRODUCER/COMPOSER

INDEX